Monty
A Biography of
Field Marshal Montgomery

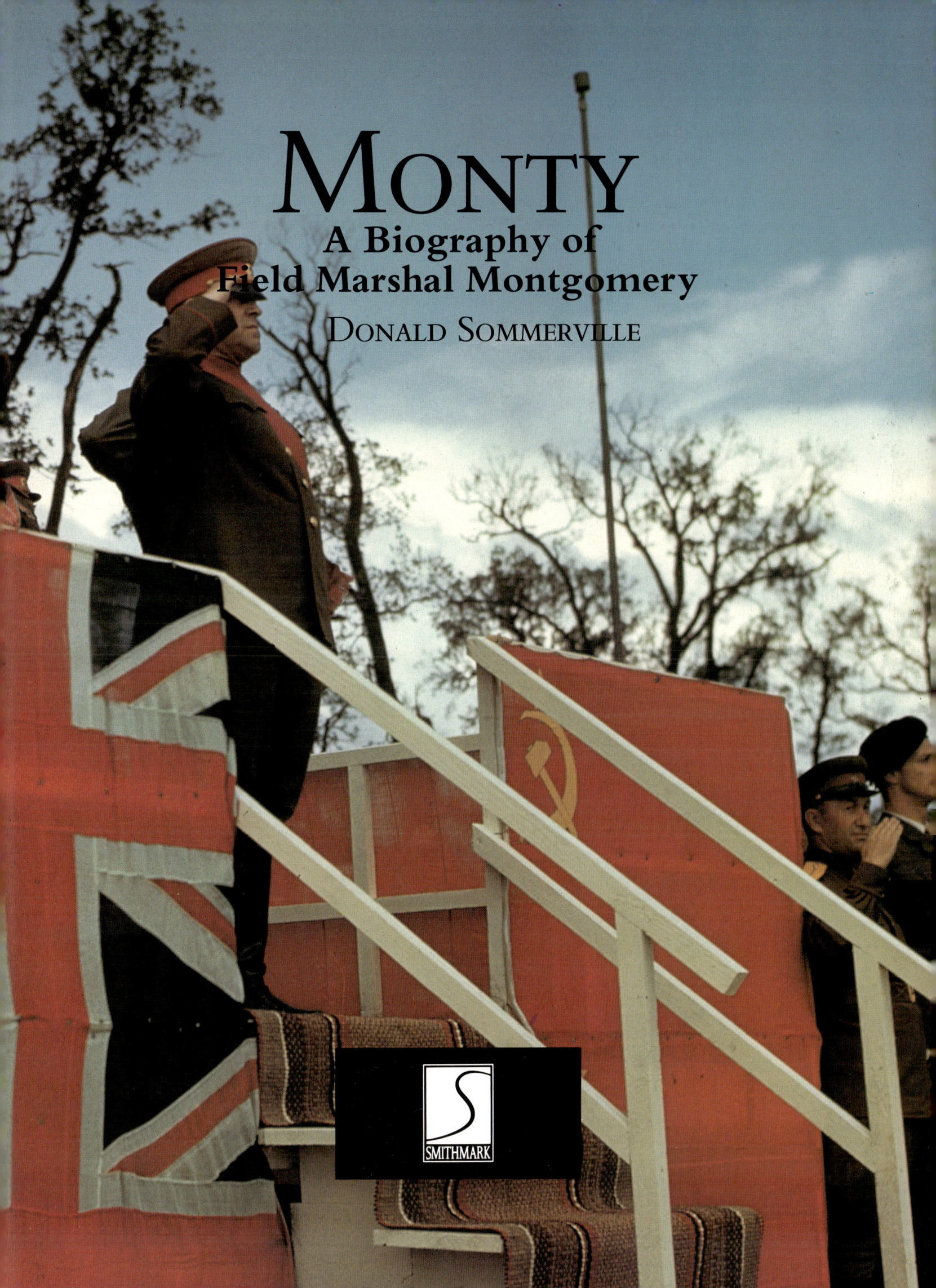
MONTY
A Biography of Field Marshal Montgomery
Donald Sommerville

Copyright © 1992 Brompton Books Corp.

All rights reserved. No part of this publication may be reproduced, stored in a retrieval system or transmitted in any form by any means, electronic, mechanical, photocopying or otherwise, without first obtaining written permission of the copyright owner.

This edition published in 1992
by SMITHMARK Publishers Inc.
16 East 32nd Street
New York, New York 10016.

SMITHMARK books are available for bulk purchase for sales promotion and premium use. For details write or telephone the Manager of Special Sales, SMITHMARK Publishers Inc., 16 East 32nd Street, New York, NY 10016, (212) 532 6600.

Produced by Brompton Books Corp.,
15 Sherwood Place,
Greenwich, CT 06830

ISBN 0-8317-5761-2

Printed in Hong Kong

10 9 8 7 6 5 4 3 2 1

The right of Donald Sommerville to be identified as the author of this work has been asserted by him in accordance with the Copyright, Designs and Patents Act 1988.

Page 1: *Monty sits in the grounds of his Hampshire home, outside one of his wartime caravans, with the original memorial from Luneberg Heath.*

Page 2-3: *Monty and the Soviet Marshal Zhukov take the salute at a victory parade in Berlin.*

CONTENTS

Left: *A file of Eighth Army infantrymen pass their leader, Sicily, August 1943.*

Preface
6

CHAPTER ONE
GO AND SEE WHAT BERNARD IS DOING
9

CHAPTER TWO
LEARNING, TEACHING AND TRAINING
23

CHAPTER THREE
COMMANDING THE 3RD DIVISION
32

CHAPTER FOUR
DO YOU HAVE 100% BINGE?
43

CHAPTER FIVE
EARNING LAURELS IN AFRICA
53

CHAPTER SIX
A DAY'S MARCH NEARER HOME
78

CHAPTER SEVEN
WE WILL SURELY MAKE HARD CHEWING
105

CHAPTER EIGHT
A GOOD AND SIMPLE PLAN
123

CHAPTER NINE
UNREPENTANT ADVOCATE
163

CHAPTER TEN
A VERY FULL LIFE
181

Index
189

PREFACE

Left: *Monty in late 1944. His usual headgear was a black Tank Corps beret with two badges but he was also colonel of the Parachute Regiment and occasionally wore a beret with their badge and his own general officer's badge added.*

Right: *The D-Day command team. Back row from left, Bradley, Ramsay, Leigh-Mallory, Bedell Smith; front row, Tedder, Eisenhower, and Monty.*

Right below: *King George VI visited Monty in Holland in October 1944. Air Marshal Coningham of Second Tactical Air Force was also present to welcome the King.*

When writing about military affairs, especially those as exalted as General Montgomery's activities during World War II, it is very easy to forget the reality behind such inevitable simplifications as 'Eighth Army encountered heavy resistance.' Even out of battle Monty's men met plagues of flies and suffered desert sores in North Africa, encountered choking dust and thirst in Sicily, mud and rain in the Italian hills, and yet more mud and freezing cold in north-west Europe. Inadequate food was the lot of the front-line soldier everywhere; malaria incapacitated more men in Sicily than enemy action, and trench foot put thousands more in hospital in Italy, Belgium, and Holland.

Overall battlefield casualties for the Western Allies in World War II were much lower than in World War I, but for the combat soldier prospects were nonetheless as grim as ever. In British divisions which served throughout the campaign of 1944-45 in France and Germany, over half of the ordinary soldiers became casualties. Another calculation, relating to a single Scottish battalion in the same period, showed that of over 50 officers who had at one time commanded one of the 12 infantry platoons, half were wounded, one quarter killed, others became sick and only one in twenty survived intact. Always there was fear, suffering and discomfort. As one Canadian in Holland described it in the last bitter winter of the war:

Do you know what it's like? Of course you don't. You have never slept in a hole in the ground which you have dug while someone tried to kill you . . . a hole dug as deep as you can, as quick as you can. . . . It is an open grave, and yet graves don't fill up with water . . . and you don't feel the cold, clammy wet that goes into your marrow. . . . When [the infantryman] is mortared or shelled he is deathly afraid and in the daytime he chain-smokes, curses or prays, all of this lying on his belly with his hands under his chest to lessen the pain of the blast. . . . The next time you are near some muddy fields after a rain take a look in a ditch. That is where your man lives.

Preface

It is all too easy in a military biography to subsume this human reality into a simple statement, such as 'Montgomery halted his advance because of bad weather.' Another form of simplification common in military histories like this may also offend. The forces led by Montgomery in the desert in 1942 are often described as British, being under British command, but in reality included Australians, New Zealanders, Free French, Greeks, soldiers of the Indian Army – who might be described nowadays as Indian, Nepalese and Pakistani – plus South Africans and a small number of Americans. Such simplifications, of either kind, are not intended to belittle the experience of the ordinary soldier, or to underestimate the full contribution of any given nationality.

Rather, the leader's role and effectiveness have been separated out from the totality of events of which they were part, in order to examine them more clearly. Montgomery's life is in itself of great interest, but it is particularly illuminating to compare Monty's various leadership techniques with those encountered in modern life.

Chapter One
Go and See What Bernard is Doing

Left: *Captain Montgomery wearing the red collar tabs and armband of a staff officer, France 1917.*

Above: *Men of the British Expeditionary Force arrive in France in 1914.*

Bernard Law Montgomery ended his career as a field marshal and a viscount and probably his country's most famous soldier since the Duke of Wellington. This simple statement of facts establishes him as a man of unusual accomplishments. He was also a highly individual man with a complicated personality, often difficult to understand, sometimes difficult to like. Yet, at first sight, Montgomery's upbringing and career do not instantly reveal these facets of his character.

Monty was born on 17 November 1887 in a vicarage in south London. His father, Henry Montgomery, was a devoted parish priest in the Church of England who was shortly to be promoted to become Bishop of Tasmania, a post he would fill with equal commitment to pastoral care. The Montgomery family was staunchly Protestant Anglo-Irish (or more accurately Scotch-Irish) with a substantial estate at Moville, County Donegal, but with no great financial resources, following mismanagement by preceding generations. Montgomery's grandfather, Sir Robert, was a nationally known figure, a hero of the Indian Mutiny, and later highly successful as Lieutenant-Governor of the Punjab. Henry Montgomery had been educated at Cambridge University, where he had been a moderate but respectable scholar and a noted sportsman. On leaving Cambridge he entered the church and in 1876, after various posts, became curate to the Reverend Frederic William Farrar, whose daughter, Maud, Henry was to marry in 1881.

Farrar was one of the most famous men of Victorian England and indeed was well known throughout the English-speaking world. He had long previously published the best-known of his many books, *Eric or Little by Little*, which, with such as *Uncle Tom's Cabin* and *Tom Brown's Schooldays*, was regarded as one of the classic illustrations of how manly Christian conduct could be a guide and inspiration to all. Farrar was a brilliant preacher and was known and respected by many of the leading scientific and literary figures of the day. In his earlier days he had been a fine teacher, critical of hidebound methods, and later became highly controversial for his unorthodox views (particularly regarding the theological doctrines of salvation and damnation in which he was notably more liberal than many of his contemporaries). Bernard Montgomery would later say, 'I do not care for the Farrar blood' but there was probably more of his Farrar grandfather in his makeup than he cared to admit –

Left: *Bishop Montgomery, Monty's father, in later life as Prelate of the Order of St Michael and St George.*

Above: *Monty's mother at the age of 14 when she became engaged to be married. Her fiancé was more than twice her age.*

Left: *The Montgomery family home, New Park, Moville, County Donegal. This now lies in the Republic of Ireland but the Montgomery family's sympathies were with the Protestants of Ulster and they did have a peripheral part in the illegal importation of arms to support the Ulster cause shortly before World War I.*

Below: *Monty's mother and father with Sibyl, their first child, pictured in their Kennington vicarage in 1883. Sibyl died young, during the family's period in Tasmania.*

interest in instruction, skill in public presentation, and unconventional ideas. It could also be said that there was a degree of ambiguity in his sexual attitudes, seen in Farrar's stories of schooldays and his relations with his pupils. Certainly the Farrar family had complicated and repressed attitudes to sex which probably had their impact on Montgomery – two of his Farrar uncles, both clergymen, were at the centre of scandals, one involving his female secretary and the other, completing the caricature, with a choirboy.

Farrar's daughter Maud was 12 when Henry Montgomery became his curate. She was 14 when they became engaged, and not yet 17 and literally only a couple of weeks out of school when they married. Henry Montgomery was nearly 34. Such a disparity would certainly cause comment now but was far less unusual in those days. Around the time of his engagement Henry was advanced to become vicar of the south London parish of St Mark's, Kennington, and the vicarage there was to be the family home until 1889 by which time there were five children of whom Bernard was the fourth. In September 1889 the family set sail for Tasmania where Henry had become the island's bishop. Bernard was not yet two and would spend the next 12 years of his boyhood on the island, apart from a brief period spent back in England in 1897.

Bishop Montgomery was not the dominant figure in the household. He was very much occupied by his church work and usually spent around half the year away on arduous travels about his extensive diocese. While Bernard clearly adored him, he seems to have had comparatively little influence on Bernard's upbringing.

Bernard's relationship with his mother was very difficult. She had been taken young from the lively, literary Farrar household to a lonely London vicarage with a new husband who was undemonstrative of his affection and often absent on parochial duties. Soon burdened not only with her own young family but also looking after the children of various relatives (a responsibility that continued in Tasmania), Maud coped by establishing a highly regimented household. A routine of schoolwork, prayers, Sunday services, and domestic duties was established for the children, and maintained by the administration of frequent corporal punishment. Among other things her children were not permitted to develop an Australian accent, tutors being brought from England to ensure that they were properly taught in this respect.

Bernard was the bad boy of the family, rebelling against his mother's discipline and often being punished for it. He summed up his mother's attitude to himself as being 'Go and see what Bernard is doing and tell him to stop it.' One revealing anecdote tells how Bernard was caught smoking and was closeted with his father for a long session of prayerful advice from which the outcome was repentance on one side and forgiveness on the other – but his mother waited outside to administer a sound thrashing to complete the lesson. On the one hand Bernard seems to have been a thoroughly poisonous little boy, rude, rebellious and disobedient, leading a group of young friends in forbidden and dangerous games, or at one point chasing a young girl around the house with a carving knife. Equally it is quite easy to see in all this the unloved child desperately craving for recognition and attention.

In 1902 the family returned to London because the bishop had accepted a new appointment as Secretary of the Society for the Propagation of the Gospel in Foreign Parts. Bernard was sent to St Paul's School, then in Hammersmith near the family's home in Chiswick. One of Bernard's older brothers, Donald, won a scholarship; Bernard did not. On his first day at the school Bernard opted,

Two views of the young Bernard Montgomery, aged 2 (above) and aged 4, with a hat to protect against the Australian sun.

without consulting his parents, to enter the school's army class. This decision did not commit him to an army career but the curriculum was more practical and scientific than the 'classical' syllabus of other classes in the school. The decision provoked a furious argument with his mother but Bernard would not change his mind. It was probably the first contest of wills with her that he had won. He was a rather mediocre scholar but did very well at sport, reaching the cricket 1st XI and captaining the rugby XV. His nickname was 'The Monkey' and an issue of the school magazine gives an interesting sketch of his style on the rugby field, 'vicious, of unflagging energy' and likely to commit such 'inconceivable atrocities' as stamping on opponents' heads. Even allowing for the exaggeration of what was meant as a humorous piece, it is not an attractive portrait.

Whether it had been his intention from the first is not known (he does not say, in his *Memoirs*, when he decided to become a solider), but Montgomery was now determined on an army career. He worked harder in his final months at school and in the autumn of 1906 he was 72nd out of 177 successful candidates in the entrance examination for Sandhurst. (A dozen years before, Winston Churchill had only succeeded at the third attempt at this examination and that after a special course of tutoring.) Montgomery was soon doing very well. After only a short time he was promoted to lance-corporal and gained places in the College's hockey and rugby teams. By his own admission this success went to his head. At the time off-duty activities at Sandhurst were little supervised and conducted by the cadets in an atmosphere of vigorous horse-play which often crossed the narrow border into viciousness. Montgomery became the ring-leader of a gang of bullies and was soon in serious trouble. While accomplices held their victim and threatened him with bayonets, Montgomery set his shirt-tails on fire. The victim was hospitalized and Montgomery would have been expelled but for the personal intervention of his mother with the Commandant. Montgomery was reduced to the ranks and missed the possibility of graduating in January 1908, instead having to stay on for a further six months.

Gentleman-cadet Montgomery had learned his lesson and realized that he should work very much harder. His family was not, by an army officer's standards, well-off and Montgomery could not expect a substantial allowance. In those days an officer, even in an unfashionable, county infantry regiment, would struggle to pay his mess bill, never mind other expenses, out of his pay. Pay in the Indian Army was higher, as were the allowances for overseas service in the British army. Montgomery, therefore, set his mind on gaining the high academic standing that would win him a place in the Indian Army. Instead he graduated a very disappointed 36th, six or eight places too low on the list. He had, however, already had contacts with the Royal Warwickshire Regiment. On 19 September 1908 he was gazetted into that regiment and was soon en route to join its 1st Battalion at Peshawar on the North-West Frontier of India.

An officer's life in India could be fairly comfortable and relaxed but the Warwicks' keen new sub-altern worked hard and remained predictably enthusiastic about sport. He learned both Urdu and Pushtu, although Indian languages were not compulsory in the British rather than the Indian Army. He passed examinations in the management of mule transport and in signalling and was put in charge of training a new force of battalion scouts. There is no evidence to support the guess but might

Top: *Monty at cricket practice at St Paul's School. Cricketing expressions remained among his favourites in later life. In particular he promised to hit Rommel for six out of Africa.*

Above: *The Sandhurst rugby XV, 1907. Monty sits aloof second from left in the back row. A common gibe against Monty was that he was only a good team player when he was captain.*

this last 'posting' not have been designed to keep the eager young nuisance quiet and out of people's way? The story is also told that, the battalion having moved to Bombay and Montgomery being the Sports' Officer, he incurred the displeasure of his superiors by disobeying instructions and fielding the strongest possible eleven for a soccer match against a side from the visiting German armoured cruiser *Gneisenau*. The Warwicks happened to have a very good team at the time and for diplomacy's sake the authorities had wanted a reasonably close game. Monty's selection won 40-0.

Whether out of his disappointment at not making the Indian Army or from his observations of life in India (as he claimed himself), or a combination of the two, Montgomery certainly developed a strong prejudice against officers from the Indian Army, believing them to be lazy and inefficient. This belief would affect his later career substantially, particularly in his dealings with Auchinleck and various of his own subordinates in the Eighth Army.

Montgomery's battalion returned to Britain at the end of 1912 and he had by then been promoted to lieutenant. Montgomery's continued hard work was rewarded by appointment as the battalion's assistant adjutant and his military education continued, helped by a captain in the battalion who had just returned from the Staff College. Monty was probably very fortunate in this contact, because, by the outbreak of World War I a few months later, fewer than 450 officers in the whole army were able to describe themselves as psc (passed Staff College).

When war came in August 1914, Montgomery served briefly as adjutant of a specially formed composite battalion but returned to his own regiment as a platoon commander in time to land in France on 23 August. He was involved in a minor attack on German positions during the Battle of Le Cateau three days later and in the very confused retreat and almost equally confused advance that followed. Montgomery performed his duties well and by early October he was a temporary captain and company commander in the rapidly developing trench system of the Aisne sector. The Warwicks were then transferred with most of the British forces to the Ypres area and on 13 October, once again a platoon commander, Montgomery was badly wounded, being shot in the chest and left leg. While recovering in hospital Montgomery learned that he had been awarded the Distinguished Service Order, an unusual award for his rank and sometimes regarded as being a 'near miss' for the Victoria Cross. Then or in later life there would be no question of his personal bravery.

It is interesting to note that Montgomery's own account of the remainder of his World War I service takes up little more than two pages in his *Memoirs*, and of this more than half is devoted to second-

The influence on Monty of his experiences during the First World War was naturally immense. For Britain it had meant raising and training a mass army as exemplified by the famous recruiting poster of Lord Kitchener (top left). The angular, mechanical, futuristic style of Nevinson's 'Troops Resting' (bottom left) suggests the depersonalizing effects of war which Monty tried to mitigate as a senior officer. Henry Dunn's 'Machine Gun Emplacement' (above) is both memento mori and, depicting American troops, a reminder of the coalition nature of the war. Finally, John Nash's 'Over the Top' (left) conveys the brutal reality of attacking prepared defences.

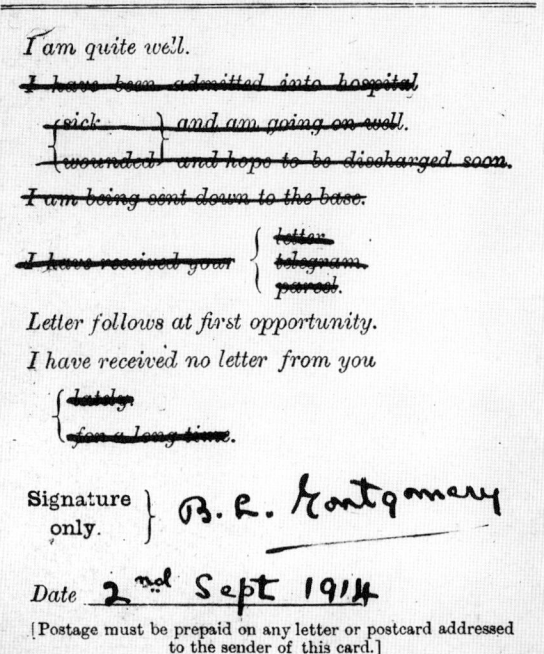

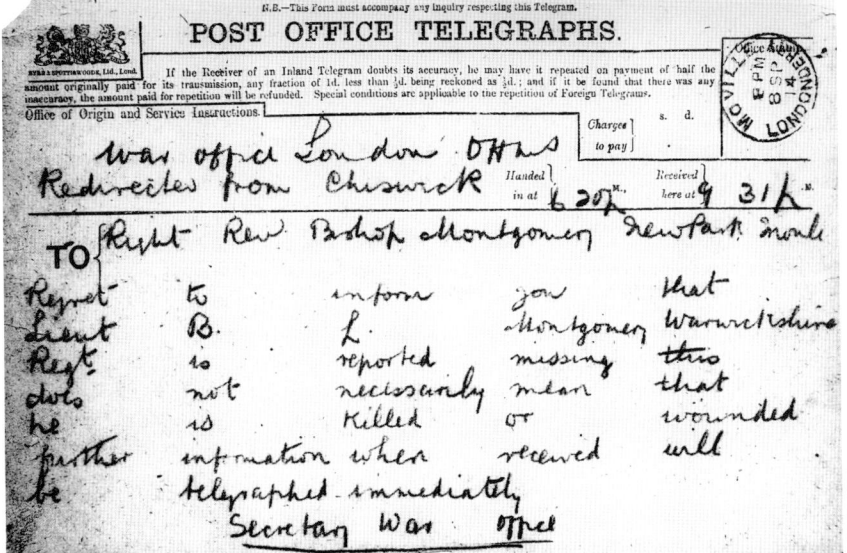

Above: *In the chaotic aftermath of the Battle of Le Cateau Monty was reported missing but by the time this telegram was sent he had already dutifully contacted his family by field postcard (top).*

hand anecdotes to illustrate how higher officers were out of touch with conditions at the front. It is also interesting that his letters at the time do not generally hint at this sort of criticism although views of this kind were clearly to have become part of his makeup before he himself reached high rank during World War II.

Monty returned to duty in February 1915 as brigade-major (effectively chief of staff) of the 112th Infantry Brigade (later redesignated 104th Brigade), with his promotion to captain made substantive. A number of New Army battalions of Kitchener volunteers trained with the brigade before it and Montgomery were sent to France about a year later. Montgomery served in this post in France for almost another year, including substantial periods at the front at the height of the Somme offensive.

At the end of January 1917 Montgomery was promoted in responsibility (he remained a captain) to GSO 2 (General Staff Officer, Second Grade) on the staff of the 33rd Division and in July became senior GSO 2 on the staff of IX Corps, even though both of the others in his grade were majors and Montgomery was still a captain. He was finally promoted brevet major in June 1918 and in July moved, as a temporary lieutenant-colonel, to be GSO 1 (chief of staff) of 47th Division. He would finish the war in this post.

In each of these jobs Montgomery was intimately involved in all the details of his trade, from the routine (but vital and by no means straightforward) staff work of supplies and march tables, discipline and administration, to planning and preparing for operations and co-ordinating infantry, artillery and other arms. It is worth noting that his principal responsibility at IX Corps was training and that for much of the time IX Corps was part of General Plumer's Second Army, well known even then for preparing its attacks in meticulous detail and executing them methodically stage by stage. Two additional points are of interest regarding aspects of his service as GSO 1 of 47th Division. One of the principles of command that Montgomery unwaveringly operated as a senior officer was that the principal staff officer of the Operations section should be a true chief of staff (that is to say with clear executive authority, regardless of rank, in the absence of the commander), with the officers of other branches of the staff – such as administration – reporting to him. This was not standard practice in the British army of 1918 (or 1942) but was the system operated by General Gorringe of 47th Division (and could only be workable when the GSO 1 retained the full trust of the general). Secondly, at 47th Division Montgomery was concerned to develop improved means of communication with the front line; he achieved this by establishing special teams, using the clumsy and unreliable radios of the day, whose duties were analagous to those of the liaison officers whom he employed during World War II.

Montgomery's next two appointments really formed part of the aftermath of World War I, so will be mentioned here. In the spring of 1919 he went to Cologne, where the British occupation army had its headquarters, and served there as a GSO 2, once more in the rank of major. Finally from September to November 1919, he commanded, very successfully, a battalion of the Royal Fusiliers. After Christmas leave, spent with his parents, he entered the Staff College at the start of 1920.

Already we are beginning to see some of the personality traits which would become more pronounced in Monty's later life. By his own account and in the unanimous judgment of his family and

Above: *Men of the 10th Battalion, the East Yorkshire Regiment, marching to the front a few days before the opening of the Battle of the Somme. This battalion, the Hull Commercials, was one of four raised from that city to join Kitchener's New Army and fight on the Somme.*

Left: *Captain Bernard Montgomery wearing the single ribbon of his DSO, shortly before he returned to France at the beginning of 1916.*

Left: *Minister for Munitions Winston Churchill attending a parade of 47th Division in Lille in October 1918. The divisional GSO 1, Lt-Col Montgomery is at front left. The two would not have their first proper meeting until 1940.*

Below: *This British ration dump at Rouen in 1917 symbolizes the way in which warfare in Montgomery's time developed into a truly material struggle.*

contemporaries, he devoted himself fiercely to his chosen profession from the moment he entered it, and with redoubled concentration after the premature death of his wife. As a young man he played a wide variety of sports, and seems to have been a useful performer in several, but no account of his life records him as having any other significant leisure interests. There is also the suspicion that his sporting exploits were motivated substantially as a means to the end of physical fitness, which he certainly valued very highly as a military virtue.

Montgomery was not alone among his comtemporaries in his considerable devotion to the study of his profession and later in his skill and ass- duity in disseminating the fruits of his researches. Alanbrooke, for example, his superior and mentor throughout World War II, developed his knowledge and career at least as conscientiously and effectively as Montgomery. He too suffered the personal tragedy of the untimely death of his (first) wife – with the additional burden of having been the driver of the car in which she was fatally injured. Yet, unlike Montgomery, he retained and developed other interests – in bird watching and photography, for example – and more importantly had the emotional maturity to overcome his grief, finding and giving happiness in a second marriage.

Monty's response to the sudden and early death of his wife, whom by all accounts he adored, was to withdraw into himself, insisting that no family members or friends attend the funeral.

Montgomery's relationship with the military world was rather more obsessional and blinkered than Alanbrooke's. His brief wooing of the 17-

year-old Betty Anderson in the 1920s seems to have consisted largely of lecturing her on military technique and tactics. Some critics might be tempted to cite this as an example of the ineptness of a confirmed bachelor and misogynist in female company, but Monty's single-mindedness extended to other areas: around the same period other officers are on record as having regarded it as something of an ordeal to sit with Montgomery at breakfast and endure even then his expositions of the military art.

Montgomery was certainly not the sort of 'decent chap' who has traditionally risen to high rank in the British army. Equally he did not share the reticence in spoken communication, verging on inarticulacy, which was common in officers of his generation, of whom Wavell is a notable example. Montgomery did share some minor habits of speech with others of his calling. 'Good morning, good morning, the general said' goes Sassoon's poem, and Montgomery, too, would often repeat such introductory remarks or comments. But however much of a bore he may have seemed to colleagues over breakfast in the mess, there is no question that, when instructing officers, issuing orders, or giving morale-boosting talks, he spoke with great clarity and forcefulness. From his letters, and his autobiographical and historical works, it is clear that the rhythms of his speech are reflected in his writing style, with short paragraphs and shorter, punchy sentences. They are predominantly composed of firm statements of fact and opinion, untempered by the doubts and qualifications with which this text, for example, is supplied.

Self-confident, then, in speech and on paper, but what of that other aspect of public presentation, dress and appearance? Montgomery was never fond of drill or ceremonial and once he became a senior officer he was equally unconventional in his attitude to uniform. He was one of the first senior officers to break with tradition and wear the utilitarian wartime battledress regularly, and his later gimmick of wearing a beret with both his own general's badge and that of the Tank Corps is also well known. And he was confident enough on this subject to dismiss a mild rebuke delivered by King George VI in person!

This book obviously features many photographs of Montgomery so a verbal description of his looks is rather superfluous. It is often said, however, that an artist's portrait can tell far more about its subject than any photograph and it is no surprise that Montgomery was a much-painted man. Equally revealing, perhaps, there is also a record of Montgomery's own opinions about some of the portraits. In the course of preparing this book I have seen a number of different portraits of Montgomery (more than can be reproduced in these pages), which all seem to share certain features. Whether the result was liked by the subject or not, each artist has portrayed a calm and thoughtful

man, perhaps a little distant, often a touch sad or melancholy. The portrait by Augustus John, which Montgomery disliked so much he refused to pay for it (he disliked John too: 'He's dirty, he drinks, and there are women in the background.'), has the thoughtfulness overlaid by hints of arrogance and disdain. By contrast the portrait by Frank Salisbury, which Montgomery displayed in his home for a time, or that by James Gunn of 1944, of which Montgomery said 'The best picture he has ever painted . . . will create a sensation at next year's Academy,' both radiate confidence, certainty and self-satisfaction. Interestingly, one of the most favourable views of Montgomery is one painted by General Eisenhower in 1951 in which the familiar

Above: *British heavy guns in action during the Somme battle in 1916.*

Below: *Monty (front row, centre) as temporary CO of the 17th Royal Fusiliers in 1919. Also in the picture is Alan Brooke (front, right), who like Monty had finished the war as a GSO 1 (in a specialist artillery post) but unlike Monty was successful in securing a nomination to the first post-war Staff College course.*

ascetic, angular features are softened into a greater appearance of benevolence. Eisenhower certainly had had ample opportunity to see the less pleasant sides of his sitter's character but perhaps his decision not to convey these is more to do with the limited skills of the amateur artist than his considered view of the man.

Mention of Eisenhower also introduces another theme which recurs at various points in Montgomery's story – his difficulties in his dealings with his equals or those in authority over him. Beginning with his turbulent relationship with his mother to his celebrated disagreements with his supreme commander in 1944-45, Montgomery at times seemed almost to take a perverse delight in making trouble for himself. Similar criticism has also been levelled at Montgomery for the brusque and unfeeling way he sacked subordinates whom he felt to be inadequate. This seems unfair. A 'good chap' might have done this more tactfully but it can certainly be argued that in wartime there is no room for such niceties. What is certainly true is that he could be astonishingly rude and insensitive in his private life. His brother Brian reports that, on leave in Ireland before what was likely to be a long posting to India, Montgomery refused to take his wife on a shopping trip to London since 'all any woman needs is one serviceable gown and a waterproof hat.' Such chauvinist brutality, too, from a man who was very obviously and very deeply in love. His relationship with his brother Brian was good also for much of their lifetimes, and yet, after promising to be free to attend Brian's wartime marriage, Montgomery went instead to a football match. Such bewildering and surely unneccessary unkindness also occurred in his professional life. The best known example here is his treatment of General de Guingand, his wartime chief of staff, on whom Montgomery relied and who saved Montgomery from likely dismissal on at least one occasion. Various incidents can be recalled but one of the most petty and yet most wounding was when de Guingand was not invited to join any official party to attend the post-war victory parade but instead had to buy tickets to a viewing stand for his wife and himself.

What has equally attracted attention is the nature of Montgomery's relationship with younger men. He gathered a lively team of young liaison officers to his headquarters during the war and in their company seems to have been particularly charming, friendly, and solicitous of their welfare. In later life he also cultivated the close company of younger men and in particular developed a curious sentimental friendship with a young Swiss boy. The likeliest explanation for this behaviour is that it was a reflection of Montgomery's emotional immaturity and inability to relate to others on equal terms, preferring instead relationships which, as the senior partner, he could control. It is possible that, on

Above: *Monty with Lucien Trueb, the young Swiss boy he befriended shortly after World War II. For several years Monty arranged to have Trueb join him on holiday and they also corresponded regularly but, although they kept in touch later, they saw little of each other once Trueb had grown up. Monty told Trueb's parents that their son reminded him of his favourite younger brother Desmond who had died in 1909.*

Montgomery's side, there was an element of homosexual motivation but even if this suggestion is accepted, there is no doubt that no form of homosexual activity involving Montgomery ever took place.

In another sense sex was certainly a source of some difficulties for Montgomery. In November 1939 following an increase in the incidence of men in his division contracting venereal diseases, Montgomery issued advice which would seem frank and explicit even in these days of 'safe sex' advertising. The order came to the notice of senior chaplains at headquarters (who believed abstinence was the only acceptable answer to the problem) and without Brooke's intervention (he was then Montgomery's corps commander) Montgomery would have been dismissed. With hindsight it seems remarkable that such a triviality could threaten an able and respected senior officer's position at a time when the army was at short notice to take part in a major campaign.

Reading between the lines of the offending order one definitely senses a deliberately cheeky and provocative tone. It is clear that throughout his life Montgomery enjoyed his reputation for controversial behaviour and speaking his mind whatever

Left: *The painting of Monty by Frank Salisbury which its subject liked well enough to display in his home. It gives a good impression of his 'Jack Russell alertness', a comparison used by several writers about Monty.*

Below: *A rather mellower Monty, as painted by Eisenhower.*

the situation. (A minor confirmation of this can be found in the quotation from the Bible which Montgomery chose to use at the beginning of his *Memoirs*, 'Yet man is born unto trouble, as the sparks fly upwards.' He had also considered *The Sparks Fly Upward* as a suitable title for the book.) In this and, it will be argued, in many other respects, his personality and character expressed themselves very openly in his generalship, the more so perhaps in that the narrow confinement of his interests to military affairs left him no other outlet for his wishes and feelings.

Montgomery therefore shows himself to be a man with little time for the niceties of life, impatient with social conventions and norms, obsessive in some respects (something which lasted throughout his life, as his attitude to gardening exemplifies: he would have his garden kept immaculate, but would not allow 'messy' flowers inside his house). Yet, it is too easy to portray Montgomery as a man of eccentricities and unpalatable idiosyncrasies; these uncomfortable snapshots can be balanced by those which show another side to Monty. All those who knew him well agree on the strength of his love for his wife, and confirm that he became a much more rounded and pleasant character under her influence. Again, there is the picture of the aged field marshal obviously moved whilst visiting military cemeteries long after the war and viewing the graves of those who had died in his battles. Reflections and doubts concerning the costs in human casualties seem to have haunted Montgomery in his decline towards senility and death, the final sad paradox in the life of a man once famous for his vitality and confidence.

To understand this extraordinary man, it is necessary to consider in more detail his rise through the ranks, and the considerable achievements to which that would lead him.

Chapter Two
Learning, Teaching and Training

Left: *British troops in Dublin, centre of Republican unrest in Ireland in 1920. Monty arrived in Cork in January 1921, when the troubles were at their height.*

At the end of World War I it was obvious that the British army would be drastically reduced in size. Montgomery was more than ever determined on developing his army career and he was certain that to do so he must first improve his military education and go to the Staff College at Camberley. He was overlooked for selection for the first post-war intake in 1919 and originally was not included for 1920 either. However, he took the chance of attendance at a tennis party to make a personal appeal to Field Marshal Robertson, British Commander-in-Chief in Germany, and this did the trick. How much Montgomery actually gained from his time at the Staff College is a matter of debate. His obituarist in *The Times* described the Staff College as 'an establishment at that time virtually innocent of any element of intellectual inquiry' and by his own admission Montgomery was far from an ideal pupil, highly critical of much that he was involved in. Some of his contemporaries certainly thought he was far too full of himself and complained that he never stopped talking.

It is not known whether, with these handicaps, Montgomery did well at Camberley (at that time students were given no indication) but it seems likely that he did since, on completion of the course, he was given a sought-after appointment in Ireland as brigade-major of the 17th Infantry Brigade at Cork, involved in the fight against the nationalists of the IRA. It was a particularly responsible appointment because the brigade had an unusually large number of units within its command. Above all, like many a counter-insurgency campaign before and since, it was a difficult and often vicious struggle. Although Montgomery was more than prepared to take strong measures he was also concerned with decent and correct behaviour and was remembered in those terms in the later recollections of one of the IRA leaders he had opposed. A truce between the British and Irish came into force in July 1921 but Montgomery's remaining ten months of Irish service were scarcely easy, with the British army often caught at least in the crossfire of the developing split between the pro- and anti-Treaty factions that would lead to the Irish Civil War.

In May 1922 Montgomery joined the 8th

Above: *Mrs Betty Montgomery in 1930. Other pictures of her, and various of her own artistic works, were destroyed with the rest of Monty's belongings in an air raid in 1941.*

Below: *Students and instructors at the Staff College in 1920. Monty is in the third row from the front, fourth from left. Monty described himself as 'critical and intolerant' at this time and the humour section of the college magazine speculated that he did not even stop talking during the two minutes' silence on Armistice Day.*

Infantry Brigade at Plymouth, again as brigade-major, and began to develop in earnest his skills as a trainer of troops. He had still more scope in this direction in his next post as GSO 2 with a Territorial Army division in York, writing and issuing a variety of instructional pamphlets, organizing courses for officers preparing for Staff College, and a variety of other activities. It was at this time also that he met and took under his wing the then Lieutenant Francis de Guingand.

Monty finally returned to regimental duty in March 1925 as a company commander with his old battalion. (It was in fact during the leave preceding the move to this post that the abortive courtship of Betty Anderson, mentioned in the previous chapter, principally took place.) There is no doubt that Montgomery transformed the training programme of the regiment greatly for the better during this appointment and equally no doubt that he alienated a good number of the battalion's officers in the process by the tactless way in which he achieved this.

The next move was his selection in July 1925 to become an instructor at the Staff College. The same month he was finally promoted to a substantive majority. The Staff College posting was to begin in January 1926 and once again Montgomery took leave before beginning his new job. He went on a skiing holiday to Switzerland, choosing to stay in the same hotel as young Betty Anderson. When she once again rejected him he was introduced to another guest, a Mrs Betty Carver. She was a widow (her first husband had been killed in World War I) with two sons aged eleven and thirteen, and was herself more or less the same age as Montgomery. She moved in literary and artistic circles and was a keen and able amateur painter and sculptor. Various members of her family were in the services including her brother, Percy Hobart, who was a noted student of armoured warfare.

The development of the romance between Betty Carver and Montgomery is a little unclear. They seem not to have met for a further year but both again chose a Swiss winter holiday at the same time and resort, which can hardly have been a coincidence. Their courtship certainly flourished during the coming months and they married on 27 July 1927, an occasion which gave Montgomery an opportunity for another example of eccentric behaviour. Montgomery would tell no one what arrangements had been made for a wedding reception or similar celebration, merely insisting that it was all in hand. Instead the family and guests saw the bride and groom simply climb into their car outside the church and drive off on honeymoon.

There is no doubt that the marriage was happy and successful. Outwardly Bernard was very much in charge, running and organizing everything and even raising the eyebrows of friends by taking over much of the 'women's work' of managing the household. In part Betty welcomed being relieved of many chores and worries but the reality was that she had far more influence than was immediately apparent. Often Bernard would publicly 'change his mind' on some matter on which he had announced a decision – after a private talk with Betty. Montgomery certainly seems to have benefited by a broadening of his horizons and in his social skills by his contact with his wife's literary and artistic friends. Their joint hospitality in the coming years as the colonel and his lady seems to have been genuinely appreciated by Montgomery's juniors and gave him a better opportunity to develop the informal teaching and man management skills that would be an important aspect of his generalship. Although it seems likely that part of Montgomery's primary motivation in seeking a wife when he did was his recognition that shortly he would be in need of a suitable hostess to support his position, equally there is no question that he lost his heart to her very thoroughly indeed.

In later life one of Montgomery's stepsons made the interesting and plausible speculation that

Above: *Vigilant British soldiers in Dublin. Monty arrived in Cork less than a month after the Black and Tans devastated the city centre, and less than two months after his own first cousin was killed by the IRA.*

Betty's calming and civilizing influence might have saved Montgomery from the worst consequences of his trouble-making and non-conformism and from earlier development of the undoubted weakness of his character. Other officers of independent mind and insubordinate attitudes like Fuller and Percy Hobart were to wreck their careers around this time; Bernard did not – quite – as shall be seen.

Betty and Bernard had one child, David, born in August 1928. While taking David to the beach one day in August 1937 Betty was bitten or stung on the foot by an insect. The wound became swollen, infected and very painful and she became very ill. She died in hospital on 19 October in her husband's arms. The passage in Montgomery's *Memoirs* in which he discusses his wife's death is sparsely but movingly written and the letter he wrote to his stepson Dick (by then an officer serving in India) is still more expressive of his sorrow and loneliness. Montgomery's first response to the loss was to withdraw into himself, ensuring that no family members or friends were present at the funeral at which he broke down completely. His brigade-major, who was present, even worried briefly about his sanity and safety until a phone call a few hours later in which Montgomery promised to be back at work in the morning. From then on his devotion to his duty was absolute.

The exclusion of family and friends from Betty's funeral was in fact the first of a series of episodes in which Montgomery distanced himself from his relations. As a young officer he had corresponded regularly and frankly with his parents and had often visited the family home and other relatives during the war and in the years since. There had been occasional upsets with his mother to be sure, but there also seemed to be a degree of mutual respect. His much-loved father had died in November 1932 at the age of 85 and Bernard had somehow come to believe that incompetent nursing by his mother had hastened his death. Bernard served overseas for most of the time between then and his own wife's death after which contact with his mother was virtually cut off. Jocelyn Carver, wife of Betty's son John, had helped attend Betty during her fatal illness and also helped to look after young David then and during the following few years. By the time of his posting to Egypt in 1942, however, Monty had decided that Jocelyn Carver was also unsuitable to care for his son. Consequently, during his school holidays, David usually stayed with a headmaster friend of his father's, Tom Reynolds and his family. Reynolds was made David's guardian and was strictly and repeatedly ordered by letter thereafter to allow David no contact with his grandmother or other members of the Montgomery family. It was as though, having had his heart broken, (and in charity his critics must accept this as the only possible description of his reaction to his wife's death) Bernard was cutting away every pos-

Above: *Monty with his son David (and teddy bear) in Egypt in 1933.*

Left: *An undated picture of Lt-Col Montgomery from around 1930.*

sible emotional connection which might hurt him. Even his concern for his son, such as it was, could hardly be described as the normal action of a loving father.

Obviously this discussion of his private life has jumped ahead several stages in Montgomery's career, which was left with his posting at the Staff College about to begin. Both at the time and certainly in retrospect, Montgomery regarded his spell instructing at Camberley as not only an opportunity to teach but also as a chance himself to study and learn. His three years overlapped with many other notable and talented officers. Colonel Alan Brooke was the chief instructor for a time and they seem to have come to know each other well and formed a high opinion of each other's abilities. Others worth mentioning who would figure later in Montgomery's life were Paget and O'Connor (fellow instructors), and Alexander, Dempsey, Leese, Nye and Tuker, who were among the students. Again, too, there were additions to the growing store of Monty anecdotes – one student

receiving zero out of a possible 500 marks for his answer to a problem because he had demonstrated his unfitness by disobeying the clear but simple instruction not to write in the margin.

Montgomery had been promoted brevet lieutenant-colonel during his time at Camberley but briefly returned, nonetheless, to his regiment as a company commander in 1929. Clearly, however, he must have been making his mark for, later that year, he was appointed secretary of a committee working to prepare a new edition of the *Infantry Training Manual, Part II*, the army's official textbook of infantry tactics, an edition which would still be in force at the beginning of World War II. Montgomery had little patience with his drafts being revised by committee and in the end contrived that the manual as printed was principally his own work. It is interesting to note that the manual has little to say on the subject of following up a success - an aspect of generalship which many would describe as Montgomery's weakest.

Montgomery returned to his regiment in the summer of 1930 as second-in-command and in January 1931 he took the battalion overseas as a substantive lieutenant-colonel and its commander. Their destination was Palestine and Montgomery became the senior officer in what was then a fairly peaceful country. He seems, however, to have neglected some of his regimental duties because of this added responsibility. Reinforcements brought from the Warwicks' 2nd Battalion were not easily integrated and Montgomery caused further problems by introducing, more suddenly and tactlessly than was sensible, his own new system of selecting and promoting NCOs.

The battalion was dispersed among various posts in Palestine and it was not until transfer to Egypt almost a year later that Montgomery could really show what he was made of. Achievement in command at this level has long been regarded as one of the hallmarks of a first-class officer and was then virtually indispensable to future advancement to senior posts. Montgomery's record would be mixed. In the small change of military life he was unconventional and a rather poor performer. He abolished compulsory church parades and had little interest in other aspects of drill and turnout. His autocratic style seems to have produced a variety of minor disciplinary crises (notably when he gave the ill-considered order that all ranks were to buy the regimental magazine) but his scruffy battalion certainly performed well on exercise and even his detractors agreed that he was a brilliant instructor. The battalion became particularly known for its skill in night operations. Some accounts suggest that this was inspired by instructions from Montgomery's brigadier; others that it originated with Montgomery himself. Either way, Montgomery was correctly to emphasize night operations and training for the remainder of his military career.

Perhaps the highlight in this respect was the exercise in which Montgomery was appointed to lead the brigade with a certain Major de Guingand as brigade-major. Their joint plan for a night move won them an overwhelming 'victory'.

Montgomery's confidential reports at the time are all highly complimentary but equally refer to 'a certain high-handedness' or a need to 'cultivate tact, tolerance and discretion'. He was definitely recommended for promotion and his superiors thought him best suited to a training or instructing post, but his grade of 'above average' rather than the highest 'outstanding' from his brigadier clearly reflected that officer's reservations about him.

At the beginning of 1934 the battalion was transferred to Poona in India, a station which placed an unusually anachronistic emphasis on ceremony, tradition and the social aspects of soldiering. Even worse, the local commander was the author of Part 1 of the *Infantry Training Manual* – the handbook on drill. Montgomery was on duty there for less than three months before going on leave but even in that short time there were a number of confrontations in which he showed a highly insubordinate attitude. Had he been longer on this station, he might well have ended his career.

Instead, while he was on leave in March 1934, he was offered an appointment as Chief Instructor at the Indian Staff College at Quetta and promotion to colonel. This was a three-year assignment and perhaps something of a sideways move (some contemporaries were already brigadiers) but, bearing in mind the situation at Poona, Montgomery wisely accepted it. Montgomery departed from Poona with a surprisingly favourable report and left behind a scandal concerning falsifying the results of the battalion's marksmanship tests.

Once again a teacher, Montgomery predictably won further commendations, both from his seniors at the time and in the retrospective recollections of his students. Montgomery and his wife were certainly very happy during this posting. Again, too, Montgomery made extra efforts to assist deserving and promising officers, ensuring for example that de Guingand was given a place at the college before he passed the age limit. Montgomery was particularly insistent on one theme during his teaching: that war with Germany was coming and that students must do their utmost to prepare themselves as fully as possible for that eventuality. The comparatively even pace of life at Quetta was only seriously disrupted by the disastrous earthquake there in May 1935. Thousands died in the town but the college, a little distance away, escaped almost completely and all personnel were for a time involved in relief work.

Montgomery finally left India in May 1937 with a promotion to command the 9th Infantry Brigade, stationed back home in England, at Portsmouth. He took up this post at the beginning of August and was already making an excellent impression in exercises when Betty became unwell. After the tragic hiatus of her final illness, the training and instructing were resumed as effectively as ever, most notably in the summer of 1938 when Montgomery organized and commanded the army side of the only significant amphibious warfare exercise conducted by the British services between the two World Wars. Montgomery was full of all the lessons to be learned but others, like Wavell, who was then GOC Southern Command, noted with dismay the ramshackle nature of the affair with almost all the troops landing from rowing boats as they might have done centuries before. To put this in context one can note that Hitler had already annexed Austria and in a couple of months more would cripple Czechoslovakia.

Left: *The military commentator Basil Liddell Hart. He and Monty met and corresponded during the 1920s and maintained a somewhat off-and-on friendship into later life. Among other matters, Liddell Hart wrote to Monty suggesting that his draft* Infantry Training Manual *should deal more extensively with exploitation, a criticism that Monty chose to ignore.*

Far left, top: *Lt-Col Montgomery, Senior Officer, Palestine, salutes King Feisal of Iraq at a parade in Jerusalem in 1931.*

Far left, below: *Monty, seen here in Alexandria with two of his wife's friends, the writer A P Herbert and his wife Gwen, who had helped Betty to settle in Chiswick, where she and Monty had conducted their courtship.*

Below: *Monty drills with his son and another officer outside the Chief Instructor's residence at Quetta, India.*

Despite the good impression he had made during the various exercises, Montgomery was again also in serious trouble. Without permission he had leased army land to a fairground operator in order to raise money for his families' welfare fund. Whether this represented genuine concern for his men or a deliberate provocation of the army's bureaucrats is open to speculation. Wavell, who recognized Monty's talents, kept the case open for long enough to allow Monty's next posting, to command 8th Division in Palestine, to take effect and finish the matter. Wavell, it is worth noting, would also be instrumental in Montgomery's subsequent move (effectively another step up) to command 3rd Divison.

Palestine in late November 1938, when Montgomery arrived, was far from the peaceful station of a few years before. Legal and illegal Jewish immigration had helped provoke an armed rising by elements of the Arab population. Montgomery was one of two divisional commanders in the country and soon took the lead in creating a firm and effective policy to defeat the rebels. By the spring of 1939 he had his area very much under control.

Shortly before he was due to return to Britain for

Below: *By November 1938, when this picture was taken, Palestine was policed by two British divisions, not the single battalion employed when Montgomery first served there. The other divisional commander in 1938 was Richard O'Connor who would serve under Monty's command as a corps commander in 1944-45.*

his next command, Monty was taken seriously ill. The doctors suspected tuberculosis and when he had to be carried aboard ship for the voyage home, it seemed that his career was over. Instead, apparently by simply putting his mind to it, Montgomery threw off whatever type of infection it was and walked off the ship in England, claiming to be completely cured. The general who was leaving 3rd Division had gone on a long leave before his formal transfer to his next post and Montgomery therefore pestered various authorities to be allowed to take over early. He had in effect done so on a semi-official basis, when full mobilization was ordered in late August. Formally this meant that all pending appointments would be frozen and, since another officer had already taken Monty's old job in Palestine, he would go into the reserve of officers waiting for employment. More desperate lobbying followed and Montgomery finally took command of 3rd Division on 28 August 1939. Britain declared war on Germany on 3rd September.

It is worthwhile pausing at this point to see where Montgomery now stood in his profession. Perhaps the best summary was the later recollection of General Wavell, describing attitudes to the then Brigadier Montgomery. 'Monty's name had come up several times in front of the selection board; everyone always agreed that he ought to be promoted, but every other commander who had a vacancy for a major-general had always excellent reasons for finding someone else more suitable than Monty.' As has also been shown, it was not just his superiors he could offend. The senior officers and the sergeants of the Warwicks had had little affection for him as a battalion commander and his less able students had often felt the force of his inability to suffer fools. On the credit side, those in a position to know agreed that he was a superb teacher of officers and men and entirely practical in his views on the management of battle. His World War I record showed that he was brave in action and suggested that he had the temperament to stand the mental strain of combat service and command. He had some important friends in high places and had just come under the command once again of Brooke who would be the most important of all. He also had a good knowledge of a wide selection of junior officers which would later be valuable in picking staff and other subordinates.

Montgomery had prepared himself relentlessly for war and had even confided in friends years before that he believed that he was somehow destined for the highest commands. He had in fact reached what would probably have been his ceiling in the peacetime army. From now on, however, as he set off for France, ability in war would outweigh any comparative defects of personality.

Above: *General Wavell who was instrumental in securing important promotions for Monty in the years leading up to World War II.*

Left: *Prime Minister Chamberlain returns from Munich and his meeting with Hitler to proclaim that he had secured peace.*

Chapter Three
Commanding the 3rd Division

Right: *Members of the BEF embark for France in September 1939.*

Adiscussion of the events from September 1939 to the fall of France can do little better than to begin with Montgomery's own scene-setting comment: 'In September 1939 the British army was totally unfit to fight a first-class war on the continent of Europe.' As he quite correctly went on to point out in his *Memoirs*, British policy until the last months of the interwar period had envisaged participation in a European war being limited mainly to the actions of air and naval forces. There was to be no 'continental commitment' of a large army, a policy motivated mainly by an understandable and laudable unwillingness to repeat the high casualties of World War I. But this betrayed a failure to comprehend that these casualties were to a large degree an inevitable comcomitant of the very substantial achievement of the British army in 1916-18 when it played the leading role in Germany's defeat.

For these reasons, as well as for economic reasons during the Depression years, the British army had been kept small and its equipment much neglected. Adequate light machine guns, anti-tank and field artillery weapons, to give some important examples, were only in the process of being introduced in 1939. Britain had pioneered the tank but now lagged behind in both quantity and quality. Indeed, throughout the war no British-made tank was anything other than second-rate. Montgomery's division went to war with requisitioned laundry vans (pilfered en route by French dockers) forming part of its transport. Again, though Britain had a larger motor industry than Germany in 1939 and would motorize her armies far more completely than the Germans ever attempted to do, the quality and reliability of many of the auxiliary vehicles were poor (a problem which would also have its effects on Monty in 1944).

The organization of the British army had been substantially disrupted in the months leading up to the war. It was inevitable that the great increases in army strength being put in hand would lead to considerable administrative complications but the doubling in size of the Territorial Army, followed quickly by the introduction of conscription (both in the spring of 1939), had been managed according more to the views of the politicians than to the practical concerns of the army's administrators. Perhaps even worse in the short term was the disruption of the army's high command, with many of the top officers exchanging jobs at a time when continuity was vital. Lord Gort, who had been Chief of the Imperial General Staff at the outbreak of war, became Commander-in-Chief of the BEF, a position in which he would prove to be inadequate. (Montgomery's description of Gort is totally apt: 'a man who did not see very far, but as far as he did see he saw very clearly.')

The new CIGS, Ironside, was also the wrong man for the Whitehall job, especially after Gort had taken two important heads of department from the War Office for his staff in France. Montgomery himself, as we have seen, was starting his third job in two years while his superior, Brooke (in command of II Corps of which 3rd Division was part), had only been in his post for a month and had held three further positions in the previous three years.

The British army was small. Only four divisions crossed to France initially and even by May 1940, when France had 100 and Germany almost 140 divisions in the field, Britain had deployed only ten (plus three divisions of untrained troops who had been sent to France for construction duties). The clear and inevitable consequence of this disparity was that France effectively dictated Allied strategy. Even more than the British, the French were still suffering from the effects, real and perceived, of World War I. Conscious of their smaller manpower than Germany's and with no wish to repeat the casualty rate of their offensives of 1914-16, the French during the 1930s had built the powerful fortifications of the Maginot Line along the Franco-

Top: *General Ironside, British Chief of the General Staff, navy minister (as he then was) Winston Churchill, General Gamelin, Allied C-in-C, and General Gort, commander of the BEF, pictured in January 1940.*

Above: *British troops begin their journey to France.*

Right: *Air raid precautions in London during the Phoney War.*

Above: *Building rather fragile-looking anti-tank defences across the Rouen-Amiens road in northern France.*

Below: *A cartoon of December 1939 has the British troops imitating a popular song of the time and hanging out the washing on the Siegfried Line (the German border defences).*

theless in November 1939 the Allied Supreme War Council (i.e. Britain and France) adopted as their war plan a scheme for the strongest parts of their northern armies to make an advancing right wheel into Belgium to take up a defensive line on the River Dyle east of Brussels in the event of a German attack. The assumption supporting this plan was that Germany would inevitably attempt to repeat the strategy of 1914's Schlieffen Plan with a strong right wing sweeping round through Belgium towards northern France. What the French high command neglected was the section of France's frontier opposite Luxembourg and the southernmost part of Belgium. This was the wooded and hilly area of the Ardennes which in a stunning example of military folly (to be repeated in 1944) was regarded as being entirely unsuitable terrain for a German attack.

the Franco-German border. But instead of using this resource to economize on manpower and create mobile reserves, the French army had become entirely dominated by thoughts of defence. Insufficient money had been found to extend the Maginot Line along France's border with Belgium and Luxembourg and by 1939 it was virtually certain that if Germany attacked it would be in this area. The best trained and equipped French forces were accordingly sent to the northern armies and the BEF was also deployed there.

The British and French rightly judged that Hitler would have no respect for Belgian or Luxembourgeois neutrality (nor for Dutch neutrality in the event). The Belgians were afraid to do anything that might provoke German hostility, however, and therefore would not even consider any form of military co-operation talks with the Allies. None-

Before looking in more detail at Montgomery and the BEF, two further deficiencies in the French organization should be mentioned. The C-in-C, General Gamelin, was elderly and out of touch in every way with the realities of modern warfare – literally so in that the radio and telephone equipment of his headquarters was so scanty as to be almost non-existent. Even more astonishingly, so many forces were to be committed to the advance into Belgium that there would be no significant strategic reserve.

The BEF had its own problems, as we have seen, and Montgomery at least was doing his best to address these. Even before crossing to France at the end of September 1939, Montgomery had conducted a variety of small-scale exercises for his division and had ensured that returning reservists had been given at least some refresher training. He was already drawing lessons from these experiences and translating them into strategies for the future. Characteristically, also, he had lectured the battalion commanders and other senior officers on his basic operational policies. This emphasis on keeping his subordinates informed was from now on to be a cornerstone of his generalship.

The winter months of 1939-40 may have been the Phoney War or Sitzkrieg to cynical commentators but it was far from an idle time for Montgomery's 3rd Division. Almost alone among the Allied commanders he devised and carried out an effective programme of rehearsals for the forthcoming advance into Belgium and, with impressive prescience, he also practised the retreats and complicated changes of direction by night that would be the main story of the campaign for the division and the BEF. Brooke, who was certainly the most effective of the more senior British officers, was enormously impressed by his subordinate, describing in glowing terms how Montgomery grew into his job, seeming to become more and more able with every passing day. Brooke's later advocacy in favour of appointing Montgomery to the Eighth

Above: *The German tank forces in 1940 included a large number of powerful tanks of Czechoslovak design and manufacture (as seen here in France) which had been taken into German service after the destruction of their country of origin.*

Left: *A common sight during the Phoney War were propaganda banners at border points to appeal to the enemy troops. This German example proclaims Hitler's supposed peaceful intentions towards France.*

Above: *British vehicles, probably from Monty's 3rd Division, in the streets of Louvain, May 1940. The nearest carrier mounts an anti-tank rifle. Even by 1940 these were inadequate in the infantry anti-tank role.*

Army would be based squarely on the good opinions he formed of him during the Phoney War period, which were confirmed in May 1940.

Montgomery's divisional exercises, however, were principally devoted to problems of movement. This was correctly judged to be one of the first things that a division should practise as a formation, but it is revealing of the low standards of training of even the regular divisions of the BEF that proficiency in these basic techniques could not be relied on.

It was Montgomery's obvious efficiency that prompted Brooke's intervention in the venereal disease scandal alluded to in Chapter One. Once again Montgomery had played with fire in what could almost be described as an adult version of the attention-seeking mischief of his childhood days. Again, typically, he meekly acknowledged the justice of Brooke's ferocious reprimand – he would always be more respectful of seniors who were quick to assert their authority and whose abilities he esteemed.

The 3rd Division and its commander continued with the programme of exercises and work on the frontier defences throughout the bitter, unusually severe, winter of 1939-1940. The Prime Minister, Neville Chamberlain, came to visit and in a breathtakingly naïve conversation with Montgomery expressed the opinion that Germany would not attack. Montgomery disagreed. He was equally shocked during a visit to slovenly and inefficient French units on the Maginot Line and made his feelings known to Brooke. Brooke had already formed identical opinions of the poor morale and capabilities of much of the French army but for Gort at headquarters such ideas constituted not so much realism as rather unwelcome pessimism when what the situation demanded was wholehearted co-operation with an ally.

Gort had plenty of additional problems. He never achieved a satisfactory organization for his headquarters to balance the extensive bureaucratic requirements of administering and expanding the BEF against the need for a far smaller and more mobile operational command post to respond in the event of active operations. Communications were woeful between GHQ and units of the BEF and were often poor between departments within GHQ itself. Communications between Gort and his various masters were also dreadful and French security restrictions prevented any radio command exercises being organized. Brooke had had to fight hard to get permission for Montgomery to carry out his movement schemes but Gort did not follow this excellent example and failed even to organize any map exercises.

Gort, it must be said, had a difficult position in the Allied chain of command. In some respects he was obviously answerable to London and had the right of appeal to London if he believed that a French order was dangerous to the existence of the BEF. Gort was under the immediate control of General Georges, commanding the French armies on the north-east front, but Gamelin also issued some orders directly to Gort. There was also a third level, under Georges, that of General Bilotte who commanded the French 1st Army Group and had co-ordinating responsibility for the actions of the BEF. The situation could be summed up by saying that there was no clear chain of command and that the physical means of communication were so poor that any consultation or passing of orders would have to be done by personal visits between one commander and another.

Above: *British troops cross the border into Belgium in May 1940.*

Viewing this depressing background with the benefit of hindsight, it is no surprise that the campaign of 1940 developed disastrously for the Allies. We now know, however, that it was only in the air that the German forces enjoyed a significant numerical and qualitative advantage in terms of manpower and equipment. The fall of France is often described as a victory for Germany's tank forces but it is worth remembering that the French had more and rather better tanks than Hitler's armies in 1940. The secret of the German success was instead to be found in the organization of the panzer forces. In practice this entailed the concentration of the tanks into powerful armoured divisions and groups of divisions, and the intimate co-operation within them of their tank and infantry components, all in close contact with the supporting and dominant Luftwaffe.

Naturally, as one divisional commander of roughly 140 on the Allied side (counting the Belgian and Dutch forces), it was not given to Montgomery greatly to affect the overall course of events, but to understand Montgomery's role, it is important to get an overview of the situation. The German offensive began on 10 May 1940 with powerful tank forces driving west through the Ardennes, coupled with subsidiary but powerful assaults farther north into Belgium and Holland. The Dutch surrendered on the 15th around the time when the French and British forces, which had moved according to plan into Belgium, were beginning to meet the advancing Germans. A little to the south, however, the German tank forces were already across the Meuse at Dinant and Sedan and were bursting out of their bridgeheads there in what would prove to be a lightning drive to the Channel coast. They would reach the Channel on the 20th and the Allied armies would be cut in two. The British and French to the north fell back to the coast under attack from the east and south. Finding themselves trapped by the advancing Germans, the Allies were saved from annihilation when, between 26 May and 4 June, 226,000 British soldiers and 112,000 French were evacuated from Dunkirk and the beaches nearby. The Belgians capitulated on 28 May. The Germans then completed the débâcle by attacking south into the rest of France. The French government agreed an armistice on 22 June.

What did Major-General Montgomery do in the days between 10 May and the morning of 1 June when he left Dunkirk aboard the destroyer *Codrington*? The planned advanced into Belgium went virtually perfectly with 3rd Division taking up positions around Louvain. The first German attacks on Montgomery's front were carried out on

Below: *A German photo of a knocked-out French B 1 tank in the streets of a French town.*

Above: *Lines of troops await evacuation from Dunkirk.*

Above right: *British troops disembark from a crowded destroyer in a British port after the hazardous trip from Dunkirk.*

Bottom right: *The shrinking perimeter around Dunkirk.*

the morning of 15 May. To put this fully into context, it was on this same morning that Churchill was awakened by a phone call from French Premier Reynaud saying that the battle had been lost following the German breakthrough at Sedan and that the Dutch armed forces had that same morning surrendered. Already Montgomery had begun his routine of travelling round his units for much of the day, leaving his staff to work on the details of administration; he would return to his HQ in the evening to issue orders and then, after dinner, retire early to bed, with strict instructions that he was not to be disturbed except in a real crisis. Montgomery himself tells the story of how angry he was to be woken one night during this period to be told that the Germans were moving into Louvain. He claims to have reprimanded the officer who woke him, issued the briefest order to throw the Germans back and then gone back to sleep. The 3rd Division did indeed defend its position at Louvain successfully during the 15th and 16th.

Montgomery's insistence in keeping himself fresh and alert was to become almost proverbial. There is no doubt that in this and all his later campaigns he would succeed in remaining confident and decisive when other senior officers would become worn down by strain and lack of sleep. Perhaps the only surprising thing about the Louvain incident was that the staff officer had decided to wake his general at all. Monty was already notorious for instantly sacking those who did not measure up to his expectations. The corollary of this, of course, was that his method of command relied on delegation of responsibility and allowing people to do their jobs so that he could do what he thought was his. Horrocks, who would be one of Montgomery's most trusted and important subordinates for most of the later part of the war, was then a battalion commander in 3rd Division and subsequently wrote of how impressed he was by the clarity of any orders he received from Monty and by the inspiring air of confidence that Monty imparted.

With Allied forces in disorder on each flank and some parts of the BEF defending less ably than Brooke's II Corps, retreat from Louvain and the line of the Dyle was inevitable. Now Montgomery's winter exercises came into their own. By 23 May 3rd Division had pulled back in a series of well-managed and hence largely uneventful moves to the old positions on the French frontier around Roubaix. There were still hopes that an attack southward by the BEF and French forces would succeed in breaking through the German encirclement but these were never realistic. On the 25th Gort finally abandoned the idea and the Dunkirk evacuation was on.

It is generally believed that Brooke's generalship, made effective in large part by the high quality of Montgomery's 3rd Division, was principally responsible in the coming days for ensuring that the BEF could be successfully evacuated, despite the crisis caused by the final disintegration and surrender of the Belgian forces. The most obvious achievement of Montgomery's division was on the night of 27/28 May when it completed perfectly one of the most difficult manoeuvres which any formation could be asked to perform. The division was required to leave its existing positions and move by night, along minor roads a short

distance behind the front line, negotiating crowds of stragglers, deserters, refugees and broken-down and abandoned vehicles, crossing the communications of the front line units behind which it was passing, ultimately to take up new positions and be in good order to defend these by morning. Brooke's comment on the successful completion of the move by Montgomery and his staff was simple: 'he had, as usual, accomplished almost the impossible.'

By 29 May 3rd Division was forming part of the Dunkirk perimeter and perhaps the clearest evidence of its commander's control was that he still had under command over 13,000 men from an establishment of some 14,000. On the 30th Montgomery was appointed to the temporary command of II Corps (Brooke had been ordered to go home) despite being the most junior of the corps' major-generals. Gort, too, had been ordered home and at his first conference as corps commander Montgomery had the nerve and confidence to take Gort aside and warn him that his choice of successor was unwise. Montgomery suggested that General Alexander would do a far better job. Alexander in fact took over on 31 May and most commentators would agree that Monty had been right, for Alex's calm style played an important part in the success of the final days of the Dunkirk evacuation.

Montgomery spent his last hours near Dunkirk helping to organize affairs on the beaches and then, once his men were away, in the early hours of 1 June he walked over to the harbour at Dunkirk and his rescuing destroyer. In the middle of the afternoon on that same day he reported to the War Office in London.

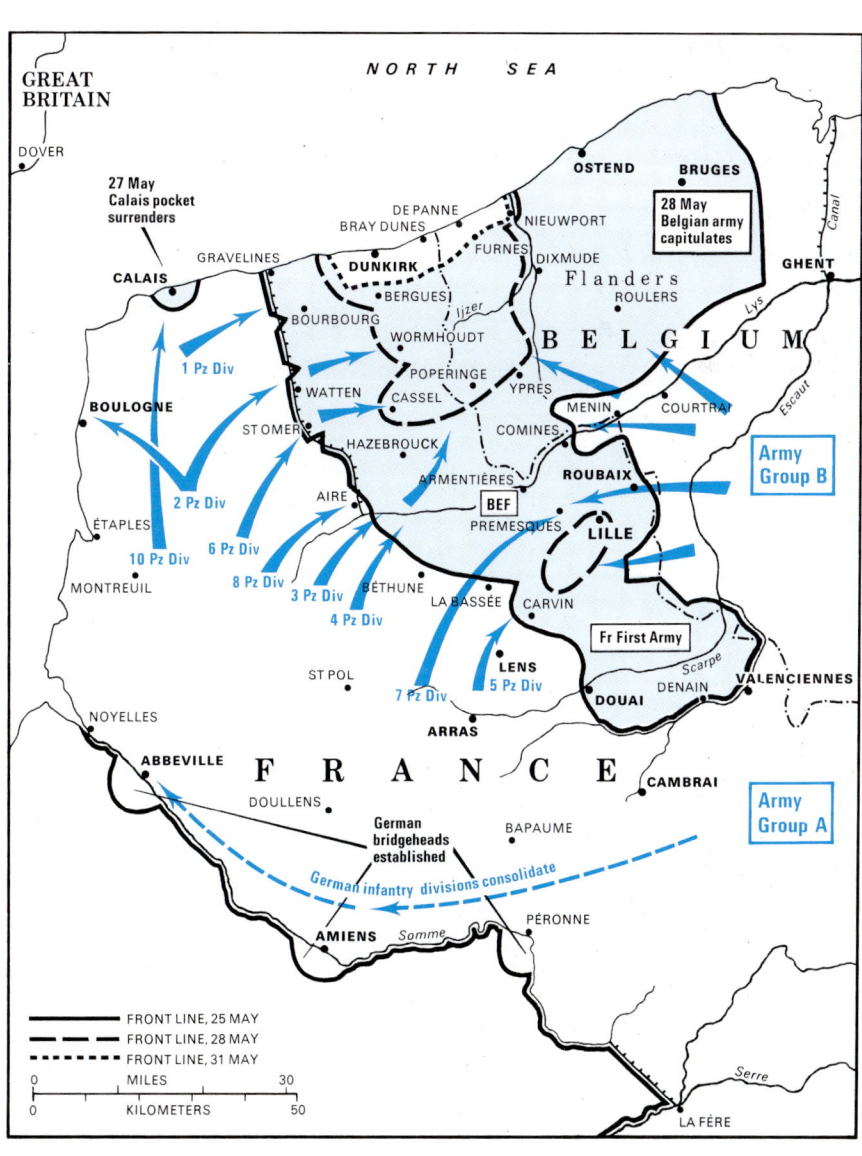

Chapter Four
Do You Have 100% Binge?

Left: *Anti-invasion defences, southern England, 1940. Monty generally opposed the creation of this sort of fixed installation.*

Monty

Montgomery may have impressed those who had dealings with him during the disaster in France with his freshness and calm in the face of stress and defeat, but he belied that appearance by his rash and outspoken conduct on his return to London. In an interview with the CIGS (now General Dill) the day after he got back from Dunkirk, Montgomery was deeply critical of Gort's performance in command of the BEF and, by his own account, laughed out loud at Dill's description of how serious Britain's position was. It was perhaps appropriate to speak frankly in a private meeting with the professional head of the army, but from other reports of the time Montgomery was clearly letting his low opinion of a variety of senior officers become well known.

Fortunately, there was no questioning the effectiveness of his own performance in France and he was immediately re-appointed to command 3rd Division. A further tribute to the efficiency of the formation and its commander was its selection to receive priority in re-equipment from the almost bare cupboard of supplies for the army, which had left virtually all its heavy equipment at Dunkirk.

Monty and the 3rd Division were earmarked for an early return to France with the 'second BEF' which was briefly planned for and rapidly cancelled in the light of the complete and final collapse of French resistance following the renewed German attacks. In the end Montgomery was to remain in England until August 1942, preparing to defend against the threatened German invasion and at every opportunity tirelessly training himself and his various commands to the highest standards of efficiency. During this period Monty's career continued to progress. He did not remain long at 3rd Division, for on 22 July 1940 he was promoted to lieutenant-general and took over V Corps, defending the Dorset and Hampshire areas. On 27 April 1941 he was transferred to XII Corps in Kent and on 17 November that year was promoted to head South Eastern Command which he unofficially renamed South Eastern Army. He would still be in that post in August 1942 when the sequence of changes began that would take him to the desert and Alamein.

Below: *Monty takes the salute at the parade of a school Officer Training Corps in June 1942 when he was GOC South-Eastern Command.*

Do You Have 100% Binge?

The first characteristic of this whole period that immediately strikes any student of Montgomery's life was the exponential growth that took place in Monty anecdotes. He became notorious in the British army, far outside the confines of his own commands, for his energy and enthusiasm, for his bizarre exhortatory slogans and his disconcerting insistence on physical fitness. Such recollections pop up in some surprising places:

> The Corps commander was a dynamic little man who demanded a fearsome standard of mental alertness and physical fitness. Just inside his headquarters was a large notice board.... 'Are You 100% Fit? Are You 100% Efficient? Do You Have 100% Binge?' We never discovered what he meant by 'Binge' because nobody dared to ask him.

This was the testimony of the actor and raconteur David Niven (then a junior officer) while the humorist Spike Milligan has recorded his (and his comrades') contemporary distaste for compulsory cross-country runs when these were introduced in the Royal Artillery battery in which he was a gunner. Although Montgomery's later fame was principally responsible for his appearance in the memoirs of such 'hostilities only' soldiers, it is very clear that Montgomery was by now making his mark in the new wartime army as he had already done in the narrower circles of the regular forces.

To many at the time Montgomery's methods were distasteful for more substantial reasons than an aversion to physical exercise. He earned no friends in 3rd Division by briefly trying to stop all leave while the division was re-equipping after Dunkirk. Later he gave strict orders that officers' wives were not to live in the V Corps area in case the officers were distracted from their duties by worries about the safety of their loved ones in the event of a German invasion. This was much resented at the time and often secretly disobeyed. (In those more class-conscious days there was no question of Other Ranks being allowed their families nearby.) Also productive of great resentment was Montgomery's ruthless dismissal of those

---

Issued by the Ministry of Information **in co-operation with the War Office and the Ministry of Home Security**

Beating the INVADER

A MESSAGE FROM THE PRIME MINISTER

IF invasion comes, everyone—young or old, men and women—will be eager to play their part worthily. By far the greater part of the country will not be immediately involved. Even along our coasts, the greater part will remain unaffected. But where the enemy lands, or tries to land, there will be most violent fighting. Not only will there be the battles when the enemy tries to come ashore, but afterwards there will fall upon his lodgments very heavy British counter-attacks, and all the time the lodgments will be under the heaviest attack by British bombers. The fewer civilians or non-combatants in these areas, the better—apart from essential workers who must remain. So if you are advised by the authorities to leave the place where you live, it is your duty to go elsewhere when you are told to leave. When the attack begins, it will be too late to go; and, unless you receive definite instructions to move, your duty then will be to stay where you are. You will have to get into the safest place you can find, and stay there until the battle is over. For all of you then the order and the duty will be: "STAND FIRM".

This also applies to people inland if any considerable number of parachutists or air-borne troops are landed in their neighbourhood. Above all, they must not cumber the roads. Like their fellow-countrymen on the coasts, they must "STAND FIRM". The Home Guard, supported by strong mobile columns wherever the enemy's numbers require it, will immediately come to grips with the invaders, and there is little doubt will soon destroy them.

Throughout the rest of the country where there is no fighting going on and no close cannon fire or rifle fire can be heard, everyone will govern his conduct by the second great order and duty, namely, "CARRY ON". It may easily be some weeks before the invader has been totally destroyed, that is to say, killed or captured to the last man who has landed on our shores. Meanwhile, all work must be continued to the utmost, and no time lost.

The following notes have been prepared to tell everyone in rather more detail what to do, and they should be carefully studied. Each man and woman should think out a clear plan of personal action in accordance with the general scheme.

Winston S. Churchill

STAND FIRM

1. What do I do if fighting breaks out in my neighbourhood?

Keep indoors or in your shelter until the battle is over. If you can have a trench ready in your garden or field, so much the better. You may want to use it for protection if your house is damaged. But if you are at work, or if you have special orders, carry on as long as possible and only take cover when danger approaches. If you are on your way to work, finish your journey if you can.

If you see an enemy tank, or a few enemy soldiers, do not assume that the enemy are in control of the area. What you have seen may be a party sent on in advance, or stragglers from the main body who can easily be rounded up.

Left: The stark reality of the summer of 1940 in a British government public information leaflet.

Above: A woman worker in the hop fields of Kent doubles as an anti-aircraft lookout.

who, in his characteristic expression, he believed to be 'useless, quite useless'. He sacked people from V Corps HQ on his first day and then went out and sacked some more from his subordinate formations, while within ten days of arriving at XII Corps he had got rid of three brigadiers and six battalion or regimental commanding officers. Much of this was no doubt a very necessary clearing out of dead wood but some of it was probably unjust and wasteful. To Montgomery's detractors all these aspects added up to a commander weakened and distorted by publicity-seeking and the creation of what might even be called a cult of personality.

Once again Montgomery also had important quarrels with superiors. For most of his time at V Corps his boss at Southern Command was General Auchinleck. The two never saw eye to eye. Following his dismissals of the 'useless', Montgomery was now beginning to establish an extended family of favoured subordinates and he was prepared to

Above: *A group of American residents in Britain who chose to join the Home Guard.*

Top right: *Anti-invasion exercises.*

Above right: *The Auk, General Claude Auchinleck with whom Monty quarrelled in 1940.*

Left: *Under the pressure of war and the determined leadership of the more able generals like Monty, training grew more realistic. The Bren gun in this photo is clearly firing live ammunition.*

pull strings in various ways to ensure that the people he wanted indeed came to work for him, to fill the vacancies he was so often creating. Unfortunately he chose to do this by openly flouting Auchinleck's authority and trying specifically to overturn arrangements for personnel that Auchinleck had made. A further dispute occurred when, at the height of the invasion fears, Auchinleck ordered that every soldier should keep his personal weapon with him at all times. Montgomery thought this silly and in an open act of insubordination ordered that this instruction should not apply in the V Corps area.

The heart of the dispute with Auchinleck seems to have been a genuine disagreement on policy. Montgomery was convinced that the only way to defeat invasion was to build up and train mobile reserve forces ready to move rapidly against any landing that the Germans might develop. Auchinleck had laid greater stress on fortifying and defending possible landing beaches, fearing that, if the Germans once succeeded in getting a significant force ashore, the undertrained and ill-equipped British army of 1940 would never be able to defeat them. Both points of view have much to recommend them and it is difficult now to be as sure that Montgomery was right as he was himself. It is certainly true that Montgomery's preferred plan was the better one as more equipment and trained men became available (and the beach defences grew stronger) during 1941 and 1942. It is worth noting that Brooke (who commanded Home Forces from July 1940) independently agreed with Montgomery while Rommel, who would face a similar problem in 1944, would take the opposite course. As for Montgomery, a point of interest is that, once he had one significant disagreement with his superior, he had no respect left for him.

Another powerful supporter for the idea of not being tied to beach defences in a Maginot Line mentality was Winston Churchill (who became Prime Minister in May 1940). The two men actually met for the first time on 2 July 1940 when Montgomery still led 3rd Division. Montgomery carefully laid on an impressive inspection for his important visitor and also took the opportunity to argue forcefully that, if allowed to requisition some civilian buses from Brighton nearby, he would make his division much more mobile for the role he favoured. The result was one of the famous 'Action This Day' minutes by which, among other things, Churchill was transforming Britain's previously lethargic war effort. And Montgomery naturally got his buses.

This meeting was also the source of one excellent

anecdote. Montgomery drank water at dinner with Churchill that evening and, when challenged about this, told the Prime Minister that he neither drank nor smoked and was 100 per cent fit. Churchill's famous reply was that he both drank and smoked (a lot of both, as we now know) and was 200 per cent fit. Another story told of that day is that at one point Monty said to Churchill, 'I don't see how on earth we can win this war,' to which the all-too-realistic reply was, 'Nor do I.'

It was, of course, during this period that Montgomery's obsession with physical fitness really came to the fore. He says himself in his *Memoirs* that by this time his military ideas had become fixed and that the first essential to be tackled by a leader was the question of physical and mental fitness. The most obvious simple manifestation of this was his order that all officers and men, whatever their military occupation, should participate in weekly cross-country runs. Middle-aged majors and colonels with administration jobs protested that they would die if made to run. Montgomery replied that he preferred that they run and die when they could be easily replaced, rather than collapse through strain in a time of emergency when they would be missed.

Far more important than simply sending the unfit out to run was the wide-ranging programme of exercises, schools and lectures that Montgomery ensured was created in each of his commands. He noted proudly, and it was a just claim, that many of his methods spread gradually through the whole army far beyond his own areas of responsibility. The focal point of all his training was the set-piece Montgomery presentation, summarizing the lessons to be learned from what had transpired in the course of the manoeuvres. All who were present at these post mortems comment on the absolute relevance and decisive clarity of all Montgomery's remarks and how evident it was that he was constantly working to create the sort of hard-headed professionalism that he and every other good judge recognized to be essential if the war was to be won. These lectures also contributed to the fund of Monty anecdotes; for example, by his express instruction, there was to be no coughing or smoking at any time.

The exercises that Montgomery conducted

Main picture: *Churchill inspecting coastal defences in July 1940.*

Inset: *The Prime Minister poses with a Thompson submachine gun during a tour of army units.*

Above: *Soldiers from a wrecked landing craft are rescued during the Dieppe operation.*

embraced a wide variety of subjects and techniques and were clearly designed with far more than anti-invasion measures in mind. River crossings following an advance, the use of paratroops, working with supporting air forces, co-operation between tank and infantry units of varying composition, were only a few among the techniques practised, assessed, and, when perfected, studied in final form. Always emphasized was the virtue of concentration so that divisions fought united as divisions and artillery in particular was not wastefully dispersed, by either physical separation or poor communications. Montgomery's claim that his military ideas were now fixed seems unlikely because it is clear that these exercises helped his own development as substantially as that of his subordinates. One can certainly see his understanding of what is and is not practical in military reality, and his mastery of the habits of command, improving throughout this time.

The clarity of Montgomery's views and his ability to discern and teach essentials are perhaps best illustrated by the violent impact he had after his transfer to XII Corps in Kent in April 1941. As well as dismissing senior officers en masse and sending away officers' wives, he immediately overturned the previous anti-invasion policies. These had been based around a system of defence lines. For this 'Maginot-minded nonsense', Monty substituted a single, clear policy. A handful of important locations were to be held and any German incursions were to be defeated by the strong reserves created by the abandonment of unnecessary fixed positions.

We have already seen when he was a battalion commander that Montgomery's touch was not always sure in the manipulation of the morale of his men. The term manipulation is used deliberately because it is now a commonplace that a commander must be, in the jargon of modern management, proactive in this respect and always conscious of the effect on morale of his actions if he is to be successful. This was a lesson which Montgomery, so isolated by the peculiarities of his own private life, was slow to learn and only really appreciated from about this time. He had come to realize that, especially in a wartime citizen army, most soldiers would not share his own complete dedication to their work, disregarding all else.

One aspect of Montgomery's development in this respect could be seen in the conscious theatricality of his formal presentations, in which he strove to create and communicate a consistent image of control and hard-driving professionalism. He saw this as an essential first step to the actual development of these qualities among his subordinates. Related to this idea was his understanding of the importance of communication in the larger sense of keeping every soldier fully informed of his commander's broad intentions and how the individual's efforts contributed to that. Montgomery clearly realized that the national service army of 1940 onwards was composed of men who generally expected army life to be 'nasty, brutish and short' with ordinary soldiers thoughtlessly led and poorly treated. Instead Montgomery always took great trouble to ensure that plans were explained all the way down the line to every private soldier. Certainly those under his command would rarely be ignorant of why they were being asked to fight or feel that he or his staff had been careless of their lives by poor planning or administration. What was earlier described as the cult of personality created by Montgomery was part of this concern – that whenever possible the soldier's actions should be made more meaningful by being directed by a real and not a faceless individual.

Unfortunately this statement of Montgomery's military virtues cannot stand unqualified for long, as on his shoulders must rest a degree of responsibility for the poor planning and high casualties of the Dieppe raid. By 1942 the Western Allies were planning seriously for an eventual invasion of Western Europe. Fond hopes that this could begin in 1942 were soon abandoned as impractical. A number of small-scale raids had previously been carried out, mostly by British commando forces, and it was decided to extend these by a large effort with the dual purpose of investigating methods of quickly capturing a useful port, and perhaps also causing the Germans to divert some attention away from the Eastern Front where the Red Army was in need of all the help it could get. The original idea, the selection of Dieppe, and the outline plan were none of them of Montgomery's making but the troops taking part were mostly drawn from South Eastern Army and operational authority on the army side was ultimately his. The raid eventually took place on 19 August, by which time Montgomery was already installed as commander of Eighth Army in

Do You Have 100% Binge?

Egypt, but it had been scheduled, with virtually identical plans approved by Montgomery, for early July, only to be postponed by bad weather. In the event it was a disaster for a large number of reasons, the most frequently cited being the totally inadequate preliminary air and naval bombardments and many detailed faults in the preparation and equipment of the landing forces. Most authorities agree that these problems should have been almost self-evident and that the failure to address them must partly be Montgomery's.

In early August 1942 Montgomery travelled to Scotland to observe manoeuvres there but on the 7th he received new orders to return immediately to England to replace General Alexander in command of the British ground forces being prepared for the Anglo-American landings in north-west Africa that would take place as Operation Torch in November. Alexander had been transferred to be the new Commander-in-Chief, Middle East. On the 8th, after Montgomery's return to England, his orders were changed again. He was now to go to Egypt to take over Eighth Army under Alexander's command. He had not always been fortunate in the way the vagaries of military postings and seniority had allowed his career to develop but now he was being given what was clearly the best job in the army for an officer of his rank at that time. He would practically have first call on the military resources of the British Empire and had a notable opponent to face up to – it was clearly a great opportunity, if he could be successful.

Above: *Early models of the Churchill tank knocked out on the beach at Dieppe. Among the problems of the landing was the lack of proper information about the composition and gradient of the beaches, a fault that would be remedied by 1944.*

Left: *Alan Brooke, who with Alexander was instrumental in gaining Monty's promotion to command the Eighth Army in North Africa.*

Chapter Five
Earning Laurels in Africa

Left: *Unloading tanks for Rommel's forces at Tripoli. Allied interdiction on the Axis supply routes became increasingly effective as the African campaign proceeded.*

Above: *A German machine-gun team in a typical desert foxhole.*

Below: *German infantry moving up to the front across typically hard and featureless desert.*

Right, above: *Alexander (left), Churchill, Monty, and Brooke. Churchill visited Egypt to set in train the command changes on his way to see Stalin. He is here shown during his stopover on the way back when he was delighted with the improvements Monty had already made.*

Right, below: *New Zealanders man a machine-gun overlooking part of the Alamein position.*

The story of the desert war in 1940-42 was one of widely fluctuating fortunes with spectacular long advances being followed by reverses and retreats. The early summer of 1942 had been a phase of triumph for the German and Italian forces. They had first won a hard-fought and protracted series of battles on the so-called Gazala Line, west of Tobruk, and then driven forward to seize Tobruk itself along with a great mass of British supplies. The Axis strategy for the Mediterranean had then planned for forces to be diverted to capture the British-held island of Malta but Rommel, commanding *Panzerarmee Afrika*, would have none of this and hurried his forces on into Egypt, becoming at times intermingled in the chaos with the retreating columns of British and Empire troops. An attempted British stand at Mersa Matruh was soon overcome but during July, in the area around an insignificant railway halt called El Alamein, the German advance was fought to a standstill. This last series of engagements is sometimes referred to as the First Battle of El Alamein.

It was clear to Churchill and his advisers that the Gazala battles should never have been lost, particularly bearing in mind Eighth Army's substantial resources and the superiority held by the RAF over the Luftwaffe in the battle area. General Brooke, now CIGS, accordingly planned a fact-finding trip to Egypt and Churchill decided to come too, en route to visit Stalin in Moscow. The upshot of their visit was a decision to replace Auchinleck as Commander-in-Chief, Middle East, with General Alexander; General Gott, a corps commander, was to take over Eighth Army which had also been under Auchinleck's personal command. Montgomery's name had come up in the various discussions and he had initially been Brooke's and Auchinleck's favoured candidate for the Eighth Army job. No sooner was Gott appointed than he was killed when the transport aircraft taking him back to Cairo was shot down, so Montgomery finally got his opportunity.

Montgomery's arrival in Egypt on the morning of 12 August 1942 is often claimed to have signalled a profound change in the direction of Allied strategy. The most enthusiastic of Montgomery's admirers (with strong support from the Field Marshal's later recollections) describe how, on his arrival, Eighth Army was ready to retreat from any German attack, give up control of Egypt and fall back into Palestine and the Sudan. Instead, they

argue, Montgomery instantly gave orders that there should be no retreat. He then created and established the defensive plan which was successfully carried out during the Battle of Alam Halfa, while preparing from the start for the offensive that would be the Battle of El Alamein. The contrary view is that Montgomery found already established, and falsely claimed as his own, the defensive layout used at Alam Halfa and that, far from expecting to retreat, Auchinleck had already begun preparations for an offensive similar to that eventually carried out.

Finding the truth among these opposing views is not easy, for the controversy has been bitter and personal. Auchinleck threatened to sue Montgomery for libel over one of the relevant passages in Monty's *Memoirs* and the publishers had to insert a disclaimer in later editions. Similarly Churchill's publishers inserted an amplifying footnote to a passage in Churchill's *History of the Second World War* after Auchinleck's assistant, General Dorman-Smith, also threatened legal action. Montgomery's various descriptions of the events concerning his takeover of Eighth Army certainly do not show him in the best light, for they are clearly 'economical with the truth'. To add to the difficulty, Montgomery's 'detractors' also draw heavily on the testimony of senior officers who would fall from grace with Montgomery's appointment, while the officers most often quoted by Montgomery's 'supporters' are usually those he promoted and who would serve with him later in the war.

Some further background details are necessary before assessing the competing claims. General Auchinleck had hoped that the series of attacks undertaken during July 1942 (the First Battle of Alamein) would force Rommel to retreat and end the threat to Egypt, not only for its own sake but also because of the growing possibility that the German advance in Russia would break into the Caucasus and from there reach the oilfields of Iraq and Persia (modern Iran). This area, only lightly defended, was part of Auchinleck's Middle East Command and he was instructed that, if it came to a choice, it was better to sacrifice Egypt and hold Iraq. Therefore, although substantial reserve forces were shortly to arrive in Egypt, they could not necessarily be allocated to the Alamein front. Plans were indeed prepared for the worst eventuality of withdrawal from Egypt, but this was only common prudence in what was undoutedly a difficult situation. After all, work on these plans, and on defences between the Alamein position and the Nile, continued under the new command team. What is also a matter of fact is that Dorman-Smith prepared an appreciation of future events at the end of July which anticipated a German attack on the south of the Alamein line; he suggested that this be defeated by a defence based on a refused left flank and the Alam Halfa Ridge and that this defensive action be followed by training for a breakthrough in the north. This appreciation was accepted by Auchinleck and discussed with various senior subordinates in the early days of August when the very first steps to establishing a training area for the eventual offensive were also made. It is also on record that, on Alexander's appointment, Middle East Command was absolved of any responsibility for Iraq and Persia and instructed only to defeat Rommel, using all the resources already in Egypt and those shortly to arrive. The evidence, therefore, does not point to a policy of withdrawal.

Montgomery later claimed that during his private interview with Auchinleck on 12 August, Auchinleck spoke only of the plans for retreat. This seems highly improbable but it is possible that Auchinleck may have failed to make himself clear, from a combination of tiredness and strain, the fact that he and Montgomery had never got on well in the past, and perhaps from embarrassment and disappointment at being supplanted. What is inconceivable is that neither Montgomery's briefing the next day by de Guingand (then Brigadier, General Staff, or principal Operations officer, at Eighth Army) during their journey together to the front, nor Monty's briefing at Eighth Army HQ by General Ramsden, the temporary commander, introduced the existing plans.

This controversy, and criticism of the insubordinate and insensitive way in which Monty assumed command of Eighth Army earlier than he had been instructed to, have tended to obscure Montgomery's very real and substantial achievements in these early days. These began with his talk to the headquarters' staff on that first evening in charge when he established in no uncertain terms that he did not intend to retreat from the existing positions and that he would not tolerate 'belly-

Right: A German tank column passes an immobilized British Bren gun carrier.

Right below: The Bristol Beaufighter became an important weapon in Monty's armoury, even if the RAF top brass dissented as to the air force's precise role.

Below: Messerschmitt 110s and transport planes crowd a desert airstrip.

Bottom: The Allied retreat to El Alamein, where Monty took over.

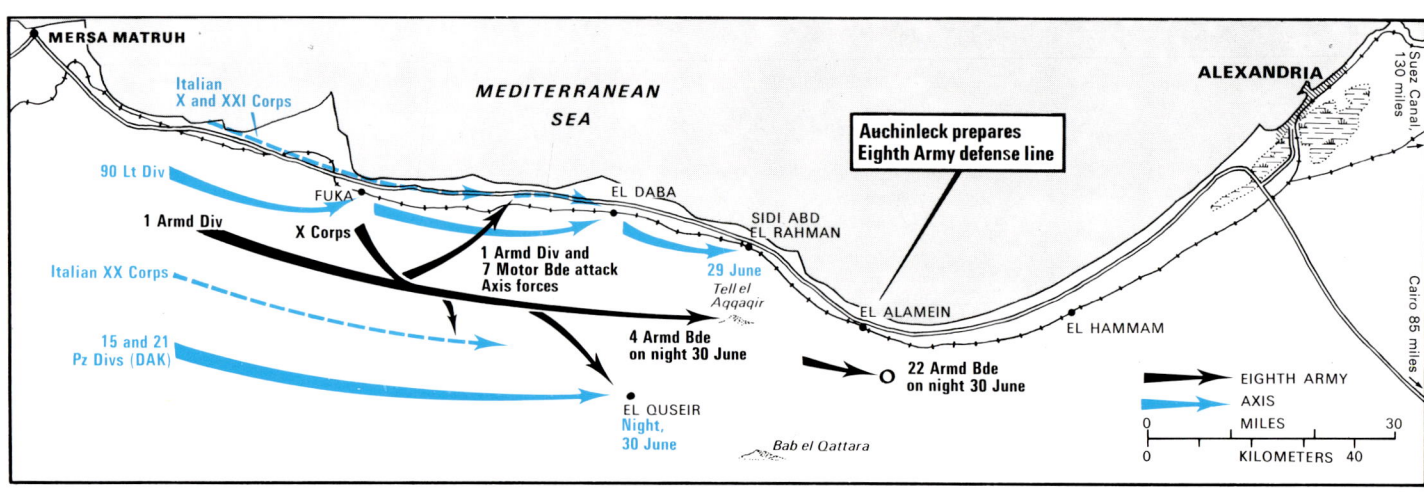

EARNING LAURELS IN AFRICA

aching' – orders were not to be queried and discussed but obeyed. De Guingand was to become Chief of Staff in the full sense, with similar authority. Montgomery had already that afternoon begun his characteristic programme of visits to subordinate formations and from these and this first talk he began deliberately to create a new atmosphere of clarity of purpose and confidence throughout Eighth Army. The new strategic priorities also enabled him, on that first day, to request that 44th Infantry Division be moved up from the Delta to the Alamein positions.

In part this new air of confidence was a product of Montgomery's deliberate self-advertisement (which those who criticized him as a showman should accept as his justification). But it also derived partly from the simplification he imposed. Auchinleck had been introducing a reorganization to combine infantry, field artillery, anti-tank and tank units into mobile battle groups. This was designed to create the sort of fluent all-arms co-operation that seemed to come as second nature to the

Left: *A Grant tank of 22nd Armoured Brigade passes a wrecked vehicle. The sponson-mounted 75mm gun of the Grant finally gave the British tank forces a weapon with the ability to fire high explosive as well as solid shot anti-tank ammunition but the vehicle's internal layout and high silhouette were far from ideal.*

Right: *Monty and Air Marshal Coningham happily co-operating early in their working relationship.*

Above: *Rommel issuing orders to one of his officers.*

German formations, but had rarely been achieved by the British. The intention was to avoid the apartheid of cavalry (now in tanks, of course) and infantry fighting separately, which had all too often resulted in infantry being left exposed and defenceless in the face of German armour. This was not a simple style of organization to operate and to Montgomery it was totally flawed because he thought, with some justice, that it would lead to dissipation of effort by groups of companies and squadrons, when divisions should fight instead as a single entity to a single plan. Auchinleck's ideas were not as obviously wrong as Montgomery claimed (they were closer to modern practice in some respects than Montgomery's) but Montgomery's were far simpler and far easier to communicate and to operate given that Eighth Army could offer only moderately trained formations at that time.

The battle-group idea had also involved preparing for a more mobile struggle than Montgomery was prepared to accept, with forward positions being given up and complicated manoeuvres being set in train along various lines to meet various possible attacks. Montgomery's realism instead took over. He wanted to fight a battle according to his forces' strengths – artillery and air firepower and resolution in defence – not the cut and thrust of manoeuvre in which it was all too clear who had been superior in the past. His alternative was that there should be no easy yielding of the outpost line while at the earliest stages of the battle the armour was to take up, and not budge from, defensive positions which Rommel would be compelled to attack. This reliance on fixed defensive positions also implied a stronger moral commitment to stand fast than did the previous plans for a battle of manoeuvre, which always seemed to carry implications of giving forces the option of tactical withdrawal. Under Montgomery this option was effectively closed for he ordered early on that most

Above: *As this photograph exemplifies, it was a crucial element of Monty's style to be seen to be in close contact with his men. One of his weaknesses was his failure to nurture a similar rapport with his senior officers.*

transport vehicles were to be sent to the rear so that units would have to stay and fight – the only vehicles to remain were to be those used in battle or for the movement of supplies.

Crucially Montgomery restored the excellent co-operation between the RAF and army that had been instituted earlier in the year and had been badly disrupted in the retreat from Gazala and Tobruk. Montgomery's first step was to move Eighth Army HQ from its bleak and fly-ridden location on the Ruweisat Ridge to a place alongside the more congenial seaside site used by the RAF. Greater comfort made in part for greater efficiency but more crucially regular personal contact between the services was the secret of close army-air co-operation. Montgomery and Coningham, the air commander, had morning and evening meetings to exchange information and co-ordinate plans, and it is worth noting that RAF observers considered Montgomery's briefings the clearest they had ever had on the army's operations.

In the meantime, as Montgomery was putting his own house in order, what of Rommel? His advance from Tobruk had not only been contrary to previously established Axis plans but against all the arguments of his logistics officers. All supplies for the German-Italian armies had to come from Europe either to Tobruk or Tripoli. Tobruk, the nearest of these ports to the front, was some 300 miles away. Tripoli was around 1300 miles distant, yet had to be used for much of the supply effort for three chief reasons: its handling capacity was larger, the routes to it were safer from Allied attack, and the sea routes to it were shorter and naval fuel was in short supply. Traditional accounts of the Alam Halfa and Alamein battles list the numerous supply ships, and particularly tankers for vehicle fuel, lost en route to British attack and ascribe Rommel's supply problem to this cause. In fact the difficulty, particularly for the earlier battle, was as much one of inability to truck supplies already in Africa to the front. Also, of course, the efficient German formations which would bear much of the fight could not expect a corresponding priority in supply allocation, compared with the much more numerous Italians.

Rommel himself was feeling the strain of his many months of continuous front-line leadership. He would be so ill during the Battle of Alam Halfa that he could scarcely climb in and out of his tank. Yet he knew that reinforcements would soon reach his opponents and that, although his supplies would remain weak, his relative strength, particularly in tanks, would probably never be better. Rommel also understood that Hitler would never permit an army undefeated in battle to make a strategic withdrawal. The only way left to resolve the dilemma was a last-chance attack to reach Egypt.

Above left: *A four-aircraft schwarm of Me 109s takes off from a desert field. The plumes of dust illustrate the difficult conditions faced by both sides in operating over the desert. Special air filters were only the simplest modifications needed.*

Above: *The Me 110 was technologically outmoded by mid 1942, but was kept on mainly as a nightflyer and was a key player in German strategy.*

The Alamein position was one of the most restricted to be found in the North African theatre, for scarcely 30 miles from the Mediterranean the Qattara Depression began. The terrain there was genuinely impassable to large bodies of troops or motor traffic so, unlike in many of the earlier desert battles, there was no ultimately open southern flank. Between Qattara and the sea were various ridges and depressions and, particularly in the southern part, some areas of broken ground. The front lines between the sea and the Alam Nayil Ridge had been strengthened during and since the July fighting and one of Montgomery's first concerns was to increase this in line with his no-retreat policies. The most obvious step in this direction was his allocation of one of the brigades (132 Brigade) of 44 Division to the 2nd New Zealand Division who were holding the area between Ruweisat and Alam Nayil. South of Alam Nayil the front line defences could not be as formidable but the minefields were substantially extended. This sector was covered by the light armour and motorized infantry units which were all that were now left of the famous 7th Armoured Division. Information from decoded German signals confirmed on 17 August that Rommel's plan was to attack in this southern area and then turn in on Eighth Army's rear. This made the defence of the Alam Halfa Ridge vital. Montgomery had been shocked to find a totally inadequate garrison there on his arrival – the remaining two brigades of 44th Division were soon installed – but more importantly positions were prepared for the tanks of 22nd Armoured Brigade at the west end of the ridge. Until almost the eve of Rommel's attack when the 8th Armoured Brigade arrived to rejoin Eighth Army, the 80-odd Grant tanks of the 22nd Brigade were the principal tank strength. 8th Armoured Brigade also had the powerful Grants and after their arrival 22nd and 8th Armoured were put under the command of the newly activated 10th Armoured Division with a total strength of 160-170 tanks. In support to the north of Alam Halfa was the 23rd Armoured Brigade with about 120 of the less powerful Valentines.

The Battle of Alam Halfa would principally be fought on the British side by units of XIII Corps which was commanded, from 15 August, by General Horrocks, one of Montgomery's favoured subordinates specially brought out from England. Montgomery's first intention had been to appoint Horrocks to the new 'mobile corps' he was forming but it was revealing of the atmosphere still prevailing at the time that Horrocks said he was not suitable because his infantry regiment background would be unwelcome in a formation which would be composed principally of former cavalry units. Montgomery accepted Horrocks's point. Horrocks also had some difficulty, once appointed to XIII Corps, in getting his authority and ideas over fully to Generals Freyberg of the New Zealand Division and Renton of 7th Armoured, with whom Montgomery also argued. Horrocks was able, with Montgomery's strong urging and support, to conduct brief exercises to rehearse the move of 22nd Brigade to its defence positions and of 23rd Brigade to come to its support: rehearsals which were exactly to mirror the moves required in the battle.

Most soldiers of Eighth Army had heard little about Montgomery before his arrival. Brigadier Roberts of 22nd Armoured Brigade had known only of his enthusiasm for physical training (and did not like the prospect) and failed to recognize him when first they met. Montgomery had by then acquired the Australian style hat which he gradually decorated with badges from the units he so assiduously visited. A faintly ridiculous gimmick, maybe, but Monty rightly appreciated that he would have to make himself a distinctive part of the desert scene if his authority and influence were to reach every level of his command. He later wrote that his intention was to become for Eighth Army 'both master and mascot'.

Montgomery had again adopted his habit of going early to bed, and himself tells of the anger over being awakened unnecessarily to receive a routine situation report. However, it is interesting that one senior officer recalled a conversation shortly before the Alam Halfa battle in which Montgomery complained of not being able to sleep well through concern that Rommel's attack would not take the anticipated route. Monty's public stance, of course, was of confidence, exemplified in his Order of the Day of 20 August in which he made his policy of no withdrawal absolutely clear to all ranks. This was the first of many special orders Monty would issue and in typical style it stressed 'stout hearts', 'determination', and 'duty' and called finally on the Almighty for aid. Such messages are often described as having an inspiring effect, and Monty certainly believed in them, but it is difficult to gauge how influential such rhetoric would have been on a tough and cynical front-line soldier.

Montgomery need not have lost any sleep, for the expected attack got under way just before midnight on 30 August. Rommel had about 230 German tanks going into action, of which about 70 were the effective Mark III 'Specials' with the longer 50mm gun and about 30 more were the Mark IV 'Specials' with the new long 75mm. On the left, north, wing was the German 90th Light Division, then the Italian XX Corps (who would make little positive contribution to the attack), then the two Panzer Divisions, 15th and 21st, of the famous *Deutsches Afrika Korps* with two reconnaissance units completing the line-up on the right. The aim was to penetrate some 30 miles east during the night before being ready at dawn to drive north behind the whole of Eighth Army.

From the outset things went wrong for the Germans. They were bombed by the RAF even while they were forming up to start. The British minefields were far more elaborate than expected and the two light brigades of 7th Armoured Division ably fulfilled their delaying functions. By the middle of the night the RAF was putting in further telling attacks. General Nehring, commanding the DAK, was wounded and General Bismarck of 15th Panzer was killed, which contributed to the confusion. Consequently the attackers only reached the east side of the British minefields after dawn, by which time they should, according to plan, have been miles farther on.

Rommel's plan had undoubtedly been over-

Below: *'Master and Mascot'. Monty in his famous Australian hat with his collection of badges.*

Above: *Desert warfare was not conducted simply in wide open spaces. Seen here are the classic elements of a fortified desert position – an anti-tank ditch (still an obstacle although it has become partially filled by soft sand), barbed wire, and a real or dummy minefield.*

Left: *Generalleutnant Nehring, commander of the Afrika Korps in the Battle of Alam Halfa, until he was wounded.*

ambitious and he now swung in the other direction, wishing to call off the attack. Instead he was persuaded to allow it to continue but with the intended turn north to begin as soon as the tanks were refuelled and rearmed – a move which would take the advance straight to Alam Halfa, the strongest part of the British position. After the delay for refuelling and a brief sandstorm, it was not until the early evening that the Germans finally attacked 22nd Armoured Brigade. There were significant casualties on both sides and one brief spell when it seemed that the Germans might break through. Reserves were brought forward and the defence held, with the new 6-pounder anti-tank guns, which were now in general use, playing an important part.

At nightfall the German tanks drew off but they had no respite, being bombed and shelled all night – to the satisfaction of the British defenders on the Alam Halfa Ridge who could overlook the whole affair. On the next day, 1 September, the Germans made new attacks to the flanks of 22nd Armoured Brigade but these were again beaten off. Montgomery tried to bring 8th Armoured into line with 22nd Armoured, since there was now little likelihood of Rommel renewing the drive to the east where 8th Armoured had been posted, but this

Left: *Monty issuing instructions on 20 August 1942. On the right is Brigadier Roberts of 22nd Armoured Brigade and behind Monty's outstretched arm is Lt-Gen Horrocks. Monty's favourite ADC, John Poston, has his back to the camera.*

Below: *Monty and Alex during their first days in the desert.*

Left: *German machine-gunners making good use of natural defences provided by the craggy landscape.*

move was held off by the customary efficient German anti-tank screen. By that evening fuel for the Panzers was still more desperately short and the next morning Rommel gave orders to retreat. As the historian Ronald Lewin later commented 'For the Afrika Korps it was a final stroke of bad luck that Montgomery refused to pursue.'

In fact this comment over-simplifies a complicated and controversial sequence of events. Some other writers believe that Montgomery missed an important opportunity to follow up the German retreat and perhaps even make the Second Battle of Alamein unnecessary. Instead Montgomery ordered that his main tank units should hold their positions, fearing correctly that an open battle would give Rommel a second chance he did not deserve. Though short of fuel, Rommel's tank units were far from being crippled and on the British side only 22nd Armoured Brigade, whose tanks were almost worn out, had any real previous battle experience. Montgomery did plan for the New Zealand Division to attack south across Rommel's lines of communication and the poor result of this limited advance proves that Montgomery was correct in not pursuing more forcefully.

Above: *A Grant tank. Although this type was powerfully armed the main gun was set so low that most of the tank had to be exposed rather than kept in the favoured 'hull down' position during engagements.*

The attack was carried out by one New Zealand Brigade and one from the raw 44th Division on the night of 3/4 September and it was badly mismanaged. The troops were withdrawn to their original positions the next day after incurring in this brief flurry half of Eighth Army's casualties for the whole battle. By 6 September all the German and Italian troops had completed their retreat and their sick and disillusioned commander would soon be ready to return to Germany for medical treatment.

Montgomery had won his first battle and won it without ever being budged from his main positions. He may not have been the first to appreciate what positions he should fight from, but the battle had definitely been fought his way. The confidence that the men of 10th Armoured Division and 44th Infantry Division had drawn from the sight of the helpless Afrika Korps being bombed and shelled in its leaguers south of Alam Halfa would soon spread throughout the army; Montgomery, it seemed, was a general who lived up to his brave fighting talk. Rommel singled out the British air superiority as the crucial factor but could not be aware that working with his supporting air force was one respect in which, at this time at least, Montgomery was his superior. With Rommel away ill in Germany and 'Eastern Front' men being brought in to replace the battle casualties and sick among the 'old Africa hands', the Afrika Korps was losing to some extent its sense of solidarity and easy co-operation. Such a sense of community and united effort was now growing at Eighth Army, thanks to Montgomery's efforts. This was an important pointer for the next battle.

Before he left for Germany on 23 September, Rommel put in hand the defensive scheme that would still be in operation for the Alamein battle. A deep and elaborate defensive network was created involving the laying of half a million anti-tank and anti-personnel mines, booby traps, and miles of barbed wire. Rommel, like Montgomery, had been an expert on infantry tactics and, as would also be seen in 1944, was inventive in his use of defensive devices. His forces would remain short of fuel and other supplies, he knew, and he and his German staff had little respect for the fighting power of their Italian allies. The front-line deployment therefore alternated German and Italian infantry to stiffen the defence. One German (15th Panzer) and one Italian (*Littorio*) armoured division were held in reserve in the north and a similar force (21st Panzer and *Ariete*) in the south – a dispersal believed to be necessary because fuel shortages would prevent a concentrated armoured reserve moving together to a threatened point. Also held in reserve in the northern sector was the German 90th Light Division.

It was clear that Montgomery intended to attack, but when? The final straw that had confirmed Churchill in his decision to sack Auchinleck was his refusal to begin an offensive any sooner than mid-September and Churchill was now outraged that Montgomery did not intend his attack to start until the full moon towards the end of October. Montgomery convinced Alexander that he could guarantee a victory for his better-prepared army at the later date and Montgomery had his way.

Montgomery's relationship with Alexander

Left: *Monty flanked by Lt-Gen Sir Oliver Leese, Commander of XXX Corps (left), and Lt-Gen Herbert Lumsden, Commander of X Corps.*

Below left: *From the air supposedly indistinguishable from a truck, but in fact a disguised Crusader tank.*

Before Alam Halfa Montgomery had appointed de Guingand as Chief of Staff and brought Horrocks to command XIII Corps, and now made other senior changes. Leese came from England to take over XXX Corps (Ramsden was brusquely dismissed in typical Monty fashion) and Brigadier Kirkman arrived to be Eighth Army's senior artilleryman. Somewhat against his will Montgomery promoted an 'old desert hand', Lumsden, to head the new X Corps; but in general the effect of these personnel appointments was to break up, for the better, established cliques which had been partly responsible for the lack of cohesion in previous operations.

The creation of X Corps was the most important of Montgomery's organizational changes. On his first day in Egypt he had a staff officer begin plans for the assembly of what he called a 'corps de chasse'. The purpose was to establish a group of tank divisions and motorized infantry capable of fighting a mobile battle as effectively as the Afrika Korps. This can now be seen as a mistake on Montgomery's part because it tended to preserve the separation between the British tank units and Eighth Army's infantry – some of which, to compound the problem, came from the Dominions or the Indian Army.

formed an important support to his early successes. Alexander had been a student of Monty's at the Staff College and this teacher and pupil relationship seems to have helped matters during the war, even though Alex was now senior. Certainly Alexander was the ideal superior for Monty, protecting him from interference from above and ensuring that Eighth Army was amply supplied in every way. It is likely that Alexander had more input into affairs than Montgomery would have cared to admit but Monty was definitely master in his own house.

Montgomery's plan for the Battle of Alamein rejected the customary desert pattern of beginning with outflanking moves to the south. The southern sector, allocated to XIII Corps, was to provide only diversionary attacks with the aim, at best, of passing light forces through the Axis lines to harass their rear areas. Instead the main attack was to be in the north with penetrations driven through the German and Italian defences between the Miteirya Ridge and Tell el Eisa. These eminences were only a little higher than the surrounding flat and open terrain but such positions were to be important tactical features of the coming battle.

Montgomery's initial plan was for the infantry divisions of XXX Corps to fight into and, if possible, through the German defences on the first night and then for X Corps to pass forward by the same routes to a position dominating Rommel's lateral communications in the rear. Rommel would be forced to counterattack and be defeated in the subsequent tank battle. Few of Eighth Army's senior officers liked the plan. The infantry commanders, like Morshead of 9th Australian Division or Pienaar of 1st South African Division, believed that the tanks would lag behind and leave their troops vulnerable as had often happened in the past, and the tank men like Lumsden and Gatehouse of 10th Armoured Division had no wish to push ahead of the infantry into what they were convinced would be a deadly anti-tank defence.

On 6 October Montgomery decided to make a substantial change to his strategy. The initial infantry attack and armoured advance were to be as before but now the tanks were to halt as soon as they had passed through the German defences and not drive on into the rear. Once halted they were to act as a shield behind which the infantry would gradually destroy ('crumble' was Montgomery's word) the Axis front line units. Rommel would be forced, therefore, to attack the armoured shield with his own tanks, under unfavourable terms, and be defeated.

Considerable effort was put into a deception plan to hide both the date and location of the attack. A dummy water pipeline (laid at a rate which implied November completion) and other measures suggested that the attack would be in the south while in the north the most elaborate schemes were put in hand to conceal the preparations. Dummy trucks

Below: *The most feared adversary for Allied tanks throughout the war, the famous 88 in action.*

and tanks were built in forward locations at an early stage to accustom German reconnaissance to their presence. When the assault units moved up, the dummies were rebuilt in the rear where the attackers had trained. Thus, in theory, no change would be observable. Another trick was to disguise something important as something less significant. Thus piles of supplies being stocked for the attack would be built in the shape of trucks and camouflaged as trucks would be, with guns also being transformed into less-threatening vehicles in this way. There is unfortunately little evidence that the Germans were deceived regarding the direction of the attack but security was good and, just as on the eve of D-Day, the German commanders were sending 'situation unchanged' reports only a few hours before the start of the battle.

Training, of course, was a priority throughout September and October. Montgomery himself devised and issued voluminous and comprehensive training instructions and saw to it that these were developed at every level. Platoon, company, battalion and all senior commanders had to produce and execute training programmes tailored to the type of operations to come. Particularly important was training in mine clearance. A special area was set aside for this training and parties from each assault division were instructed in a newly devised drill for the task. Many of the mine clearance men would have to use the most basic method of prodding with bayonets but some 500 newly-produced mine detectors were issued along with 120 miles of tape and almost 90,000 lamps to mark cleared lanes and other routes.

It is worth remembering, however, that the amount of training possible was limited. The Australian and South African divisions had to hold part of the front line as well as prepare for the attack. They were only, therefore, able to send back a brigade at a time – the Australian brigades in turn being relieved by brigades of 51st Highland Division so that, in a compensating benefit, these could gain some front-line experience. Much was also expected of the new Sherman tanks, some 300 of

Below: *With the arrival of the 6-pounder anti-tank gun the British at last had a respectable infantry anti-tank capability*

Above: *A 25-pounder battery blasts away during one of Monty's night barrages.*

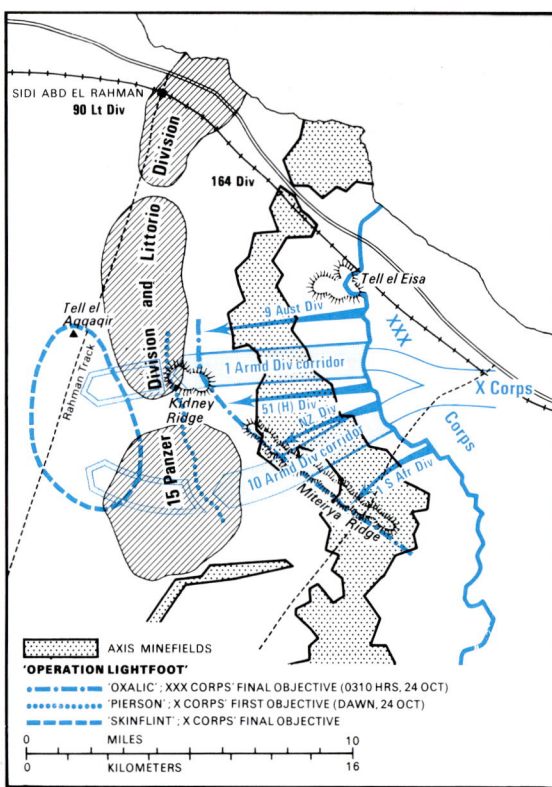

Right: *The Alamein plan as it stood at the opening of the battle.*

which arrived in Egypt from early September. After delays for minor modifications, however, many of these were not actually issued to fighting formations until well into October (some only the day before the battle started), which obviously left little opportunity for familiarization.

Montgomery also put into effect his declared intention of ensuring that every soldier knew what was expected of him. At first the lowest level to which the plan was released was that of divisional generals and their GSO 1s and officers commanding Royal Artillery. Although exercises at lower levels involved models of the attack areas and other specifics, these were not identified, neither were timings given. All officers down to lieutenant-colonel were briefed by 10 October; company commanders were told on the 17th; other officers on the 21st and all troops on the 21st or 22nd – except for those who were on patrols or outpost duty where capture was a possibility. Montgomery himself addressed meetings of every officer from lieutenant-colonel upwards on 19 and 20 October. His notes for the speeches survive and are remarkably accurate in their prediction of a 10-12-day battle of attrition and the need to keep pressure on the enemy to capitalize on material superiority. Many of Monty's listeners seem to have been impressed and heartened to hear such a confident and comprehensive description before the event rather than in a congratulatory post-mortem. Taken as a whole, Montgomery's performance in raising the morale of his army has been called 'a brilliant exercise in calculated leadership' – and this from one of the historians most critical of his abilities.

Part of Montgomery's briefing was a recital of the substantial resources of Eighth Army. Montgomery's figures and those of every other historian differ in detail but the comparative position seems to have been roughly a two to one Allied superiority. There were about 50,000 German and 54,000 Italian troops facing just under 200,000 of their enemies. On the eve of the battle Eighth Army had something over 1000 tanks with the forward units (including 285 Shermans and 246 Grants) and perhaps another 1000, mostly older types, under repair or in reserve. The Italians had about 300 of their very weak tanks and the Germans about 200 altogether – of these only 30 were Mark IV Specials and fewer than 100 Mark III Specials. The Allied artillery amounted to just over 900 guns but all except 52 of these were 25-pounder field guns. The Axis forces had around 500 guns, less than half of them German, and although they had a slight advantage in the heavier calibres, they had none of the abundance of ammunition that Montgomery could count on. The strength of the Afrika Korps in the past had often been its anti-tank defence and this now consisted of some 850 guns, 86 of them the feared '88s' along with about 360 of the good German 50mm or ex-Russian 76.2mm which were also powerful weapons. Eighth Army possessed 850 of the very adequate 6-pounders and over 500 of the older 2-pounders which were still useful. These were distributed on a lavish scale not only to the anti-tank units but to infantry and motorized battalions as well.

Montgomery's main attack opened at 2140 on 23 October with 456 guns on the XXX Corps front bombarding all known German and Italian artillery positions. After a quarter of an hour there was a five-minute pause, then the bombardment resumed to lead the attacking infantry into the enemy defences. The assault divisions were 9th Australian on the right moving on Tell el Eisa, then 51st Highland, 2nd New Zealand, and 1st South African on the left towards the south end of Miteirya Ridge. The New Zealanders had a complete armoured brigade (9th) in close support and each of the other divisions a tank regiment. Their task was to fight their way through the Axis positions to a line code-named 'Oxalic' by the early morning of the 25th. Following behind were the two active armoured divisions of X Corps, 1st and 10th. (A third armoured division, 8th, was also part of X Corps but at this stage was not a complete formation.) Each of the armoured divisions was to clear a corridor of three or four lanes through the minefields and pass beyond the Oxalic line to positions, 'Pierson', a mile or two beyond by dawn on the 24th. In retrospect it can be seen that Montgomery's change of plan to set the more limited Pierson objective for the tanks meant less of a difference in practice than he expected, since it would prove difficult enough to reach even that far. What was undoubtedly true was that the operation of two army corps in the same confined area was a serious mistake, certain to increase the difficulty of managing what was sure to be a complicated action.

Fortunes during the first night were mixed. The Australian attack went almost according to plan. The Highland Division, despite the anachronistic inspiration of being led into battle by its pipers, did not do so well in its more testing assignments. Broadly speaking, only intermediate objectives and not the final line were reached and some defensive strongpoints remained unsubdued as the attack passed by. The New Zealanders did better with some of the supporting tanks being on the Miteirya Ridge at dawn and some of the South Africans were also on or near their objectives by then. The armoured divisions did less well. 10th Armoured Division had its four lanes cleared through to Miteirya Ridge by early in the day but had few tanks forward at first, while 1st Armoured Division

Below: *Overview of the development of the Battle of Alamein.*

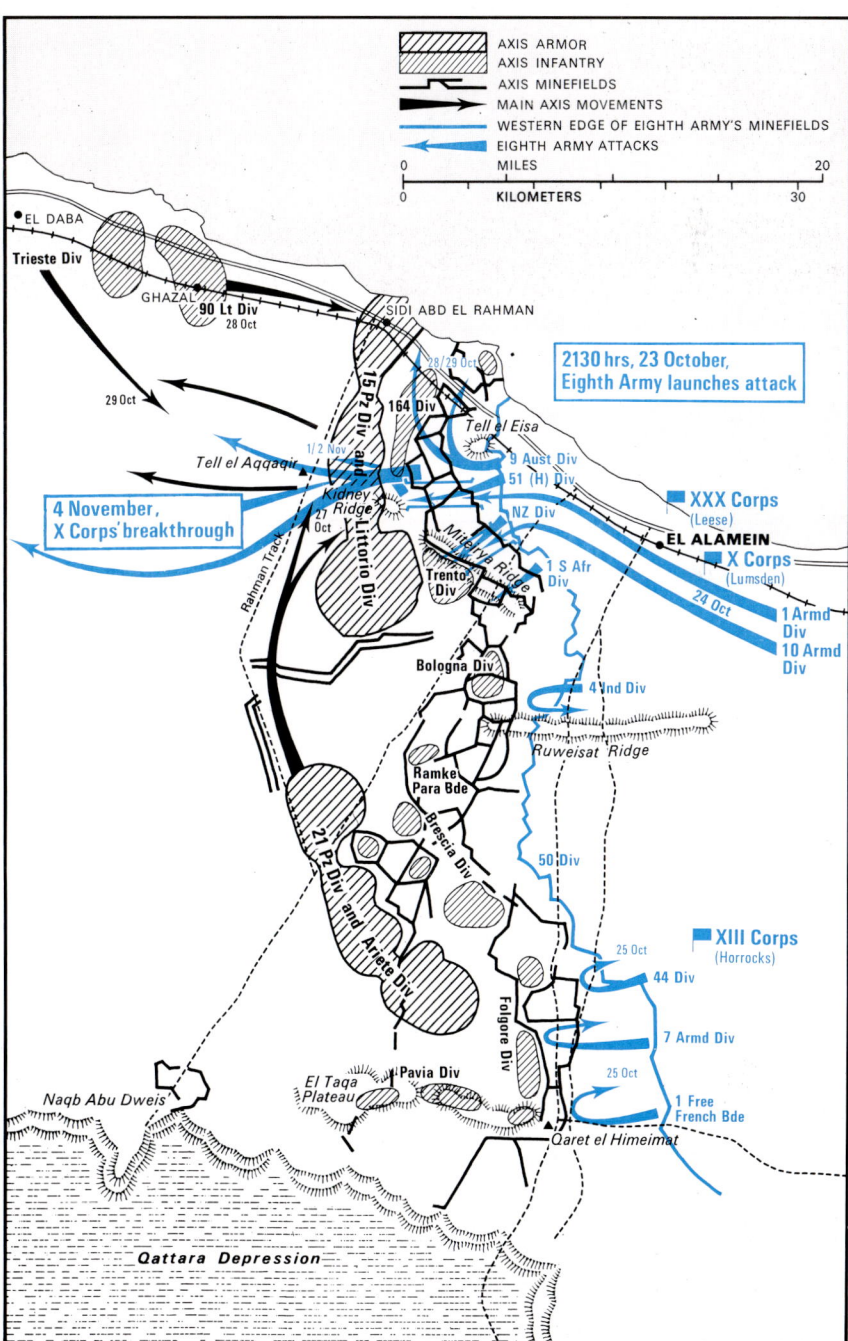

had one good gap in operation by dawn but its two others not until later in the morning. With units from many formations horribly intermingled, confusion was increasing. The minefield gaps were at certain points less than 10 metres wide. The area's topography was featureless with precise navigation hard enough at the best of times, but now if a single vehicle strayed off line it could take with it the tape and lamps marking a route, and even without enemy action the British bombardment and advance had raised great quantities of dust. As one soldier-historian said, 'The whole area looked like a badly organized car park at an immense race meeting held in a dust bowl.'

Fortunately for the Eighth Army their opponents were also disorganized. Rommel's deputy, Stumme, died of a heart attack in the early hours of the battle when on a reconnaissance visit to the front line, made necessary by the disruption caused by the British bombardment. Rommel was summoned back but he recorded that, as he left Germany, his opinion was that 'there were no more laurels to be earned in Africa.' General Stumme's death was beneficial for Montgomery because the German staff did not know of it for some time and von Thoma, commanding DAK, chose not to make an immediate counterattack in the uncertain situation. Also, before setting out on his reconnaissance, Stumme held back his artillery fire for a time because of fears of ammunition shortage. This, too, was probably an error.

The story of 24 October was largely of attempts to sort out the chaos in the 'car park'. Montgomery issued and re-emphasized orders to complete the clearance of the 1st Armoured Division corridor and for 10th Armoured Division to push on to 'Pierson' to permit the New Zealanders to 'crumble' to the south. Despite every effort only modest gains were made and during the night of the 24th/25th an important turning point was reached. The advancing armoured brigades of 10th Armoured Division were halted on the Miteirya Ridge by a combination of new enemy minefields, artillery fire, and air attack. Their commanders wished to call off the advance rather than be caught at dawn in exposed positions where they could expect heavy casualties. The divisional commander and Lumsden concurred.

Montgomery was asleep when news of this proposed departure from his orders reached Eighth Army HQ. The sequence of de Guingand's reactions confirms Montgomery's good judgement in selecting him. He recognized that this was a matter for the Army Commander and therefore called Leese and Lumsden to a conference - and only then woke Montgomery to explain what was happening. At the conference Monty gave very definite orders for some of the tanks to keep pushing forward and privately made it clear to Lumsden that he could do what he was told or be relieved.

On the ground Montgomery's firmness had, in fact, little effect, for the armour proved unable, as its commanders had rightly feared, to remain west of the ridge. Why then is this conference regarded as so important? Montgomery had been exactly right in his early warnings against 'belly-aching'. There would be little of it after this assertion of authority and the armour would increasingly take a willing part in all-arms actions which the Germans had long since shown to be the most efficient way to fight. Perhaps even more important than the reiteration of Montgomery's desired style of fighting in the abstract sense, is the opinion, later supported by Leese and de Guingand among others, that without this unequivocal order to advance the whole offensive might have stalled into stalemate. Unfortunately, from the developments that took place and the fuller information that became available to Montgomery on the 25th and 26th, it seemed that this was only too real a possibility.

As well as the main attacks in the northern sector, Montgomery's offensive had also begun with secondary assaults in the south. The attack here was led by 7th Armoured Division (now commanded by Harding after Renton had been sacked) with newly devised 'flail' tanks to front the advance. These were soon knocked out, or broke down, and as a result only one of the two main minefields was crossed on the first night. A repeated attack on the second night got little further and, after this, fighting in the southern sector effectively died down. Montgomery at first kept 7th Armoured Division in the south, later claiming that this was necessary if his dispositions were to remain balanced (another favourite expression and something of an obses-

Below: *No shortage of ammunition for this 5.5-inch gun. Monty had comparatively few weapons in the heavier calibres like this at Alamein but the slight Axis advantage in this respect was negated by their ammunition shortage.*

sion). This was an error since there could be no possibility of an Axis attack in this area. It was not until after the German 21st Panzer Division had definitely moved north that 7th Armoured Division was also summoned to join the main battle. A point of more general importance is the confirmation that this southern action gives of how difficult it was to break through the Axis defences and how wide of the mark are criticisms of Montgomery's slow and methodical plans.

During the 25th it started to become clear to Montgomery that he would have to recast his plans. Despite his forceful orders 10th Armoured Division could clearly go no farther and, as a consequence, any southward 'crumbling' by the New Zealanders should also stop. To the north some gains were made during the day by the Highlanders in the area of a feature known as Kidney Ridge and plans laid by Montgomery's order for an attack by the Australians on the night of 25th/26th on a low hill west of Tell el Eisa known to Eighth Army as Point 29. 1st Armoured Division was also heavily engaged during the day and 15th Panzer, facing the northern advance, was now down to fewer than 40 tanks with well over 70 lost. Montgomery's own tank losses were now up to around 250 but many of these were being recovered and repaired.

The night attack by the Australians on Point 29 was successful and the combination of this drive to the north and advances around Kidney Ridge caught and held the attention of Rommel, newly returned on the evening of the 25th. He therefore began to bring both 90th Light from reserve behind the coastal positions and summoned up 21st Panzer, so far lightly engaged, from the southern sector opposite XIII Corps. Montgomery's core plan, to drag the German reserve forces into a 'dogfight', was now working, although this was far from obvious at the time.

Above: *Training for the advance and breakthrough.*

Below: *A German tank crewmember surrenders as his vehicle is charged by an Eighth Army infantryman.*

In fact Monty spent much of the 26th pondering how he might resuscitate his offensive. Growing infantry casualties were a particular concern but he still had up to 900 tanks fit for battle. Despite the fact that his tank advances had clearly lost momentum Montgomery decided that X Corps must continue to press in the Kidney Ridge area while the infantry of XXX Corps consolidated their gains, reorganizing and resting whenever possible. In the evening of the 26th he amplified these plans by a decision to pull the New Zealand Division into reserve, filling the gap this created by extending northwards the frontages of the South Africans and 4th Indian Division to the south. The Australians were to prepare another northward attack for the night of the 28th and the final blow was also to be in the coastal sector, delivered by the New Zealanders freed by this regrouping.

While this was all going on various units of X Corps were fighting fiercely around Kidney Ridge (known rather confusingly to the Germans as Point 28). Here, throughout the 27th, a single motorized battalion with support from part of an anti-tank unit (with together a total of 19 6-pounder anti-tank guns) held off attacks from most of 15th Panzer and *Littorio* as well as parts of 21st Panzer and *Ariete*. At the end of the day the British riflemen brought only one anti-tank gun out of the action but they had knocked out at least 37 enemy tanks – a remarkable achievement in what has since become one of the most famous minor actions of the war. A minor action in one sense maybe, but Rommel had intended his efforts in this area to be part of a major counter-attack. Instead his losses were a real body-blow, reinforced by news that still more tankers of precious fuel had been sunk en route to Tobruk.

The ferocity of Rommel's attacks, however, did convince Montgomery to make yet another sensible adjustment to his plan on the 28th. To the consternation of Churchill and others in London, Montgomery began to pull 1st Armoured Division into reserve, leaving the infantry of XXX Corps to hold the whole northern front. Other infantry units were ordered up from XIII Corps to reinforce the New Zealand Division and 7th Armoured Division, too, was finally brought northwards. To Churchill the withdrawal of the armour made it seem as if Montgomery was abandoning the battle and his anger was only just held down by Brooke, the CIGS, who privately had his own doubts. This would not be the last time that Brooke proved to be Montgomery's staunchest friend and defender. Brooke is often described as the best chief of the General Staff Britain has ever had and his support for Montgomery was based, as has been seen, on a very high estimation of Monty's military abilities – a compliment indeed from such a source.

The night of the 28th saw the renewed Australian attack north of Point 29. Some ground was gained

Top: *Australian troops advance through a dense smoke screen.*

Above: *Wendell Willkie (a former candidate for the US presidency) visited Monty on 4 and 5 September as the Battle of Alam Halfa was coming to an end.*

Top right: *Monty in the top turret of a Grank tank. He is seen here with the two-badge beret which became his usual headgear for the remainder of the war.*

Right: *Australian troops move in on a German position.*

in fierce fighting but more importantly Eighth Army intelligence learned on the morning of the 29th that all the German army formations with Rommel were in action in the north. With advice from his own staff and from Alexander's Chief of Staff, General McCreery, Montgomery after some reluctance made a decisive alteration to his plans. The Australians would make a further coastward drive on the night of the 30th/31st but the New Zealand attack, now to be known as 'Supercharge' would be aimed farther south, again in the Kidney Ridge area with the intention of hitting the weaker Italian units. Rommel, already almost in despair at his losses and dreadful fuel shortage, would finally be caught off balance.

The Australian attack once again threatened to cut off part of the German 164th Division, who were only able to return to their own lines after a fierce counter-attack during the 31st. If any formation of Eighth Army did most to win Montgomery's battle it was the Australians in these repeated northward lunges. Freyberg, preparing for Supercharge, requested from Montgomery, and was granted, a 24-hour postponement to complete his preliminary manoeuvres. Finally, at 0105 on 2 November, the last act at Alamein began with, in effect, a repeat of the first night – infantry advances after a fierce artillery barrage. Again the following

tank forces were delayed and the leading brigade, 9th Armoured, took very heavy losses with over 70 of its 84 tanks knocked out during the 2nd. By the end of the day, however, two other armoured brigades had also been deployed into action and, though they too had suffered heavily, Rommel was reduced to fewer than 40 tanks and was ready to retreat.

Rommel gave orders that night to retire to Fuka and the withdrawal was detected by Eighth Army intelligence the next morning and confirmed later in the day by decrypted German signals. During the 3rd Rommel was dismayed to receive, however, an order from Hitler telling him to stand fast, which he initially tried loyally to implement. Attacks that night by the Highlanders and an Indian brigade finally allowed the British armour to move ahead into open country. The Battle of El Alamein had been won and Montgomery's reputation had been made.

In many ways the story of the battle could be written around the theme of the astonishing resistance of the German forces in the face of their enemies' crushing material superiority on land and in the air. As the whole future course of the war would prove, it would always be desperately difficult for an Allied general to dislodge German forces from a defensive position. Montgomery's achievements should be viewed in this light. Certainly his plans had gone astray at more than one point – often avoidably in, for example, the confusion

Earning Laurels in Africa

Above: *Guarded by Scottish soldiers, a column of German prisoners goes into captivity.*

Above left: *Happy headlines in a British newspaper.*

Left: *A wounded German officer is guarded until medical help arrives.*

caused by his decision to operate two army corps in the same area – but he had certainly 'gripped' his battle (another favourite expression), imposing his ideas on reluctant subordinates and reducing Rommel for most of the time to a hurried series of expedients in his efforts to shore up his crumbling front line.

Montgomery's critics pay less attention than they should to the real weaknesses of his forces. Memoirs like Keith Douglas's *Alamein to Zem Zem* illustrate only too vividly the essential amateurishness of many of Eighth Army's units, both at the front and in supporting positions. Impressions such as these can be confirmed by a reminder of how often during the battle there were arguments between units as to their exact locations. It is equally misleading to describe the German army as invariably efficient and professional (and the performance of their Italian allies varied from brave and effective to bungling) but the overall comparison is clear.

Montgomery had to win a decisive victory. This was in every political and strategic sense a necessity for Britain and the Allies at this point in the war. It was a prerequisite for the forthcoming invasion of north-west Africa and the capture of advanced airfields to help efforts to re-supply Malta. With these imperatives there was no justification for Montgomery taking any risks during the battle, and every reason to fight in a conservative style, as he did, exploiting fully his army's strengths. His greatest achievements were not in any battlefield manoeuvre or tactical innovation but in the positive attitudes he created beforehand, plus the force of his will that ensured that these were generally maintained. In the past Eighth Army had had formations (like 9th Armoured Brigade on 2 November) which took catastrophic losses. Previously this had often occurred casually and for no significant tactical gain. On this occasion Montgomery was well aware of what the losses might be but rightly judged that these were necessary and inevitable in a hard-fought battle. Above all, at this point and throughout, he ensured that the bravery and sacrifice of his men were harnessed to a practical plan.

On a later occasion Brooke said privately to another general, 'Do you enjoy fighting battles? I don't. I think Monty does.' During Alamein and again in later crucial times one can detect Monty's real relish for the struggle – the lonely little man of such narrow interests but fierce competitive determination grasping eagerly the opportunity to express his personality and prove his own worth in the only field in which he had allowed himself to participate. Such happy determination and concentration had done much to win Alamein.

Chapter Six
A Day's March Nearer Home

Right: Monty chats with the commander of a Grant tank, December 1942.

Montgomery's success in winning the Battle of Alamein was absolutely clear by the morning of 4 November 1942 with only futile attempts to obey Hitler's order stopping the whole Axis army from falling into a near panic retreat. The Alamein battle should be examined in context, however, if its significance and the significance of its aftermath are to be clearly understood. There had been four weak German divisions (two Panzer) and eight Italian in line at Alamein. On the Eastern Front at the same time there were 171 German divisions, 24 of them armoured, out of a total Axis force of 232. The Soviet riposte at Stalingrad would begin on 19 November while the situation in Africa, already transformed, would be entirely reconstituted by the opening of Operation Torch on 8 November.

With the active entry of US forces into the European war and the North African theatre in particular, Montgomery's responsibilities would become more and more directly related to wider strategic issues and the wishes, needs, and prejudices of Allied generals and their political leaders and populations. These factors would make themselves felt as Eighth Army's advance reached closer to Tripoli and eventually Tunis.

In the meantime there was the pursuit from Alamein when Montgomery might hope to make his victory even more decisive. Some 30,000 Axis prisoners (about two-thirds Italian) were taken in the battle or its immediate aftermath with at least another 5000 killed or wounded and 450 tanks left on the battlefield. Eighth Army lost 13,500 men killed, wounded, and missing and about 150 tanks damaged beyond repair. The victory was then substantial enough but in assessing Montgomery's generalship it is difficult not to feel that more might have been achieved before the Eighth Army's advance next halted at El Agheila. All Montgomery's pre-battle messages and briefings had spoken of victory at El Alamein as an ultimate end in itself when it might have been more farsighted to lend some attention to the opportunities victory would bring. Montgomery's original description of X Corps as a 'corps de chasse' naturally suggested an intention of using it in pursuit operations. This intention was almost entirely nullified by the total commitment of its units to the succession of shifting blows which were used to win the battle and the mixing with XXX Corps formations that Monty's unwise structuring of his army created. The fact that such shifting blows were necessary also

Below: *Monty receives his distinguished prisoner, Gen Ritter von Thoma, at his desert HQ, before treating him to dinner. This courtesy provoked great controversy back in Britain.*

contributed to the milling, dusty confusion in the rear as support formations were also constantly on the move.

Comparing Montgomery, having just won his breakthrough, with Rommel, at those times when his past great advances began, is revealing. Time and again in those days Rommel was seen driving furiously up to dawdling units or flying over in his light aircraft and dropping peremptory messages to get moving forward or else. Instead, on the evening of 4 November Montgomery is at his HQ enjoying dinner with General von Thoma, captured commander of the Afrika Korps, and on the next day he has time to give a press conference. It would certainly be unwise to infer too much from this brief comparison and it would be incorrect to suggest that simplistic front-line leadership was as appropriate in the much larger Eighth Army of November 1942 as in the Afrika Korps in the spring of 1941 but the fact remains that there is not the same sense of urgency or grip emanating from Monty in the days after Alamein. Nor, tellingly, even in his *Memoirs* is there a description of any clear plan for the pursuit.

Indeed, when presented with the opportunity to prepare for an immediate pursuit, Monty consistently turned it down. During the last phase of the Alamein battle de Guingand had tried to collect various units as a reserve to exploit the victory when it came, but Monty prevented this, employing any formation thus available in the continuing struggle. General Briggs of 1st Armoured Division asked near the end of the battle to be allowed to restock his support vehicles with more fuel and less ammunition, ready for mobile operations, but this was denied. Similarly 4th Indian Division, little used in the battle and with ample desert experience and able leaders, prepared plans for a deep exploitation but instead was not employed in the pursuit at all.

Montgomery later claimed that the heavy and unexpected rainfall of the afternoon and evening of 6 November was all that enabled Rommel to make good his initial escape but historians now generally agree that this was nonsense and that by then Rommel had already begun to slip out of Monty's reach. After the delay caused by Hitler's 'stand fast' order the definitive retreat had started on the 4th. Throughout the 5th and 6th the leading British armoured brigades and the New Zealand Division all tried various short 'left hooks' toward the coast in attempts to cut off the enemy retreat. These had modest success as when, on the 5th, 8th Armoured Brigade destroyed a number of Italian tanks near Galal station, but progress was by and large painfully slow. Staff work was poor and traffic control lacking among the dusty, tangled paths through the minefields, barbed wire, trenches, and weapon pits. Front-line units ran short of petrol while their supports were impeded by hundreds of vehicles

Above: *Sherman tanks manoeuvring in the desert. The Sherman had good mobility and its 75mm gun was adequate when it was introduced in 1942 but it was seriously out-gunned by improved German types later in the war.*

Below: *The Torch landings.*

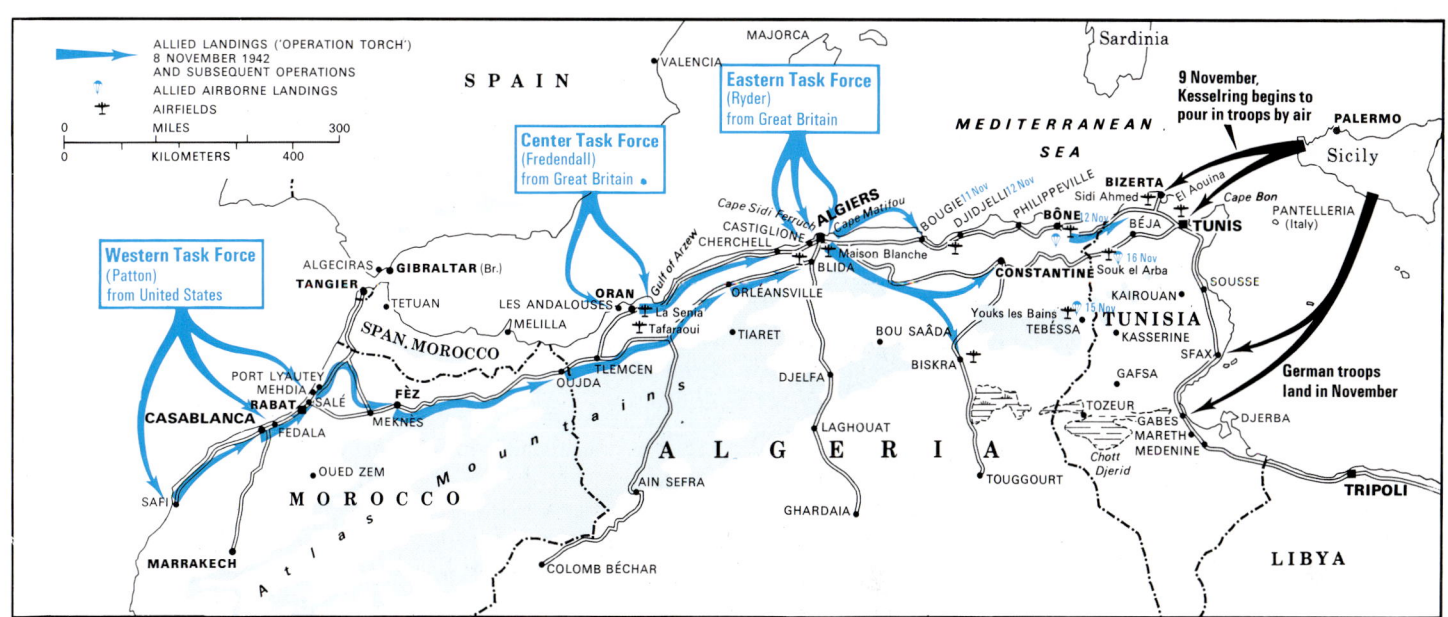

Above: *British tanks passing through Mersa Matruh during the advance from Alamein. The column of Shermans is led by a command version of the Crusader type with its main gun removed and replaced by additional radio equipment.*

Top right: *A destroyer passes astern of an escort carrier during the Torch landings.*

Right: *Monty looks out over the small harbour at Sollum near the Egyptian frontier shortly after its capture during the advance.*

which had no business to be on the congested routes. Again some of the moves Montgomery ordered had units crossing the communications of others and all the moves were too confined and unambitious. Certainly there was a lack of drive and leadership further down the line – Montgomery continued to complain with some justice of Lumsden and Gatehouse of 10th Armoured Division and would soon sack both – but he was already warning his juniors of the danger of a riposte from Rommel. In fact Montgomery knew from his intelligence that Rommel had fewer than 20 tanks left and not enough fuel even for this small number. The historian Correlli Barnett summarized the position well:

> Montgomery took Tobruk on 13th November; his eleven days for the distance from Alamein compares with Rommel's nine in the reverse direction (in June 1942), when he deployed for, fought and won a battle on the way.

It is worth adding that Rommel could not have gone faster on the retreat because of his fuel difficulties but Montgomery should have been able to find a way. Perhaps it was a time when Montgomery should have involved himself in the type of details he usually left to his staff and used his authority to see that the forward units were not hindered by the tangles to the rear. The other side of this coin would have been to have given his front line commanders more general objectives and perhaps to have pursued with a smaller and hence better supported force. This would have offended, however, against Montgomery's need always to be in control himself – his own words on this period refer to his 'precise instructions' and how he 'kept a firm hand on the battle'.

If Montgomery lost an initial opportunity to capture much of the remaining Axis force as Rommel pulled back from Egypt past Tobruk, it is also arguable that a second chance was lost to emulate General O'Connor's success at Beda Fomm in the first desert campaign by sending strong forces across the interior of Cyrenaica to cut the coast road between Benghazi and El Agheila. The first specific objective of Montgomery's advance was to seize airfields in the Martuba area west of Tobruk so that these could be used to support Malta convoys. Even before Eighth Army left Egypt it should have been obvious from decoded German signals that Rommel could have no hope of holding either these or Tobruk and that most of his retreating army

would have to continue back along the coast road. At this stage, by Montgomery's choice, it was the worn-out tanks of 22nd Armoured Brigade which provided the strongest part of Eighth Army's advance guard. It was not until 16 November, after Rommel's weakness and fuel problems had been spelled out in no uncertain terms in another decoded signal that Montgomery made a serious attempt to send 22nd Armoured Brigade to cut the German retreat from Benghazi. By then it was far too late.

Montgomery always said that one of the most important qualities in a general was the ability to plan well ahead and his admirers would with justice claim this as one of his chief virtues. Unfortunately there were also occasions when he would stick to his original appreciation of a forthcoming problem and ignore ways in which circumstances had changed. In his *Memoirs* Montgomery wrote that on arriving in Africa he foresaw that forcing the El Agheila position would be the next important and difficult operation after the Germans had been thrown out of Egypt. El Agheila had after all been the point where both Wavell and Auchinleck in the past had had their victorious advances turned by Rommel into ruinous defeat and retreat and so,

Left: *A classic image of the desert war. A Vickers machine-gun team firing at German positions near Mersa Matruh.*

Below left: *Men of a Sherman unit enjoy a brief interlude to celebrate Christmas 1942.*

superficially at least, there was cause for caution. Realistically, however, there was no likelihood of Rommel attacking. It was inconceivable that he would risk an advance when uncertain about the progress of the Allied invasion of Algeria and Tunisia to his rear and, unlike his predecessors, Montgomery was not being required to weaken his forces substantially for the benefit of other campaigns. Instead he could build up as fast as his administrative back-up allowed. Despite this, Monty even briefly suggested that the Allies should plan to capture Tripoli and the rest of Tripolitania from the west, a hope that became impractical as the Germans poured land and air reinforcements into Tunisia and halted the Allied advance there in early December.

Montgomery believed that a formal attack was needed to clear the Germans and Italians out of the Agheila position and took three weeks to prepare it. Rommel had no intention of trying to fight and even before Monty's attack began he was thinning out his front by sending back much of his Italian infantry, leaving only more mobile units as a rearguard. Monty's advance was made by 51st Division along the coast road, and 7th Armoured Division

Above: *An excellent example of how a brief rainstorm could transform mobility in the desert war. Monty himself cited this as the reason for Rommel's escape after his defeat at Alamein.*

farther inland, while the New Zealanders and a supporting armoured brigade made a wide outflanking move through difficult terrain to the south. By the time the New Zealanders reached the coast road a few miles west of Mussolini's grand triumphal monument known to the British as Marble Arch, most of the remaining Axis force, warned by the frontal attack, were already retreating. An optimistic broadcast by Cairo radio reported that Montgomery was about to capture most of the Afrika Korps but this was wishful thinking. All the Eighth Army forces were delayed by mines and booby traps and most of the Germans successfully slipped away. Montgomery might have done better to have held up his frontal attack until his turning manoeuvre was further advanced but it was always likely to be virtually impossible to catch an able opponent who was determined to withdraw rather than fight a major battle.

The next large-scale action was at Buerat 200 miles farther west. Monty very sensibly planned that once the attack began it must be provided with the resources to reach all the way to Tripoli (an additional 200 miles on) before the next pause. Despite the firm orders he received to hold at Buerat, Rommel would have done better to defend nearer to Tripoli in the area of Homs and Tarhuna, but he was also keeping an eye on the still-stronger positions to the rear, around the Gabes gap over the border in Tunisia. Montgomery's offensive began as scheduled on 15 January with 51st Division attacking along the coast and the New Zealanders and the 7th Armoured Division performing the customary inland move. Montgomery had some 500 tanks against (as he well knew) 34 German and 57 Italian and, although his manpower superiority was not nearly as great, the German positions were never strong enough to hold.

Montgomery's attack had almost been delayed, however, by a severe storm on 3 January, and subsequent poor weather, which caused great damage at Benghazi and greatly reduced the cargo capacity of that port. Montgomery had intended to have another division in the advance and also to bring X Corps forward from the Tobruk area to El Agheila to act as a 'back-stop' in the worst case. Instead, to assemble sufficient supplies for his attack, he grounded X Corps and had Horrocks organize all its transport vehicles to bring supplies forward to the front line.

Montgomery had hoped that the enemy would fight longer for the Buerat position but instead they withdrew gradually, mining and booby-trapping as they went. On 23 January 1943 Eighth Army entered Tripoli. Tripoli had been the great prize that had eluded Wavell and Auchinleck when they had commanded in the Middle East; it was the last major town of Italy's overseas empire. Although the Germans and Italians had successfully removed the great mass of stores in the town and substantially destroyed the port installations, this was a triumph indeed – compounded by the remarkable work by naval parties and Eighth Army engineers which enabled the port to dock its first ship on 3 February. Monty was the hero of the hour.

Churchill arrived in Tripoli on that same day and in an emotional speech to Montgomery's headquarters' team he added to the stream of praise:

> Ever since your victory at Alamein, you have nightly pitched your moving tents a day's march nearer home. In days to come when people ask you what you did in the Second World War, it will be enough to say: 'I marched with the Eighth Army'.

The next day there was a ceremonial parade in the city – the Highland Division had somehow managed to lay hands on their kilts – and Churchill and other senior onlookers were openly in tears. For Montgomery this display of public and Prime

Above: *Australian gunners, among the various nationalities which made up Eighth Army.*

Ministerial approval must have seemed like a complete vindication of his conduct throughout the campaign.

Churchill's presence in Africa was as a result of the major Anglo-American strategic planning conference held at Casablanca during January. Among numerous other matters, this conference decided (with more enthusiasm from the British than the Americans) that, after the completion of the war in Africa, the Allied forces in the Mediterranean theatre would next invade Sicily. Monty's part in planning and executing this operation will be described in the next chapter. In the shorter term General Alexander was soon to take over as deputy to General Eisenhower, commander of the forces in north-west Africa, with responsibility for co-ordinating their land operations with those of Eighth Army. Monty's work was indeed being tied in ever closer to a much larger scheme of things.

In the pause in Eighth Army operations which necessarily occurred while Tripoli was opened and supplies were assembled for the next advance, Monty had organized a senior officers' training conference. Various members of the top brass from Britain joined the participants from Eighth Army but there were only comparatively junior officers from British First Army in Tunisia and, according to a letter written by a disappointed Montgomery at the time, 'only one American general.... an old man of about 60.' The old man in fact would soon become much better known – General Patton. Patton was rude in public about the proceedings at the conference but privately, in his diary, gave an interesting, double-edged verdict on his host, 'very alert, wonderfully conceited, and the best soldier – or so it seems – I have met in this war.'

In fact Patton was not the only American general at the conference; also present was Eisenhower's

Above & top: *Two views of the victory parade in Tripoli. Monty saluting a tank unit and Churchill in a staff car with Leese and Monty.*

0500 hrs, 23 January 1943
Eighth Army enters Tripoli
GABES
MARETH
Mareth Line
MEDENINE
16 Feb
BEN GARDANE
ZUARA
TRIPOLI
TUNISIA
CORRADINI
HOMS 20 Jan
Castel Benito
TARHUNA
19 Jan
MISURATA
51 (H) Div
Free French Force
(Leclerc)
from Chad via Murzuk
BUERAT
GULF OF SIRTE
SIRTE
XXX Corps
(Supply line from Tobruk
operated by X Corps)
15 Jan 1943
7 Armd Div
and NZ Div
Tripolitania
NOFILIA
Marble Arch
16 Dec
EL AGHEILA
17 Dec
NZ Div
MERSA BREGA
13 Dec
AGEDABIA
23 Nov
BENGHAZI
19 Nov
BARCE
Jebel
MSUS
ANTELAT
LIBYA
900
800
700
600
500
1400
1300
1200
1100
1000
900
800

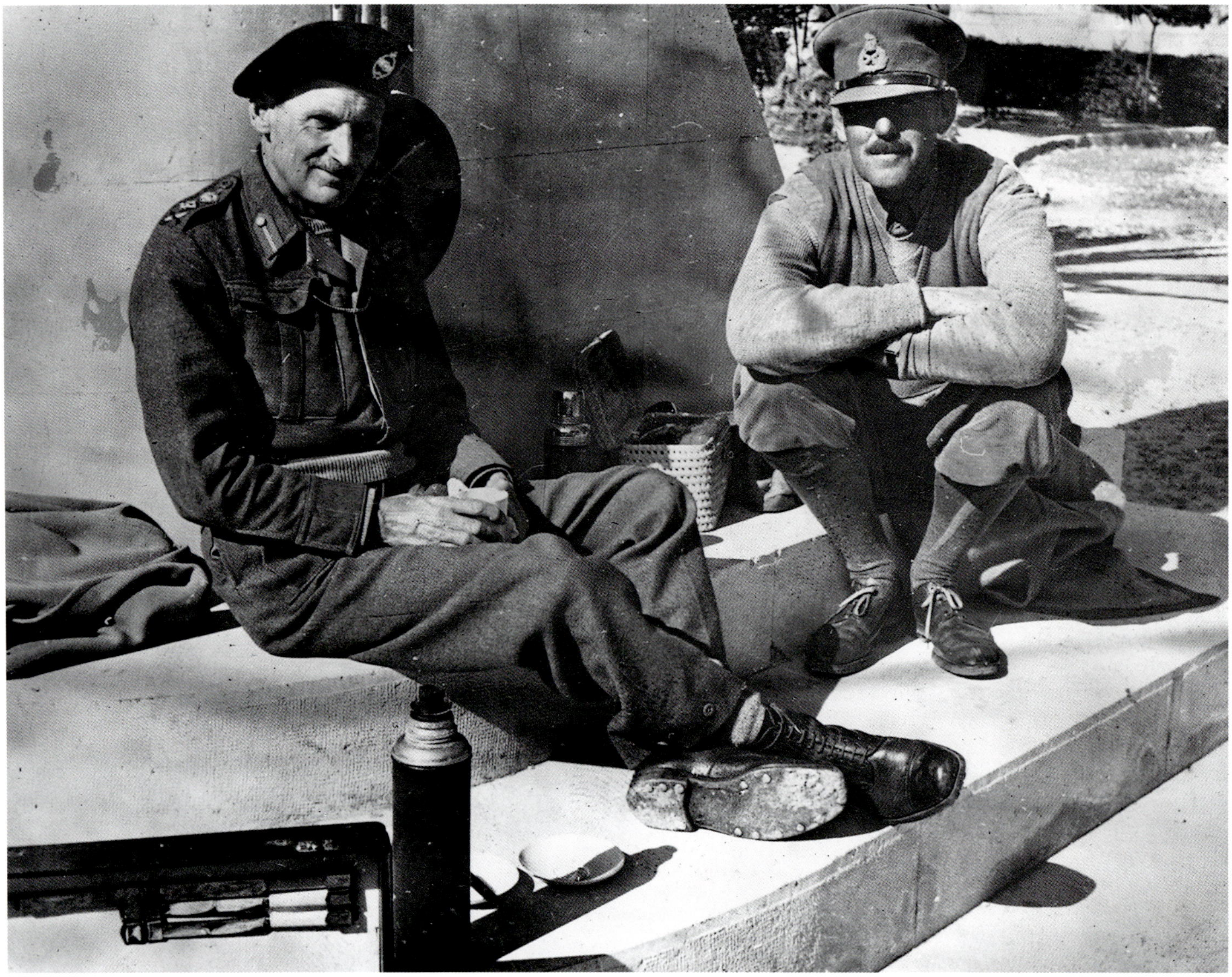

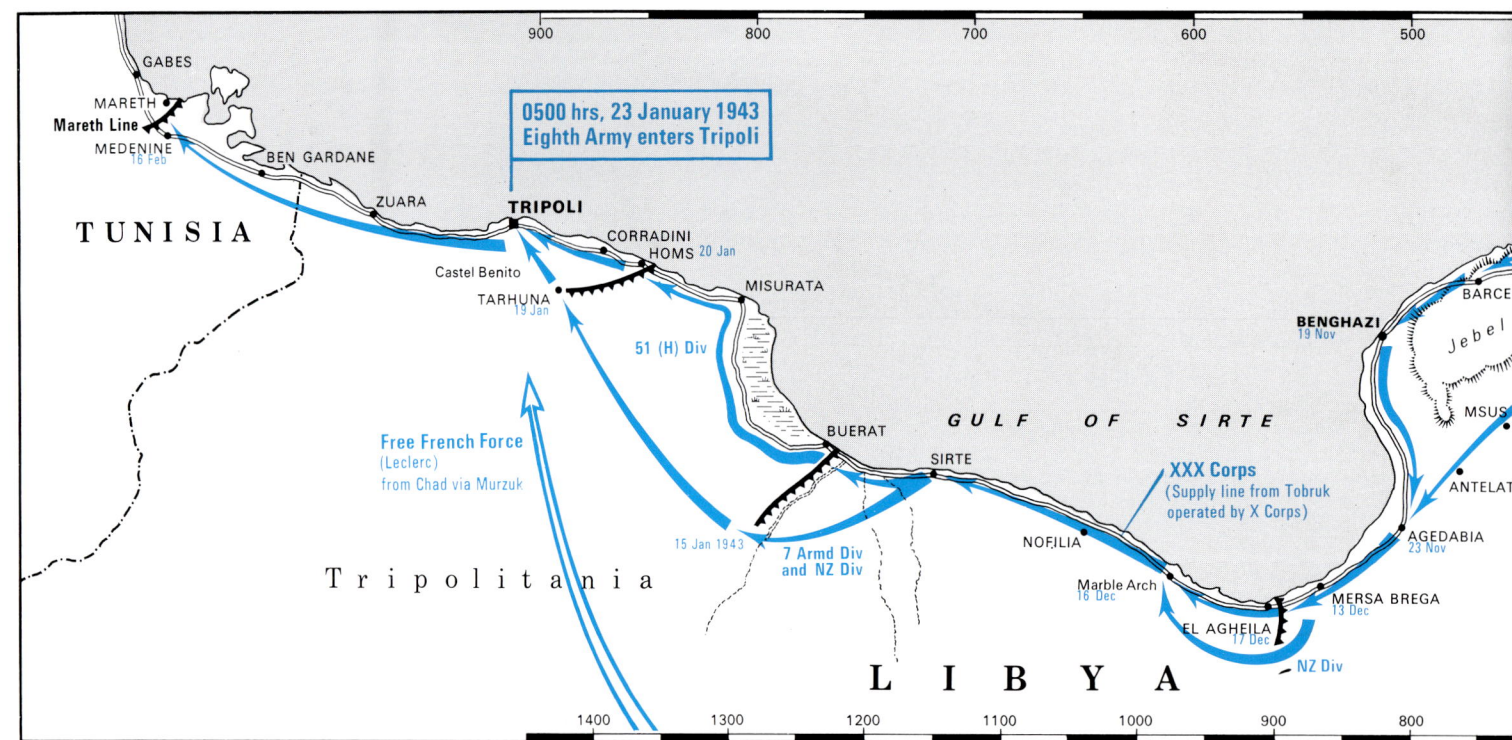

Chief of Staff, Bedell Smith. He and Monty struck a curious 'bet' which is illustrative of the development of Monty's personality. Montgomery boasted that Eighth Army would reach Sfax before a certain date in April. Bedell Smith more or less replied 'Bet you anything you like that you don't,' and Monty set the stake as a US Flying Fortress aircraft and crew to be used as his personal transport. Bedell Smith treated it all as a joke but it stopped being funny in due course when Monty claimed and eventually, by his insistence, collected the stake, ignoring the obvious embarrassment that this would cause. During the campaign in Europe in 1944-1945 Monty kept a betting book at his HQ, as there would be in many an officers' mess, in which wagers were recorded with other generals on matters like when the war would end, but these were for relatively modest sums of at most a few tens of pounds or dollars. That Monty made no distinction between the two kinds of bet, of personal money on the one hand and public property and the services of a crew on the other, is symptomatic of the way that he, even as early as 1943, was becoming distanced from the real views and personalities of his colleagues. He became increasingly forgetful of his obligation, more pressing as his seniority and fame grew, to cultivate good relations with them.

The sort of difficulties the Fortress incident hinted at were also presaged by other events soon after the capture of Tripoli. Montgomery had already heard disturbing gossip of inefficiency among the British and US forces in Tunisia which was soon confirmed in correspondence from Alexander after he took over his new posting on 18 February. Letters from Alex were hardly needed to make the point, for in the days immediately before and after his appointment, the Germans had great success in attacks around Sidi Bou Zid and then in the notorious battle of Kasserine. A combination of British and US reinforcements halted these advances fairly quickly but it was obvious that the raw American troops had not fought well at first. A quarter of a century later Montgomery wrote in his *Memoirs* that the mistakes made by the Americans were similar to those the British had made earlier in the war and that the Americans learned from them far more quickly. This just and accurate opinion was not matched in Montgomery's attitudes at the time and it would do nothing for his relations with US leaders in the coming months that his low opinion of their fighting qualities was ill-concealed. In justice to Monty it should be pointed out

Above: *Monty's personal HQ caravans are now displayed at the Imperial War Museum in London.*

Left: *Monty and Leese enjoy an informal lunch. One of Monty's quirks was generally to carry his own rations when he went to visit front line units, rather than mixing with his near-equals in the officers' mess.*

Below: *The advance from Alamein.*

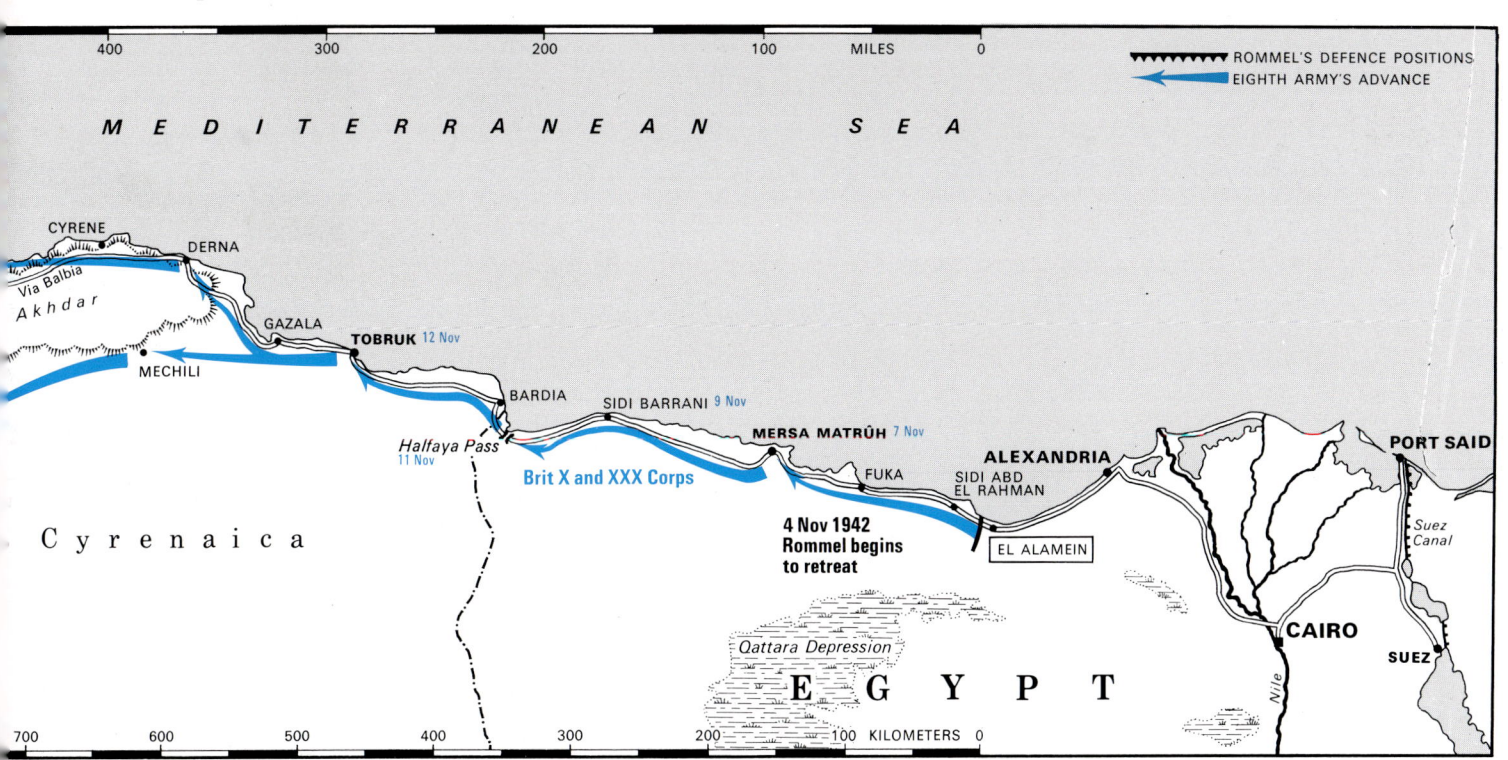

that he was no less scathing about British generals like Anderson, or various of the Home Forces visitors to his conference.

Disputes within the German and Italian high command had done little to aid their performance at Kasserine or indeed during the long retreat from Egypt. Rommel was now 'kicked upstairs' to command all Axis troops in Africa with the Italian General Messe taking over direct control of the forces facing the Eighth Army which were now known as First Italian Army. Rommel hoped to follow the reverse inflicted on US II Corps with a successful spoiling attack on Eighth Army before Tripoli was fully in use and Montgomery's forward strength built up.

Eighth Army had begun to occupy what would be its positions for the coming battle at Medenine on 16 February. Alexander sent Montgomery a message on 21 February asking that he speed up his advance as much as possible to take pressure off First Army. By the 25th definite information was reaching Eighth Army that Rommel planned to attack them next. Montgomery later wrote that his speeded-up advance had helped persuade Rommel to call off the attack at Kasserine but there is little evidence to support this.

Montgomery certainly believed at the time that he was taking a real risk in advancing so quickly and was worried that his front-line force (mostly at this stage from 7th Armoured and the Highland Division) might not be strong enough to resist an attack. More tanks and troops were rushed forward – the New Zealand Division, a Guards Brigade, tanks to bring the inactive 8th Armoured Brigade up to strength, artillery, and anti-tank guns, including a number of the very effective 17-pounders now being used in action for the first time. These had all arrived by the end of 5 March by which time Monty was hoping that his opponents would indeed attack.

The offensive duly came the next day. From before the start, when Messe and the senior German officers debated the plan (Rommel having more or less washed his hands of the affair), it was badly organized. Three German Panzer divisions spearheaded the assault in the morning but they were battered to a halt by the British artillery and anti-tank guns. After regrouping they came on again later in the day, this time with infantry leading, but this effort too was shot to pieces. Early on Montgomery spoke to General Leese, whose XXX Corps had tactical control, and announced that Rommel had made a mistake and he was going to retire to his caravan to catch up with his correspondence. (And we know he did, for several letters of that date survive). Monty was right, for the British deployment had been so well judged that the Germans lost 50 tanks and achieved absolutely nothing before Rommel called off the battle that night. Only a handful of the British tanks were engaged,

Above: *Monty in full flow at one of his characteristic briefings.*

as the anti-tank guns did almost all the execution. As Montgomery described it in one of his letters written that day, 'an absolute gift, the man (Rommel) must be absolutely mad.' Even allowing for Montgomery's material superiority, however, it was certainly an immaculately conducted defensive battle with an untypically amateur German attack being seen off in a thoroughly professional manner. A few days later Rommel was relieved and left Africa for the last time.

It was now Montgomery's turn to attack but the position he was faced with was formidable indeed. Before the war the French colony of Tunisia and Italian Tripolitania had been potential enemies and it was around Mareth that the French had chosen to build their border defences. Many of these installations were still functional (although some pillboxes, for example, were too small for the larger weapons of 1943). The Mareth Line itself ran inland for just over 20 miles from the sea to the rugged Matmata Hills which in turn were bordered to the south by the Dahar sand sea.

The line between the hills and the sea was made particularly strong by the Wadi Zigzaou, effectively an enormous, natural anti-tank ditch. The stream in the bottom of the wadi was up to eight feet deep and the wadi itself was 60 feet or more wide with steep banks of 10-12 feet. The Germans had laid over 150,000 mines in the position, dug the banks of the wadi into steeper slopes in places, and had fixed machine guns and previously arranged artillery plans to cover the practical crossing points. The line was strengthened further by outposts east of the wadi, between it and the Wadi Zeuss which lay more or less in no-man's-land separating the armies.

An offensive via the Matmata Hills was difficult but not out of the question, as there were some minor roads, but it would be a problem to generate any momentum by an attack on this route. In a creditable piece of forward planning Montgomery

Below: *German prisoners taken during the Mareth battle.*

Above: *The crew of a Grant tank watch as German prisoners are escorted through the streets of Tripoli.*

had secretly sent out a Long Range Desert Group party to scout the Mareth position while his main body was still back at El Agheila, and they had discovered that the Dahar was by no means impassable. Access to the Dahar could be gained by the so-called Wilder's Gap (Wilder was one of the LRDG officers) and from there a force could reach the Tebaga Gap. The Germans and Italians were aware of this route from a pre-war French report they had access to but had naturally fortified the direct coastal route with much more care.

Montgomery decided upon a two-pronged attack. The New Zealand Division, strengthened by an armoured brigade and other troops and artillery, would assemble west of Wilder's Gap before setting off to Tebaga and then El Hamma and Gabes, while XXX Corps, led by 50th Division, would make a frontal assault across the Wadi Zigzaou near the coast. 4th Indian Division would be in line in the centre opposite the Matmata Hills and X Corps (1st and 7th Armoured Divisions) would be in reserve behind XXX Corps.

Monty, as usual, was strong in artillery but it was only really in tanks that he otherwise had an overwhelming superiority on the ground. The garrison behind the Wadi Zigzaou was mostly Italian from the *Young Fascist, Trieste, Spezia*, and *Pistoia* Divisions but the veterans of the German 90th Light were also in line. The German 164th Light held the Matmata Hills and initially only a small force was located in the Tebaga Gap. 15th Panzer (32 tanks) was in reserve behind Mareth and 21st Panzer (74 tanks) was near Gabes but was also charged with keeping an eye on developments on the US II Corps front to the north west.

The XXX Corps attack began just before midnight on 20 March with the Eighth Army's biggest barrage since Alamein involving 13 field and 3 medium regiments. The crossing of the Wadi Zigzaou was to be won by 151st Brigade from 50th Division and it would transpire that to attack on a front as narrow as a single brigade was a serious error. Once the attack began the point of crossing became only too obvious to the enemy and quickly attracted heavy defensive fire. Nonetheless, despite casualties, the infantry did establish a significant bridgehead after using the ancient technique of scaling ladders in the actual crossing. The plan was to support them immediately with a tank regiment but despite brave efforts by the engineers only four tanks could be got across during the night after which the route became blocked. Hard fighting followed on the 21st and that night most of the tank regiment did succeed in crossing but the route was so ploughed up by their progress that no other vehicles or, crucially, anti-tank guns could follow. By the next day the Germans had regrouped and 90th Light and 15th Panzer attacked fiercely in the afternoon, knocking out most of the British tanks, and recapturing the lost Axis positions one by one. At 0200 on the 23rd General Leese of XXX Corps came to see Monty (an occasion when it was judged serious enough to waken him) to say that planned attacks could not continue and the battle was lost.

Monty later wrote that he was not too concerned by this news but other witnesses disagree, including de Guingand, who thought it was one of the very few occasions when he ever saw Monty at a loss. If Monty was downcast he had every reason to be since, largely through poor planning, one half of

Above: *A Special Air Service patrol in the desert with their commanding officer Lt-Col David Stirling.*

his twin attack had completely failed. By the morning, however, he had completely recovered his air of confidence and took steps to reinforce his other option.

Before turning to this much more successful phase of the battle, it is worth making some further observations on the frontal attack. The British Official History hints that 50th Division was left pretty much to plan its own show both by XXX Corps and Monty's HQ, which seems surprising and untypical. It has already been suggested that the front of the attack was too narrow but this would not have been open to 50th Division to change without input from higher authority. Also questionable was the decision to employ 23rd Armoured Brigade as the initial support, as that formation was equipped with elderly Valentine tanks, almost all of them the totally outdated version with the 2-pounder gun. Montgomery had hoped to move up the Shermans of 7th Armoured Division next but it is at least arguable that they should have gone in first. By the second day of the battle Monty was correctly stressing to his subordinates the need to get anti-tank guns forward, but again this should have been put in hand with more determination at the start. For all its pre-battle confidence the overall verdict on the Eighth Army performance must be that it failed badly to adapt to the changing conditions once the desert was being left behind.

Freyberg's force, designated the New Zealand Corps for the battle, had completed its assembly to the far side of Wilder's Gap during 19 March, ready to begin the long and difficult march across the Dahar. They were detected en route but despite that, and the difficult terrain, as well as some enemy resistance, they reached the Tebaga Gap (the position known to Eighth Army as 'Plum') during the 21st. Some of Freyberg's subordinates thought it worthwhile to try an immediate attack but he believed this to be too risky, particularly from his point of view as commander of what was a large proportion of New Zealand's fighting manpower. An opportunity was perhaps lost for, during the 22nd, elements of the German 21st Panzer and 164th Light moved to reinforce the Italians opposing the advance.

The next morning, as we have seen, Montgomery was faced with the problem of recasting a battle that had failed completely on his right flank and was now making slow progress on his left. He made two sensible decisions. The withdrawal of the German 164th Light from the central hills had been detected, so he ordered 4th Indian Division to push forward there, which would both threaten to outflank the coastal positions and open a shorter route toward the New Zealanders. Secondly he ordered Horrocks to take his X Corps headquarters and 1st Armoured Division to follow the New Zealanders' route and reinforce and invigorate their attack.

These moves began on the evening of the 23rd and immediately encountered problems, for as 1st Armoured Division passed through the village of Medenine, its route crossed with one of the Indian brigades. Confusion and congestion followed (an armoured division would have over 3000 vehicles) and the end result was that the progress of the Indian Division was delayed by a full day. Since the tank units and the Indian brigade were from different army corps, responsibility for co-ordinating their moves ultimately fell to Eighth Army staff and Montgomery.

This was not the only unsatisfactory aspect of the scheme now under way. While Freyberg may have been dragging his feet, he had been designated a corps commander for the operation and was of such massive seniority and so much a part of the New Zealand set-up that he could not readily be pushed aside. Yet, by Montgomery's order, a second corps commander had been sent off to join the battle. Horrocks sensibly realized the friction this could cause and arranged with the tactful de Guingand that orders should be sent to him and Freyberg jointly.

Horrocks moved off ahead of his troops and reached Freyberg at the front later on the 24th. They turned down a suggestion of Monty's that they undertake an immediate attack and instead various alternative plans were put forward. The record is not clear as to who, if any one person, devised the scheme that was finally adopted but it was certainly a bold and innovative plan. Both Horrocks and de Guingand certainly made important contributions. On the 26th there would be what de Guingand called 'a real blitz attack, using all possible air support.'

The air support plan was devised by the new commander of the Desert Air Force, Air Vice-Marshal Broadhurst, and was, to Montgomery's credit, enthusiastically supported by the army commander despite its novelty. Although Broadhurst's superiors, Coningham and Tedder, had been instrumental in improving British close air support techniques and organization during the desert war of 1941-42, and had had good relations with Montgomery during the early stages of his command, their liking for Monty had cooled dramatically since then. Now they were unhappy with, and tried to stop, Broadhurst's proposals. In particular they opposed Broadhurst's intention to have strong forces of fighter-bombers operating for a significant period at very low level. In general they did not wish to see the whole of the Desert Air Force and other units subordinated so directly to the land battle – in a less extreme version of the delusions of the 'bomber barons', they believed than an air force should concentrate on the role of winning and preserving air supremacy and not lower itself to little more than beefing up the army's artillery barrage. They believed that to devote the whole air force to this purpose was somehow a misuse of air power. It may seem a digression to discuss these points in a biography of Montgomery but the same airmen would remain closely involved with him for the remainder of the war and different versions, often repeated, of this debate would underlie the steady deterioration of personal relationships, which in due course would threaten Montgomery's position.

Above: *A battered Valentine tank. By Mareth the type was clearly outdated.*

Below: *The air force leaders who worked with and sometimes against Monty for the last two years of the war. From left, Tedder, Portal (Chief of the Air Staff), Broadhurst and Coningham.*

Above: *A British tank crew use their Honey tank as an observation post.*

Although Montgomery had wanted to attack sooner than 26 March, Horrocks and Freyberg made him wait, very sensibly, because in fact the last units of 1st Armoured Division only reached their battle positions minutes before the attack began. The attack was codenamed Supercharge, just like the final stage of Alamein, and it was set to start at the unusual time of 1530 with heavy bombing and bombardment of enemy positions. Half an hour later Freyberg's infantry attacked behind a creeping barrage with ground attack aircraft continuously overhead, bombing and strafing. As well as assisting the infantry in the usual way the creeping barrage automatically and unmistakably defined the bomb line between friend and enemy for the RAF pilots. Over 400 support sorties were flown in just over two hours. This crushing weight of attack served its purpose and the infantry fought through almost three miles to their objectives. Then it was the turn of the tanks.

Freyberg had been doubtful whether the tanks would really go through any gap the infantry won but they did. After a pause for the moon to rise, came the next surprise, an all-out drive by moonlight towards El Hamma and the coast road. At times during a remarkable night the advancing tanks of 1st Armoured Division were mingled among retreating Germans. The commander of the German 164th Light saved the battle for them. He assembled a small anti-tank gun screen (probably no more than two 88s, four 50mm and some field guns) a little south of El Hamma and behind that the 15th and 21st Panzer were able to form and hold off the attack long enough for the Mareth garrison, already in retreat, to escape along the coast.

Montgomery had won a notable victory with another large haul of prisoners, a large proportion of which were Germans. In the end it was probably the most enterprising and imaginative of his successes and one of which he was very proud in later life; he even intended at one stage during the compilation of his *History of Warfare* to feature Mareth with more emphasis than Alamein. However, he was probably wrong not to have organized a really strong attack at Wilder's Gap from the first rather than improvise one later and create a traffic jam on the way. Montgomery believed that, even after its end, the frontal attack was justified by the number of Axis reserves retained in that sector. This does not accord with the facts. If a frontal attack was needed it should have been better conducted or, if not needed, it could have been replaced with a feint. Again, Horrocks was a good choice to liven up the left flank attack, but should he not have been sent from the start on a task which was likely to require his established qualities of boldness and enterprise? Perhaps the most notable facet of Montgomery's generalship during the battle was not the ultimate plan of attack but his personal recovery and retention of control after that grim awakening in the small hours of the 23rd.

The next defence line was at Wadi Akarit, 15 miles beyond Gabes. This was the position to which Rommel had longed to retire almost from the moment he left Alamein, but Rommel of course, unknown to Montgomery, was now gone. During the 29th and 30th the New Zealanders and 1st Armoured Division had come up to the line with hopes of quickly driving through it but it was soon clear that a more formal attack was necessary. The Italian General Messe would later describe Wadi Akarit as 'not a good battle' while Monty, in his diary, called it 'the heaviest and most savage fighting we have had since I have commanded the Eighth Army.' It is interesting to contrast this with his version for public consumption in his *Memoirs*. Quoted in full his description there of the battle reads, 'We had a stiff one-day battle on the line of the Wadi Akarit north of Gabes on the 6th April, where we took another 7000 prisoners.' Of course there was far more to it than that, not all of it creditable to the Eighth Army commander.

Once again Monty could be criticized for the delay in mounting his attack, as for every day he spent preparing, the enemy defences got stronger and, as Rommel had appreciated, this position was naturally very strong indeed. It was narrow and well defined, for less than 20 miles inland were the genuinely impassable salt marshes of the Chott el Fedjadj. The Wadi Akarit itself runs inland for some four miles towards the 500-foot-high ridge, Djebel Roumana. From Roumana there is a gap of a couple of miles of better ground to the Djebel Fat-

Above: *Monty inspecting a Gurkha unit of 4th Indian Division. The Gurkhas played a crucial role in the Wadi Akarit engagement.*

nassa, another dominating, jagged ridge towering over the likely battlefield. Monty and his army were fortunate that their enemies were so concerned to defend at Mareth that they had done little to prepare this potentially much stronger position before their army retreated to it. This makes a delay in the attack seem even less advisable. Some mines and barbed wire were set out and there was an anti-tank ditch along much of the front. A number of the deadly 88s were as usual carefully deployed for anti-tank defence.

Montgomery originally planned to make his attack with two divisions, 4th Indian and 51st, the Highlanders taking Roumana and the Indians moving through the gap on the left. Neither of the divisional commanders was happy with the scheme, particularly Tuker of the Indian Division, who feared that his troops would be in danger of attack directed from Djebel Fatnassa. Together the two major-generals approached Leese and convinced him that their alternative, for the Indians to make a surprise night attack on Fatnassa, was superior. Leese persuaded Monty to change his mind and also add 50th Division to the attacking force.

After dark on 5 April the Indian troops, with the hillmen of Gurkha battalions in the lead, began silently to climb among the Italian defenders on Fatnassa. There was no bombardment and surprise was made complete because it would be another ten days before the full moon: the defenders had thought the position so strong and Monty so methodical that he would wait for that before beginning his assault. When the central and right wings of Eighth Army's attack began at 0400 on the 6th most of Fatnassa was already in the Indians' hands.

Both the 50th and 51st Divisions had hard fighting practically from the start, the 50th among the minefields along the anti-tank ditch between Fatnassa and Roumana and the 51st on the slopes of Roumana ridge itself. Nevertheless, by early in the morning it seemed there was a chance for the New Zealand Division to lead the armour of X Corps through, but again there was a delay. A number of tanks of the leading 8th Armoured Brigade were lost to the 88s, and the German reserves, 200 Panzer Grenadier Regiment of 90th Light (the remainder of 90th Light was in the defence line along the wadi) and 15th Panzer made repeated counterattacks during the day. These were fiercely resisted – like Montgomery, the Alamein veterans of the Highland Division described this as their hardest day of

Above: The eventual link-up between First and Eighth Armies.

Right: The opening frontal attack of the Mareth Line battle.

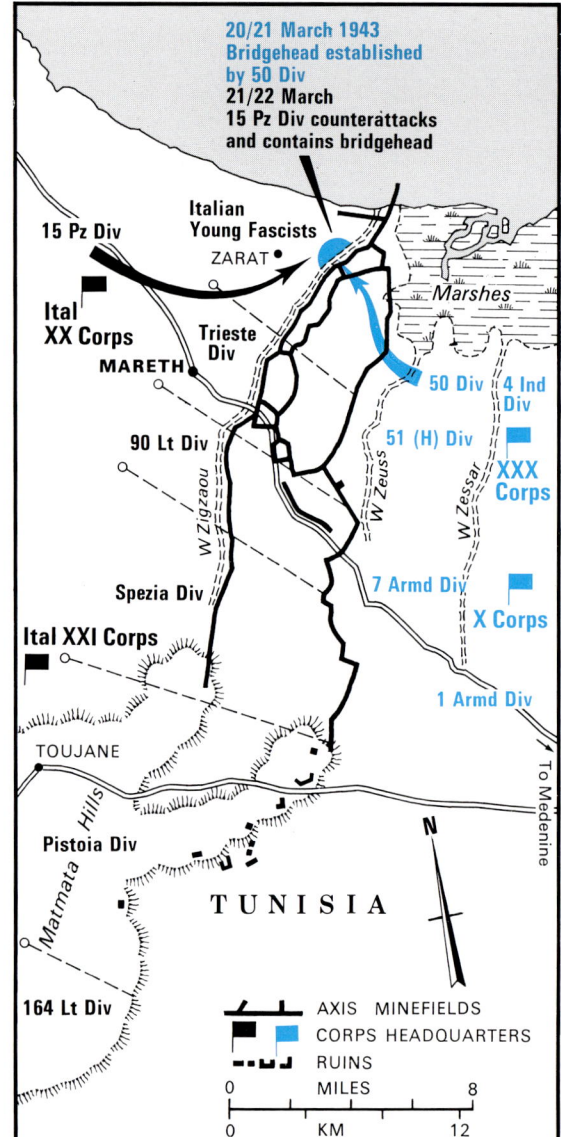

the whole campaign. By the afternoon the German and Italian generals were arguing among themselves but were sure that the battle was lost. By the next day they were in full retreat.

The Axis forces had been hampered in their defence of the Akarit line by the threat of attack from First Army, particularly the US II Corps. This formation had been commanded since the Kasserine débâcle by General Patton and its performance had greatly improved, but there was still no clear sign of the drive and enterprise that Patton was to demonstrate in the future. It is interesting also to contrast the Eighth Army's relaxed attitude to uniform regulations and methodical fighting practice with Patton's near tyranny on dress but fluid operational style. Montgomery had hoped that II Corps would threaten more substantially the rear of Italian First Army. This did not happen, although the threat did hold 10th and 21st Panzer out of the Akarit battle, a concrete illustration of how Montgomery's days of virtually independent action were over. The invasions of Sicily (Operation Husky) and Italy are the subject of the next chapter, but it should be noted here that they were introducing constraints into the African operations. First, from about this time some formations were being withdrawn from front-line duties to refit and train for Husky; second, Monty and other commanders would gradually become, if not preoccupied, then distracted by planning for the new campaign.

As the Germans and Italians retreated from Wadi Akarit and the British advanced, it was obvious that the war in Africa was nearing its end. On 7 April Eighth Army's left wing made contact with US II Corps; on the 10th Eighth Army entered Sfax (enabling Monty to claim his Flying Fortress); on the 11th they made contact with 6th Armoured Division of British IX Corps also from First Army and on the 13th the leading tanks of X Corps reached the next and last enemy defence position near Enfidaville. Over the following two weeks Montgomery would order several attacks on this strong line – each one bloody and unsuccessful. Ronald Lewin summarized the events simply, 'It is impossible to justify such a wanton waste by a seasoned commander except on the grounds that he is mad, ill, or otherwise pre-occupied.' Monty was indeed ill and had other worries but it is still an uncomfortable episode.

Before the Mareth battle began Montgomery had issued a typically forthright order of the day in which he had described Tunis as the Eighth Army's ultimate objective. In fact any sensible analysis of the terrain and distances involved would have shown that it would be far more reasonable to complete the campaign with a drive to Tunis and Bizerta from the west on the First Army front, as was eventually done. Montgomery claimed that his attacks on the Enfidaville position (after the first efforts to 'bounce' the Germans out) were designed principally to apply pressure and draw strength away from the Tunis front. Unfortunately there also remains the suspicion that Monty was hoping for a breakthrough that would allow him to win the final African prize to add to his other laurels. Alexander had told Monty, while Eighth Army was advancing to Enfidaville, that the main effort to finish off the campaign would be made by First Army. This was confirmed by the transfer to First Army of 1st Armoured Division, before the Enfidaville battle began. On the one hand Montgomery was thus co-operating fully with his chief but on the other he was driving Horrocks and his men hard in search of a breakthrough.

As at Wadi Akarit, the Enfidaville position was dominated by a series of jagged crags and ridges which gave superb observation over any potential attack routes and provided numerous defence positions which were almost impossible to hit with artillery. The defenders included what was left of 90th Light and 164th Light among the Germans and the Italian *Young Fascist, Pistoia, Folgore,* and *Spezia* Divisions. All were understrength and short of fuel and ammunition but only the most resolute would have kept fighting to the bitter end.

Montgomery's formal offensive started by the light of the moon on the night of 19 April with 5th New Zealand Brigade attacking the steep and jagged Takrouna hill and village and the Indian Division deployed to take Djebel Garci. Despite losing around one third of the attacking force, the New Zealanders captured Takrouna and held it throughout two days of aggressive counterattacks. Less progress was made on Garci but some ground was gained around Enfidaville village and along the coast. In retrospect it was a misguided effort even if, in Montgomery's defence, one accepts that it was designed to make First Army's 22 April attacks easier. Unfortunately these too were indecisive.

Montgomery was then called away to Cairo on Sicilian business but left strict orders with Horrocks to prepare to break through along the narrow coastal plain. (It is worth adding that de Guingand was also absent during these days following injury in an air accident.) Despite Horrocks's protests that any advance could only bring high casualties, there were further attacks during the nights of the 26th and 28th with the inevitable high price and limited

Top: *A German artillery position bombarding Allied lines.*

Above: *The versatile Messerschmitt Bf 110, which the Germans put to a variety of uses in the desert.*

Right: *The final moment, German prisoners in Tunis.*

Left: *Monty and Alex reflecting on recent successes.*

gains, if any. The 56th Division, a formation new to Eighth Army and without any battle experience, took part in these difficult operations and performed very badly when counter-attacked during the 29th. Montgomery says nothing whatever of these operations in his *Memoirs* and in his earlier *El Alamein to the Sangro* says only, 'I called forward 56th Division from Tripoli,' omitting to mention that the division had spent much of the previous month on the uncomfortable overland journey from Iraq to Tripoli and that its last units only reached the front from Tripoli the day before their attack.

On the 30th sense was restored. Montgomery, now back with Eighth Army, was ill, so ill that Alex came to see him to discuss future plans. At their meeting it was decided that Horrocks would take 7th Armoured Division, 4th Indian, and other units to join and lead IX Corps of First Army in the final drive to Tunis. Montgomery's account, supported by people like Broadhurst and Horrocks, implies that this decisive change was all his idea but Alexander's memoirs naturally tell a slightly different story.

All that now remained for Eighth Army was to watch their former comrades drive into Tunis on 7 May and in the following days accept the surrender of 90th Light and other long-time adversaries. It was less than a year and more than 1800 miles from Alam Halfa.

By the end of his North African campaign, Monty's public reputation was immense. Church bells had been rung in Britain to celebrate the Alamein victory and even in the USA he was re-garded as something of a hero. His reception during an incognito visit to England shortly after the end of the Africa campaign also demonstrated a staggering popularity that he claimed surprised him. The official film of Alamein, *Desert Victory*, was shown throughout the UK and in the USA and USSR to considerable acclaim. Nearer to the action Montgomery was also supportive of his own press and public relations staff whether producing army newspapers for his troops or providing him with photographs of himself to send to his various friends and official and personal correspondents. Perhaps most gratifying were the marks of official

Below: *King George VI and Monty during the King's visit to Eighth Army at the end of the African campaign.*

favour. His promotion to lieutenant-general was made permanent not long before Alamein and shortly after the battle he became a full general and was given a knighthood, that honour conferred when the King came to Tripoli in June 1943.

Public popularity was all very well but what of the genuine military criticisms already being made of Monty? These were, principally, that he was ponderously slow and over-cautious, never attacking until he had a substantial material advantage and a powerful air superiority. Rommel's private papers, which recount a series of supposed 'lost opportunities', now provide much of the ammunition for the criticisms of Montgomery, and could claim a greater degree of impartiality than some memoirs since Rommel never had the chance to adjust them for publication. Montgomery's defenders can rightly point out the great distances advanced by Eighth Army and the fact that, even with substantial administrative efforts, it was never possible to bring the whole of Eighth Army's potential strength to the front after the advance from Alamein began.

Montgomery was right to stress the importance of good administration in this and his other campaigns. He realized that his German opponents were simply too good as soldiers to be treated with anything other than the utmost respect. He was also aware that tank forces could no longer rely on the sort of technical superiority over antitank techniques which had helped the Germans win so many remarkable victories earlier in the war. He had seen how the Germans in Russia in 1941, despite fighting over far shorter distances than the North African campaign entailed, and in spite of qualitative superiority over the Russians, still failed to secure an overall victory. It was Monty's inclination, therefore, to ensure that he laid sound foundations for any tactical move, ever cautious not to squander the resources at his disposal.

Of course such comparisons should not be pushed too far, but it is certain that the collapse of their supply system was central to the German defeat in Russia in 1941. Montgomery did not have all their advantages and would not make the same mistake. Nonetheless with Montgomery there always seems to be an air of over-insurance and an administrative staff who, for all their competence, appear conservative and unambitious. When there was a hint of a crisis approaching at Medenine, for example, it became possible to rush troops, tanks, guns, and supplies to the front in very short order. Could not Montgomery have created a similar sense of urgency on other occasions?

Montgomery's concern for good administration, proper preparations, and remaining, as he put it, 'balanced' at all times has been said to have been based on an unwillingness to take risks. It would be more accurate to say that it involved accepting a different type of risk – as Monty well knew. A

A Day's March Nearer Home

Left: *A German scout group in the desert.*

Opposite, above: *The crew of a Crusader tank clean their 6-pounder gun during a pause from action among the Tunisian hills.*

Opposite, below: *A Bofors light anti-aircraft gun ready for action during the last stages of the advance to capture Tunis.*

Below: *A Bristol Beaufighter sets out on another sortie in the desert.*

Left: *General Horrocks (left), the King, and Monty, Tripoli, 19 June 1943.*

Below: *Gen Patton before he became a household name. After their first encounter he described Monty in his diary as 'the best soldier – or so it seems – I have met in this war.'*

quickly improvised attack risked repulse because it might not be efficiently carried out but a Montgomery set-piece, he was aware, would meet better prepared defenders. On the credit side, however, a properly 'teed up' attack (another Monty expression) would employ what were obviously Eighth Army's strengths – artillery and air power for example – and discount weaknesses – ability to improvise and adjust to new types of terrain and tactical problems. Finally, even if Montgomery's method was to take no chances, why should he? Until the Casablanca conference in January 1943 there was no timetable for future Allied operations and therefore no reason to accept what Montgomery saw as the real-life accompaniment of 'taking risks', increased and unnecessary casualties.

Genuinely felt criticism of Montgomery's supposed slowness was only one aspect of his personal reputation in military circles. His methods of command had increasingly isolated him from worthwhile contact with close contemporaries. He spent much of his time at his Tactical HQ, discouraging visitors, and attended principally only by his young liaison officers. These officers were employed to be

Above: *Monty during his brief visit home at the end of the African campaign. He is shown with his son and his son's guardians, Major and Mrs Tom Reynolds.*

his eyes and ears, visiting all areas of the front (more than Monty could himself) and reporting back on what they found. They were brave and able but inevitably their relationship with Monty was not on an equal basis. Although they supplied their leader's principal social contacts, they could not be in a position to comment informally on his thinking and behaviour as, for example, some of Eisenhower's or Patton's friends were.

Montgomery was often outspoken in criticism of others and his views naturally became the subject of gossip. Not all the targets for his criticism or those doing the gossiping were as generous of spirit and devoted to Allied co-operation as Eisenhower, say, and inevitably grievances were being stored up in many quarters for later use. Some, too, were a consequence of the bad feeling that arose between Eighth and First Armies, which was laid at Monty's door because he had rightly been so concerned to develop the self-esteem of his own command.

One of the undoubted compensations of Montgomery's intolerance of incompetence was that he picked his subordinates very well and, once he had confidence in them, backed them up and helped them whenever he could. Various of his senior subordinates have described, however, how difficult it was to argue with him. Monty's method was to study a problem with the aid of the staff and then himself to decide an answer. Only then would he hold a conference – to issue orders and not to discuss what should be done. All his senior men agreed that, if they wanted to change anything, it was essential to get Monty alone to put suggestions to him (exactly, it will be remembered, as his wife had done during their marriage), so that he could later announce that he had had a new idea or had changed his mind. He could take advice, but he wouldn't admit it. If this was the nature of his relationship with the chosen helpers within his circle, then it is obvious that he would not be likely to benefit from the sort of informal friendly advice from equals or near-equals that might have restrained him from rash or impolitic behaviour.

Two examples of rude and ill-considered conduct that were to occur during the forthcoming Italian campaign can be added here to the growing store of anecdotes circulating, often maliciously embroidered, about Montgomery. During the fighting in Sicily, the commander of the Canadian army in Europe, General McNaughton, arrived hoping to visit 1st Canadian Division at the front. Montgomery refused him permission to land on the island and threatened to arrest him if he tried. Again, once the fighting on the mainland was well under way, General Mark Clark of Fifth US Army arrived at Monty's Tac HQ on one occasion only for Monty to refuse to speak of him. A luckless aide was sent outside to tell Clark that Monty was away visiting the front when it was obviously not true.

Such ridiculous rudeness was only part of a more significant picture of the utmost future relevance. Some might shake their heads and think with a smile that it was only Monty being Monty, but General Brooke knew better. As he wrote in his diary around this time, 'It is most distressing the Americans do not like him.'

Chapter Seven
We Will Surely Make Hard Chewing

Left: *Scenes of devastation in the streets of a Sicilian town.*

Above: *Monty at his HQ.*

In his official report on the invasion of Sicily, General Alexander wrote that in many respects the pre-planning of the attack was of more interest than the actual operations because, or so he said, these 'proceeded according to plan.' Certainly the pre-planning was a complicated and controversial process and Montgomery was predictably in the thick of it.

Montgomery's thinking on the invasion of Italy began with the premiss that fierce resistance could be taken for granted from the German forces present and must be assumed from the much larger Italian contingent who, after all, would now be defending their homeland. The planning for Operation Husky, as the invasion was to be known, also operated under a number of general constraints which apply to all amphibious operations. The first was obviously the availability of suitable beaches coupled with a supply of the correct types of landing craft to operate over them. Air cover was vital: the landing areas had to be within fighter-range of Malta, Pantelleria, and Lampedusa (the last two islands were captured by the Allies in June). Moreover airfields ashore had to be neutralized or, preferably, captured and put into Allied service as soon as possible to offset the defending air force's inevitable advantage of having its bases nearer to the action. The army and navy also needed ports, for only in this way could sufficient supplies be landed to support the fighting. For the invasion of Sicily, predictably, these demands often conflicted and interacted in an assortment of complicated ways. For example taking enough airfields to satisfy the air force meant, first, increasing the strength of the invasion and hence finding more scarce landing craft, and second, increasing the need to capture additional ports (which were nowhere near the 'extra' landing beaches) or make other arrangements to supply the larger ground forces. In spite of the ramifications, this was the arrangement adopted.

The planning for the invasion of Sicily started with some old British staff studies. Following the decision of the Casablanca conference in January that Sicily would be the next objective of the forces then fighting in Africa, these studies were passed to the Supreme Commander, General Eisenhower, and formed the basis of the work of various planning groups that he had established. From these emerged a plan for landings over a period of several days at half a dozen locations from Palermo in the north-west of the island to others on the south coast and still more in the south-east. When Montgomery was introduced to these ideas he was horrified: the dispersion of effort, a brigade group here, another there, landings not mutually supporting, no 'master plan' – as far as he was concerned it was a lesson in how not to plan a battle and a recipe for a

Below: *Monty looks on from the right as Churchill is the centre of attention during the Casablanca conference. The others present are, from right, Eisenhower, Marshall (US Army Chief of Staff), Alexander, Cunningham, Tedder, Brooke, and British Foreign Secretary Eden.*

'first-class disaster'. Accordingly, in his habitual frank and forthright style, he set about having the plan changed.

Montgomery first expressed his dislike for the initial plans early on in March and the history of the meetings, correspondence, and arguments that followed is long and too complicated to be told in detail here, though a few points can be highlighted. First, there was the problem that all the senior commanders were busy with the ongoing battles in Africa. Next there was the simple dispersion of the various elements involved with some of the planners in Algiers, some in Cairo, some later on in Tunis, the RAF in Malta playing an important part, Monty at his front, and Alexander often with the First Army. This provided ample opportunity for simple mishaps to compound existing difficulties. When Monty was ill at the end of April he sent de Guingand to a meeting in his place. De Guingand's aircraft crash-landed and he was injured, so Leese was sent off in a hurry instead but when he arrived, not in full uniform and after finishing his journey by hitching a ride in a truck, he did not really have sufficient authority to argue Eighth Army's case with Tedder and Cunningham, the air and naval Commanders-in-Chief. On another occasion a conference could not get going because Alexander had not arrived: bad weather had grounded his aircraft. Montgomery turned this incident to his advantage by tracking down Eisenhower's Chief of Staff, General Bedell Smith, in the toilet and insisting on putting his arguments to him there and then.

This lavatory lecture in fact marked an important stage in the creation of the final plan. It had already been effectively established that the British contingent in Husky would land in the south-east of

Above: *South African Prime Minister Smuts visits Eisenhower and Alexander.*

Below: *Monty and Eighth Army staff in Malta, July 1943. Freddie de Guingand is on Monty's right.*

the island to capture airfields in the Pachino area and the ports of Syracuse and Augusta. It was now also agreed that the American landings would be in the Gulf of Gela, initially to capture airfields near the beaches there, and not in the north-west near Palermo. This decision required that extra landing and assault shipping would be found and that arrangements be made for the administrative support for the American forces to pass through the ports captured by Eighth Army in the early stages.

Montgomery had certainly caused a great deal of offence during the various arguments as when, for example, he insisted that Broadhurst and the Desert Air Force be involved as soon and as much as possible in the close support of the land battle, alleging that the officer commanding the RAF in Malta was only really knowledgeable in air defence and maritime support operations. Monty had something of a point in this but the officer concerned was the vastly experienced Air Vice-Marshal Park, who had commanded the front line units which won the Battle of Britain and whose Malta pilots had been active over Sicily at every opportunity in the past.

Montgomery also insisted from the start that the British contingent making up the Eastern Task Force for Husky should very clearly be designated as Eighth Army and commanded by his Eighth Army staff. This was a very sensible move to preserve the prestige and esprit de corps that he had spent such effort in building, and it was also valuable in that the soldiers of the 1st Canadian Division, coming from England to join the operation, were also, by all accounts, heartened and inspired to become part of such a famous fighting formation. However, Montgomery overstepped the mark by suggesting, once the plans had been adapted to his taste, that the American landings in the Gulf of Gela should also be controlled by the Eighth Army. To anyone with the slightest grasp of political realities this was clearly an impossibility, whether it was militarily desirable or not. Instead Patton's West-

Below: *The invasion and capture of Sicily.*

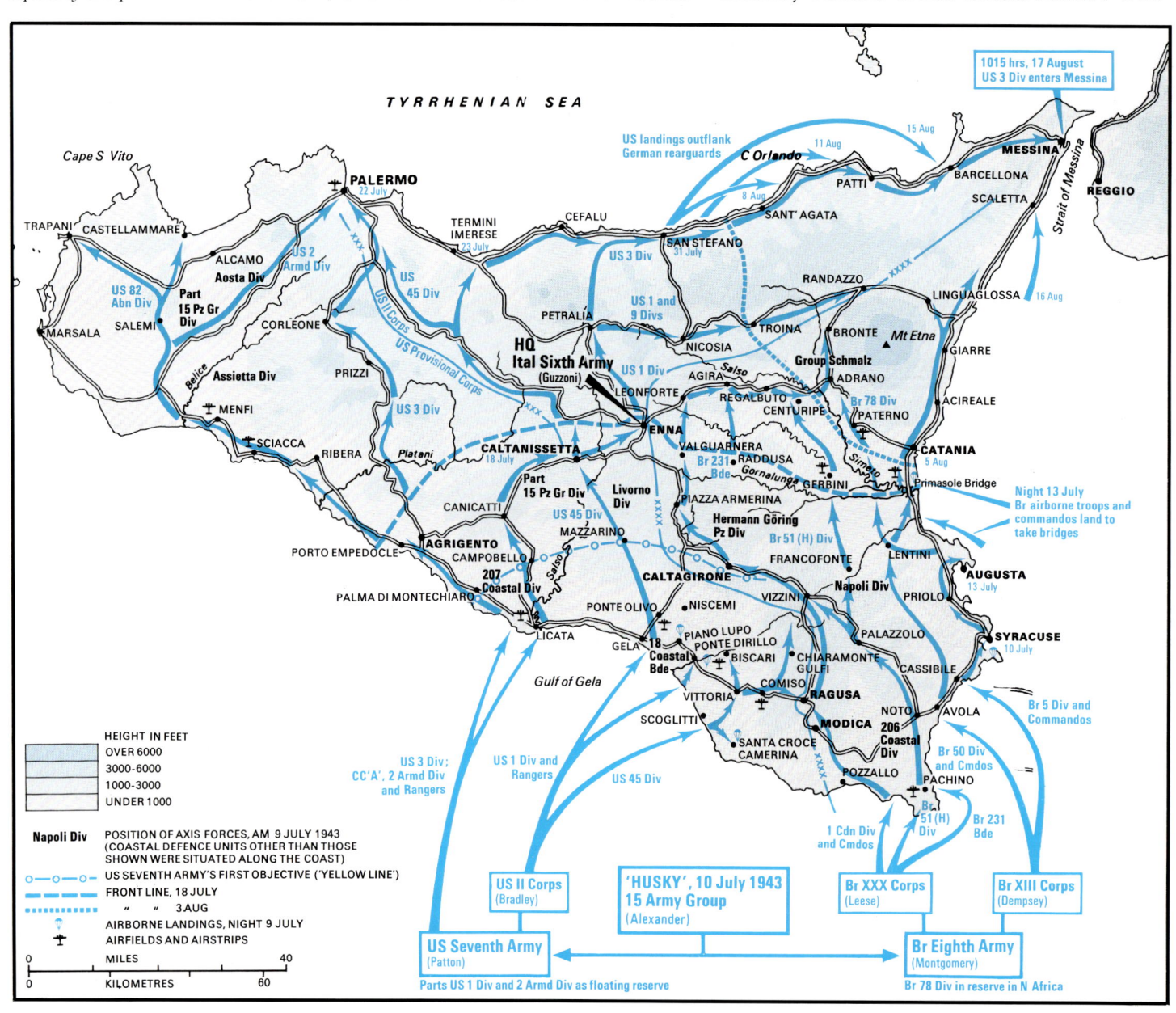

ern Task Force was upgraded to full army status (as Seventh Army).

To do Montgomery justice this suggestion was more to do with a genuine military judgement and desire for well co-ordinated operations than mere self-interest. He firmly believed that it was essential in any planning process to appoint the commander for the eventual operation at the start so that the plan could match his objectives and so that he could give firm decisions on any contentious matters. (Ideally, the commander would not be involved in other operations.) Only thus could a 'master plan' be created and held to, and the various departments of all the services do their work properly. Montgomery's constant complaint during the Sicily campaign and, even more forcefully, during the invasion of mainland Italy, was that there was no clear strategic objective and never a master plan. Monty was right in this but probably less correct to fault Alexander as he did, although this does largely explain his efforts to extend his responsibilities into areas that were clearly Alexander's. Alexander was by no means to blame, for at the heart of the problem was the dispute between the British and Americans, at the highest level, on the value of the Italian campaign in general. The details of this are beyond the scope of this book but the outcome for Montgomery was that some of his divisions would go home at the end of Husky, some during operations in the later months of the year, and he himself would be summoned back to Britain in December.

Overall, there is little doubt that Montgomery was absolutely right to do everything in his power to change the plans for Husky. One history of the

Above: *General Patton in typically aggressive pose during the fighting for Sicily.*

Left: *De Guingand, Graham (head of Eighth Army administration), Monty and Broadhurst during the fighting on Sicily. Note the cage for Monty's pet canaries hanging behind.*

Italian campaign correctly points out that 'in a seaborne invasion, to withdraw is to drown.' Husky would be the largest amphibious operation ever attempted up to that time and historical precedents, starting with Dieppe, suggested that opposed landings were a most difficult operation of war. Memories of earlier disasters on land like Kasserine, or Eighth Army's retreat from Tobruk in 1942, were also still fresh enough to douse any false optimism. No responsible leader could possibly have counted on Italian forces supplying as little resistance as they did in the event, and the first plans could scarcely have given greater opportunity for the landings to be defeated in detail. General Dempsey, who commanded XIII Corps in Sicily and was one of Britain's most able soldiers of the war, later gave it as his opinion that Montgomery's input to the planning of Husky was his greatest achievement. This may be doubted in view of Monty's similar contribution in putting 'Overlord' on the right track in 1944 and in view of the weakness and incompleteness of the Husky plan in other respects: weak because it tended to allocate a subsidiary role to Patton's forces and incomplete because it did not set out a clear pattern for subsequent operations. These faults contributed to the poor co-ordination which transpired between Patton and Montgomery.

The actual invasion began on 10 July 1943 with the XIII and XXX Corps of Eighth Army landing south of Syracuse and around the Pachino peninsula. Four divisions and commando and airborne forces were in the initial landings. The US forces, Bradley's II Corps and other air- and seaborne units, went ashore in the Gulf of Gela, around Gela itself and near Licata. About 150,000 men would be landed in the first few days. They were opposed by around 200,000 Italian troops and around 35,000 Germans in two divisions, 15th Panzer Grenadier and the Luftwaffe *Hermann Göring* Division.

Bad weather threatened to disrupt the seaborne landings, and paratroop and glider operations in both the British and US sectors were a disgraceful shambles with severe casualties caused by 'friendly' anti-aircraft fire and when gliders and paratroopers were dropped in the sea by inexperienced pilots. Nonetheless, the initial landings were successful and the important port of Syracuse was captured later on the first day.

It was obvious that the ultimate objective must be to take Messina in the north-east for this would definitely cut off any Axis forces remaining on the island. However, access to Messina would be governed by the need to bypass the dominating bulk of Mount Etna to the south of the town. This meant negotiating the rugged terrain on the island proper, with its jagged, steep, rocky hillsides and inaccessible mountain villages overlooking the few good roads. There were naturally also the Germans and their plans to consider. Hitler's first reaction,

unsurprisingly, was to order that the invaders be thrown back into the sea but this was soon modified into an intention to hold a bridgehead in the north-east of the island and this in turn became a decision to evacuate all forces. Any criticism of the attackers for failing to win a more substantial victory must take into account this combination of unfavourable geography and the Germans' defence plans. It would be very difficult indeed to prevent able and determined troops from making a controlled retreat, if that was their plan, in such awkward terrain. Montgomery often claimed that in his battles he made the enemy dance to his tune but, as some commentators have suggested, on Sicily it would be more true to say that the Germans retreated and eventually left the island in their own good time.

This conclusion is not meant to suggest that the battles were without controversy on the Allied side. Essentially one good road ran north along the east coast from the British landing areas, which

Top: *Monty is cheered by a group of Canadian soldiers after giving a speech to their battalion.*

Above: *Monty and Patton pose amicably for the camera with a map of Sicily, a picture taken in the royal palace at Palermo shortly after the Americans captured the town. Monty's Flying Fortress was badly damaged in a landing accident when he came to see Patton at Palermo on 28 July.*

Above: *Heavily laden soldiers of the Highland Division struggle ashore near Pachino.*

Dempsey's XIII Corps was using, to advance first on Augusta, captured on 13 July, and then, it was hoped, Catania and Messina. The only other significant road that could be accessible to Eighth Army was the one running from Vizzini through Caltagirone, Enna, and from there round the west side of Etna. Unfortunately, from Montgomery's point of view, this road was in the sector allocated to Bradley's II Corps. It caused enough offence to Patton and Bradley that Montgomery persuaded Alexander to adjust the boundaries in his favour, but it caused still more when troops of the Highland Divison were found to be using the road on the 13th, before the boundary change came into effect.

Montgomery's hope was to advance Leese's XXX Corps by this road to 'cut the island in half' and then move towards Messina on this axis as well as with XIII Corps. The US Seventh Army in the meantime would do little more than guard the left flank. This would never be enough to satisfy Patton and he soon convinced Alexander to make a further change and allow the Americans to advance towards Palermo; this they did with impressive speed. Unfortunately this was really a diversion from the true Allied interests, for the port facilities of Palermo were no longer essential once both Syracuse and Augusta had been taken.

Montgomery's decision to split his advance over two routes also proved unwise, as XIII Corps was halted in fierce fighting on the approaches to Catania, while XXX Corps, in spite of enterprising attacks by the new Canadian Division, was also held up. Montgomery might have done better at the start to concentrate more of his attacking power near the coast road, if the communications to that sector could have been made to support a larger force. Also, if Seventh Army had been permitted their original road allocation, they could have attacked powerfully towards the centre of the north coast and then to Messina, leaving Palermo and any enemy troops in the west of the island to be dealt with later.

EIGHTH ARMY

PERSONAL MESSAGE FROM THE ARMY COMMANDER

To be read out to all Troops

1. The time has now come to carry the war into Italy, and into the Continent of Europe. The Italian Overseas Empire has been exterminated; we will now deal with the home country.

2. To the Eighth Army has been given the great honour of representing the British Empire in the Allied Force which is now to carry out this task. On our left will be our American allies. Together we will set about the Italians in their own country in no uncertain way; they came into this war to suit themselves and they must now take the consequences; they asked for it, and they will now get it.

3. On behalf of us all I want to give a very hearty welcome to the Canadian troops that are now joining the Eighth Army. I know well the fighting men of Canada; they are magnificent soldiers, and the long and careful training they have received in England will now be put to very good use—to the great benefit of the Eighth Army.

4. The task in front of us is not easy. But it is not so difficult as many we have had in the past, and have overcome successfully. In all our operations we have always had the close and intimate support of the Royal Navy and the R.A.F., and because of that support we have always succeeded. In this operation the combined effort of the three fighting services is being applied in tremendous strength, and nothing will be able to stand against it. The three of us together—Navy, Army and Air Force—will see the thing through. I want all of you, my soldiers, to know that I have complete confidence in the successful outcome of this operation.

5. Therefore, with faith in God and with enthusiasm for our cause and for the day of battle, let us all enter into this contest with stout hearts and with determination to conquer.

The eyes of our families, and in fact of the whole Empire, will be on us once the battle starts; we will see that they get good news and plenty of it.

6. To each one of you, whatever may be your rank or employment, I would say:

GOOD LUCK AND GOOD HUNTING IN THE HOME COUNTRY OF ITALY

B. L. Montgomery.

General,
Eighth Army.

Above: *Monty's message to his troops at the start of the battle for Sicily.*

Right: *A deceptively peaceful scene as the sun rises over the Allied invasion fleet off Salerno.*

It remains doubtful if any substantially better success would have resulted from this strategy. The Germans (for they were pretty much in control of the whole defence) were retiring to the northeast of the island in any case, fighting aggressive and effective rearguard actions as they went. On 25 July Mussolini was deposed by the Italians and a new government began secret negotiations with the Allies for an armistice. For the fighting on Sicily this meant, first, that the Germans more openly took charge, and, second that on the 27th Field Marshal Kesselring, the German Commander-in-Chief in Italy, gave orders for the evacuation of the island. Eighth Army continued to have to fight hard to push forward to Catania (taken only on 5 August) and on the inland route towards Messina. By the end of July Patton's men were also driving aggressively along the north coast, with Patton determined that he would beat Montgomery to Messina. There is less evidence that Monty saw the situation as a personal race for prestige with Patton (Monty willingly offered Seventh Army the lion's share of the good roads near the north coast) but this atmosphere of jealous competition certainly existed and would be a factor in their future relationship. Race or not, Patton's men were first into Messina by a few hours, quickly followed by their commander making a hazardous triumphal entry on the 17th.

The final unsatisfactory aspect of the campaign was that some 60,000 Germans (and a rather greater number of Italians) and a great deal of equipment and arms were successfully evacuated across the Straits of Messina, despite the Allied air and naval supremacy. Bearing in mind the vehicles and other resources taken from the Italians, the German units

were probably better equipped when they returned to the Italian mainland than when they first arrived in Sicily. Of course, the failure to do more to hinder this evacuation with air and sea attacks was not of Montgomery's making, particularly since he had been very active in urging that more be done in this respect.

After the fall of Sicily some of the experienced Eighth Army and American divisions were to go to Britain, in fact to be readied to lead the invasion of France. A song written by a Scottish soldier, *The Highland Division's Farewell to Sicily*, very neatly sums up the veterans' feelings after the long struggle in Africa and the recent vicious battles.

> Fareweel ye banks o'Sicily,
> Fare ye weel ye valley and shaw,
> There's nae Jock will mourn the kyles o'ye
> Poor bloody squaddies are weary.

Were the prospects for the invasion of Italy, which was to be the next step, any more hopeful? As will be seen the Italian surrender was shortly to follow and there was the possibility that the Germans might cut their losses and pull out to the north. Unfortunately, as a letter taken in October from a dead German soldier by a young Canadian officer hinted, these were false hopes and much fierce fighting in vile conditions lay ahead.

> The Führer has ordered us to hold Rome at all costs. This shouldn't be too hard if you have any idea of the kind of country here. It is made for defence and the Tommies will have to chew their way through us inch by inch, and we will surely make hard chewing.

If the strategic background to the Allied invasion of Sicily had been confused, then the preparations for the invasion of the Italian mainland were worse. With the fall of Sicily the simple objective of making the routes through the Mediterranean safe for Allied shipping had been achieved. Mussolini's deposition and the approaches made by the new Italian government suggested that the next objective, to knock Italy out of the war, might not be far off. There was enormous political pressure on Britain and the US to open a 'Second Front' in Europe as soon as possible to aid the Russians who were still engaging the bulk of Germany's armed forces. By the early summer of 1943 it was clear that there could not possibly be an invasion of Western Europe that year. (There was only one US division in Britain by the start of May 1943.) In those circumstances the substantial forces in the Mediterranean theatre could not remain idle and so it was agreed that the Italian mainland be invaded. There was one clear physical objective – to take airfields in the Foggia area so that these could be developed as bases for Allied heavy bombers to attack southern Germany and the important German-controlled oilfields in Romania. Beyond that and the vague hope of knocking Italy out of the war, General Eisenhower was told only that certain army and airforce units and much assault shipping were to be withdrawn to the UK later in the year.

This uncertainty of purpose was compounded by the difficulty of judging the progress of negotiations with the new Italian government. They were promising to change sides but wanted to know more of Allied plans first. Some Allied leaders believed that the Italians would be able to turn on the German forces in Italy and seize control as far north as Rome, or even beyond with some Allied help. Montgomery was much less optimistic, saying that the Germans would 'stamp on the Italians' (his own words) and that the Allies could expect no worthwhile military assistance. As is usual when a pessimist is proved right, Monty's accurate prediction did nothing to improve his popularity or reputation for being over-cautious.

In this atmosphere of confusion it is no surprise to learn that the Allied staff produced a barrage of contingency plans for the invasion of Italy. Barracuda, Gangway, Mustang, Musket, Goblet, Buttress, Giant I and Giant II were some of the schemes considered and rejected. Baytown, Slapstick, Ava-

Above: *A group of Canadian infantrymen in the main street of Agira, Sicily.*

Above: *Signallers at work on radio equipment on a Sicilian airfield in August while in the background a Spitfire prepares for take off.*

Above right: *The first landings across the Straits of Messina begin.*

Right: *On the harbour at Catania waiting to cross to the Italian mainland.*

lanche and Giant III were actually carried out. Avalanche and Giant III related to sea- and airborne landings at Salerno by US Fifth Army. Baytown and Slapstick were Monty's and Eighth Army's direct concern. Even before looking at any of the details one can guess what Monty's oft-repeated complaints during the Italian campaign would be. What is the master plan? What is the objective? And from the point of view of an army commander he was exactly right. What he did not recognize at this time, or in France in the following year, was that questions of this sort at the highest level do not lend themselves as readily to black-and-white answers as battlefield problems and that it may be more constructive to work happily within a weak policy than to bombard higher authority with assessments of how they are going wrong.

Baytown was the code name for an Eighth Army operation to cross the Straits of Messina to the toe of Italy. This would be valuable in the first place to make the Straits safe for Allied shipping en route to Salerno or other parts of western Italy in due course but landing so far south was pointless in terms of a larger aim to capture Italian territory. The landing began on 3 September with a heavy preparatory bombardment fired across the Straits at what would prove to be abandoned German positions. Since he could get no intelligence to confirm that his crossing would not be opposed Monty insisted on assuming that it might be and prepared accordingly. The delay in assembling a sufficiently strong force for this led to a typical unnecessary quarrel with Cunningham, the naval C-in-C. In the event, when 1st Canadian and 5th Divisions of XIII Corps went ashore, they were unmolested and as the troops began their march inland they were passed by lines of Italians moving in the other direction to surrender. Later in the same day the Italian government signed the formal instrument of surrender, although this was to be kept secret for the moment.

Napoleon is said once to have commented that, since Italy is shaped like a boot, the way into it is from the top and this belief was confirmed by Eighth Army's experience from the start. There was little opposition to the advance but virtually every bridge, every culvert, every junction, every corniche, on the tortuous, switchback Calabrian roads had been blasted or cratered. Mines and booby traps were planted to hinder repairs or to block spots where diversions were possible, so progress was unavoidably slow with a regular burden of casualties. So many bridges had to be built that supplies of bridging material ran short, imposing further delays.

The next major developments were on the 8th and 9th by which time XIII Corps had struggled as far as Catanzaro. Early on the morning of the 9th the British X Corps, along with VI Corps of the US Fifth Army, began what was to be the most important Allied landing in Italy, Operation Avalanche, in the Gulf of Salerno. Fierce fighting would follow there for several days with fears for a time that the Germans might succeed in pushing the attackers back into the sea. The British and Americans had landed in an optimistic spirit, for the Italian surrender had been announced the day before, Marshal Badoglio the Italian leader broadcasting to confirm the news after General Eisenhower had forced his hand by going on Algiers radio first. The Germans, as Montgomery had guessed, had made plans for such an eventuality and quickly and ruthlessly took control of the whole country. A ridiculously optimistic operation, Giant II, had been planned to land most of a US airborne division at Rome to help the Italians control the city. This was only cancelled when some of the transport aircraft were already in the air, the troops later being more sensibly deployed (in Operation Giant III) to help at Salerno. The final development of the 9th was the landing by sea at Taranto of the British 1st Airborne Division (Operation Slapstick). The units landed here, and at the

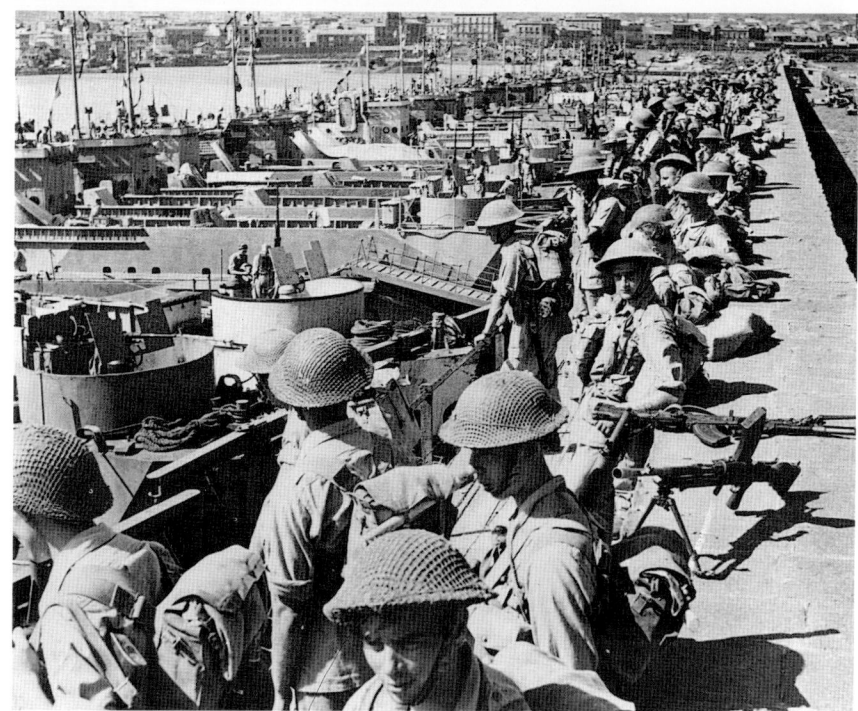

Adriatic ports in due course, would make up V Corps and would also come under Eighth Army command. At first, however, they were comparatively immobile as they were landed from naval vessels without most of their transport vehicles.

Montgomery halted the advance of XIII Corps at the Catanzaro neck on the 10th to allow his troops a rest while their communications were improved and more engineering equipment brought forward. Despite urging from Alexander, concerned about the situation at Salerno, Montgomery did not push forward again in strength until the 13th and 14th. Contact between Fifth and Eighth Army patrols was made on the 16th. On this occasion criticism of Montgomery for dawdling, although often made, is certainly unfair since he had never had the resources from the start to support a long and rapid advance. His reputation suffered further, through no fault of his own, because, in an attempt to play down the real problems of Fifth Army for inevitable German consumption, Alex's press staff overemphasized the achievement of XIII Corps,

which naturally caused considerable offence.

The true position was that the crisis of the Salerno battle was past by about the 14th with the Germans thinking about pulling back and developing a new policy. The events at Salerno, where the Allies had lost three times as many casualties as the Germans and had seemed to the Germans to be poorly trained and led and lacking in determination, convinced Kesselring that there was no need for a radical withdrawal in Italy. Instead, he argued, a fighting retreat should be made to a main defence line, the so-called Gustav Line, which would be held well south of Rome for the winter at least. Italian labour would be forced to help the Germans to fortify it and a series of advance defence lines would be occupied to hold the Allies off for as long as possible. The rivers in southern Italy tend to run roughly east or west from the central spine of the Apennine Mountains and each of the defence lines would be constructed on these successive river valleys and the dominating ridges overlooking them to the north. Fifth Army would first advance from Salerno to take Naples, then push on to cross the Volturno after a bloody struggle, and finally be halted looking across the Garigliano and Rapido below the fearsome bulk of Monte Cassino. Eighth Army would have its battles on the east side of the peninsula.

After the link-up with the Salerno beach-head Montgomery was instructed to begin operations towards the airfields around Foggia and to develop bases for Eighth Army in the ports around the heel of Italy. The Foggia area was taken fairly simply in the later part of September but creating strong forces for an advance north was not so easy. Since no proper strategy for the Italian campaign had been worked out, appropriate administrative arrangements had never been made by the Army Group staff and could not be created by Eighth Army alone. During much of the fighting in 1943, for example, broken down or damaged Eighth Army vehicles had to be shipped back to Egypt for repair because the relevant workshops had not yet been established in Italy. Supplies reached Taranto, Bari or Brindisi loaded in bulk, which meant that complete unloading and sorting was needed before what was immediately required at the front could be found and dispatched. Also much shipping space was taken up by items which were of little use

Above: *Canadian infantry take cover from sniper fire in the streets of Campochiaro, 23 October 1943.*

Left: *Monty and Mark Clark at a rare meeting in October 1943.*

Left: *4.2-inch mortars pound German defensive positions.*

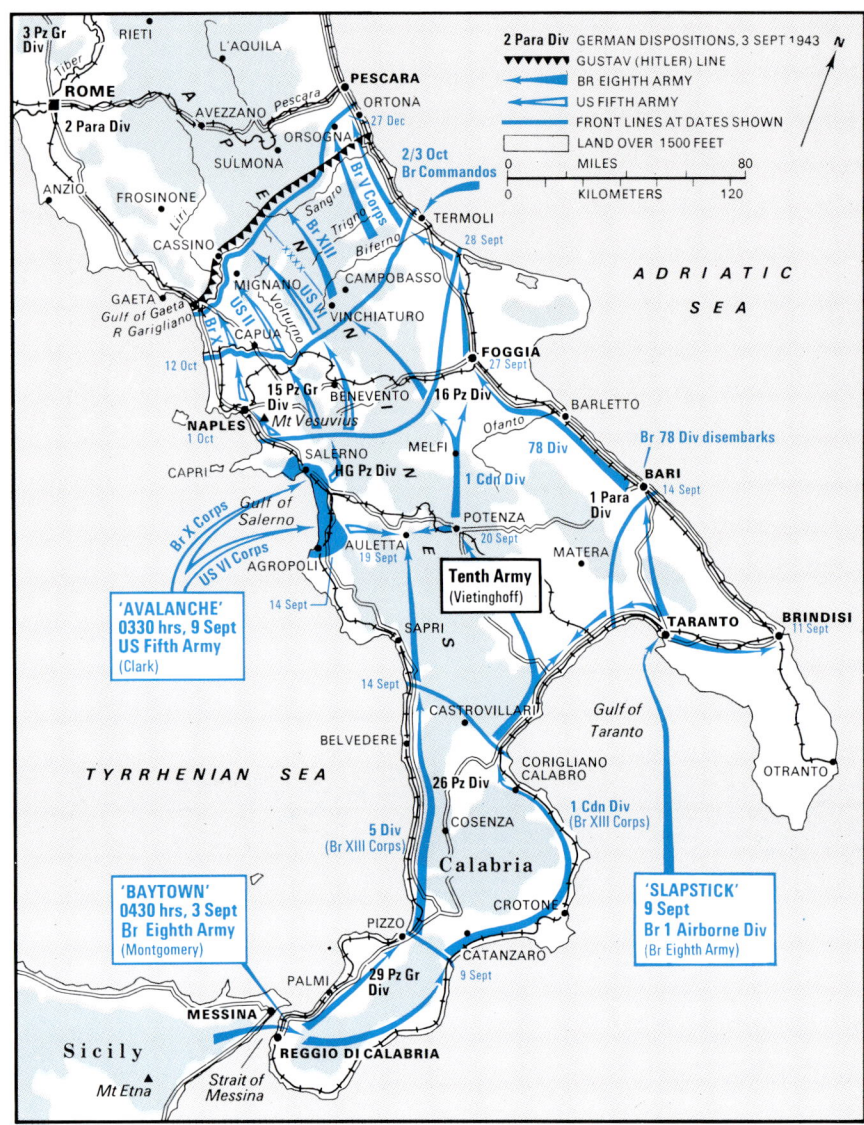

in the short term when others not supplied were in shortage. Putting together the sort of structure necessary to handle problems of this sort was much more difficult when it could not be done in advance of operations. Further difficulties were created by the limited port capacity being used both for the landing of troops and to support the substantial and growing needs of the Allied air forces who now had the bases they wanted. It became still more difficult when it was found that making any progress in typical Italian terrain demanded an even more massive supply of artillery ammunition than had been predicted.

Supplies of another sort were also soon to be a problem once casualties began to be incurred in numbers. There were very few infantry replacements available to fill the gaps in the ranks or, even more important, to supply the pressing need for good junior officers. Both the British and US armies relied more heavily on junior officers for effective tactical leadership than the German army, where far more responsibility was shared with the NCOs. The results could be serious when, for example, as Montgomery recorded in early November, no infantry platoon in 78th Division was being led by an officer.

Another concern often recorded in Monty's diaries, and which monopolizes the accounts of every soldier who served in the campaign, was the miserable, biting cold and wet weather. Weather has often been the excuse put forward for doubtful generalship but there was no exaggeration here. Early in November again, Montgomery noted that he was using six blankets to sleep at night and that his usually snug caravan was leaking. In the front

Maps: *Both the general and the detailed map give a clear impression of the way the Allied campaign in Italy was split between the two sides of the country with little co-ordination between the drives. Also clearly shown is the way the campaign for Eighth Army became a series of river crossings of successively the Biferno, Trigno, Sangro, and Moro.*

Left: *A heavy-load bridge is built across the Sangro in early December. The picture gives an excellent impression of the way the various river crossings were dominated by the rising ground to the far side and of the typical flat and marshy river valley that would quickly become inundated after rain.*

We Will Surely Make Hard Chewing

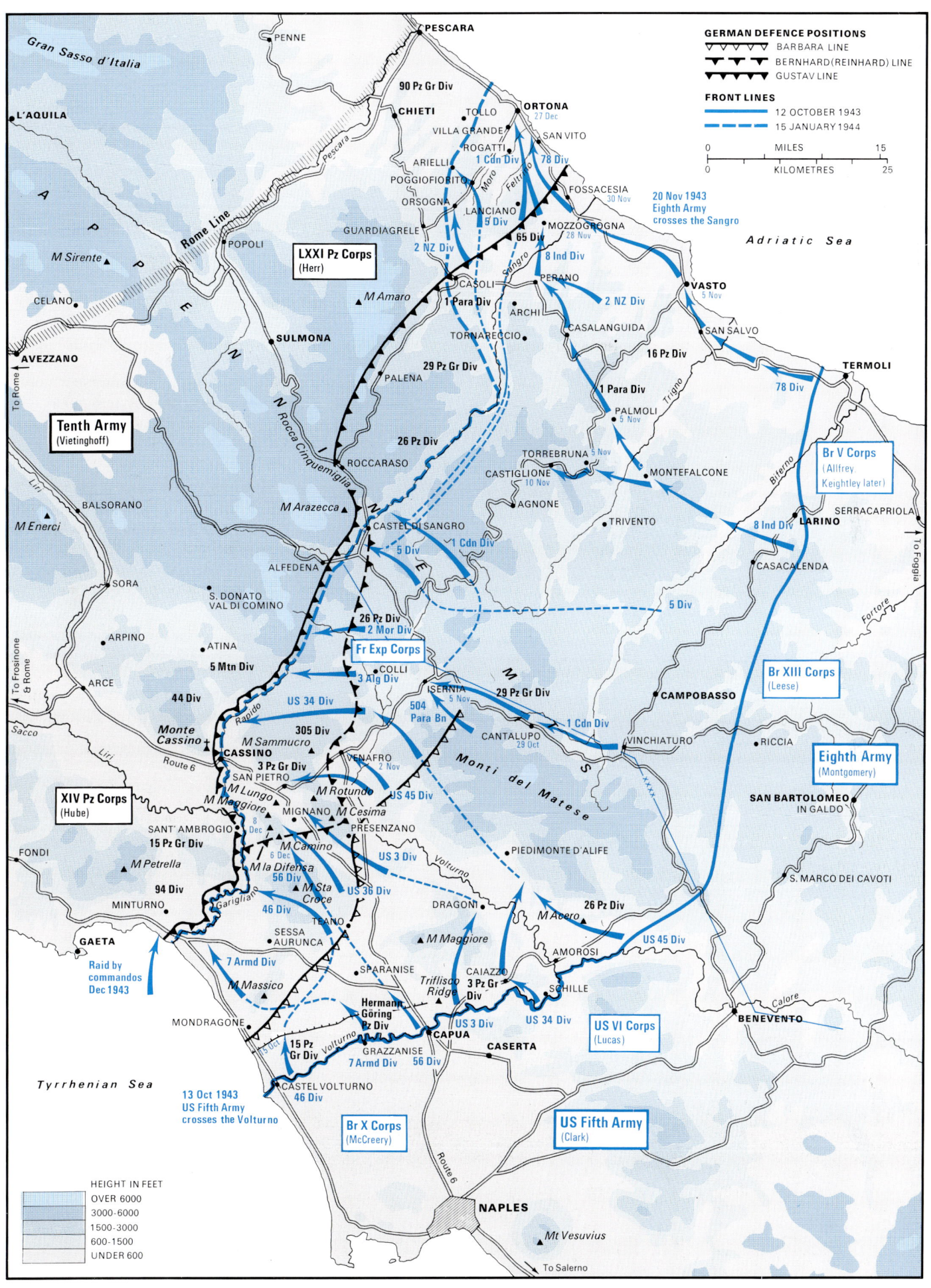

Above: *Fighting in the streets of Ortona, one of the last actions commanded by Monty in Italy.*

Right, above: *General Oliver Leese (third from right) who took over command of Eighth Army from Monty after serving under him in the desert and Sicily.*

Right, below: *Churchill, Roosevelt, and Stalin at the Teheran conference. Stalin pressed to be told who would command Overlord and a few days later Roosevelt finally plumped for Eisenhower.*

line no man could expect such comforts. Instead, even when not under fire, men died of exposure in the slit trenches, or drowned trying to cross rushing rivers on patrol or simply laboured in the deep, clinging mud trying to bring supplies up or evacuate wounded, with six men needed to carry a stretcher. Veterans of the toughest fighting in Flanders in World War I would have seen much that was familiar in the winter battles in Italy.

Looking once again at Montgomery's *Memoirs* it is interesting to note that he discusses the administrative difficulties and the bad weather to some degree but does not describe the events of the fighting in the last three months of 1943 at all.

The first major actions were to cross the Biferno River and capture the coastal town of Termoli near its mouth. A small amphibious attack by commandos and part of 78th Division landed north of the town on 3 October while other units began crossing the river to the south. As would so often be the case in subsequent Italian battles, heavy rain then fell and the river rose. During the 4th and 5th, German reinforcements arrived and it looked as if the forces who were almost cut off north of the river might be overrun. Finally a bridge was got across and a Canadian tank attack drove the Germans back – but only as far as the next river line, the Trigno.

Rome and the lateral route leading east from the capital to the Adriatic were now the objectives of the Allied armies in Italy, but as Montgomery was soon complaining, there was little co-ordination between his attacks and those of Clark's Fifth Army – 'we each do what we like, when we like.' In these unsatisfactory circumstances Montgomery had little option but to continue to drive his army forward as energetically as he could.

When crossing the Trigno, some attempts were made to deceive the Germans with a diversionary attack but this could only have limited effects on the comparatively narrow front. It also cost significant casualties and was destructive of the morale of the troops making the feint. Again, after another exhausting brawl, with vehicles now virtually confined to the roads by the mud and rain, the Germans pulled back to the Sangro.

In writing this account it is difficult not to feel the dread apprehension that must have struck the unhappy soldiers of Eighth Army as they 'squared up' (Monty's phrase) to crossing yet another swollen torrent, with beyond it the deep system of German forward positions and on the ridge some three miles back the main German defences. The operation mounted to breach the Sangro line was the most elaborate Montgomery commanded on the Italian mainland. As usual he had considered the problem well in advance and decided to attack near the coast with 2nd New Zealand, 8th Indian, and 78th Divisons providing the main thrust. Every effort was made to suggest that the attack would be by XIII Corps inland or by an amphibious operation farther up the Adriatic behind the German defences. Extensive aggressive patrolling, always hated by front-line troops, the more so in such appalling weather, was employed to discover as much as possible of the layout of the German defences. From 20 November infantry struggled gradually to expand a bridgehead on the north bank of the river despite bridges often being flooded or swept away behind them. On the 27th a large part of 4th Armoured Brigade was got across and during the last days of the month the main defence line on the Li Colli ridge around Mozzagrogna was taken.

Montgomery now reorganized to move the exhausted 78th Division inland, bring 5th Division into the battle and continue his drive. The New Zealanders fought hard to be in Orsogna on the inland flank just before Christmas while in the last week of the year the Canadians took the coastal town of Ortona. The best comment on the fight for Ortona is that it is still studied in military textbooks as a classic example of the particularly brutal form of war that is house-to-house urban battle. With these last actions the offensive was closed down.

On 23 December 1943 Monty received a most welcome signal from London that he was to return to Britain to take over the British army group preparing for the invasion of France, Operation Overlord. Before he left it was necessary first to say his goodbyes. A large gathering of Eighth Army officers, including all the seniors, was assembled in the Opera House at Vasto near Main HQ and Monty made an emotional speech, reviewing past achievements and thanking them for their support. Various accounts of the occasion have been left. Some suggest that it was genuinely moving for most of those present but others say that expressions varied from the politeness of the senior officers in the front rows to bored cynicism of the more junior at the back.

Monty left Italy on 31 December and flew to Marrakesh where Prime Minister Churchill was convalescing after falling ill on the way back from the Teheran conference with Stalin and Roosevelt. Churchill gave Montgomery a copy of the outline Overlord plan to study for the first time that evening. Monty's report was delivered the following morning and the crucial sentence read, 'My first impression is that the present plan is impracticable.' Clearly, more storms lay ahead.

Chapter Eight
A Good and Simple Plan

Left: *January 1944 and Monty is back in London. In the background is his son David.*

Above: *Allied unity is signified by the British and American flags displayed behind Eisenhower but disputes between the generals often seemed to develop along national lines.*

MONTY

Speculation as to how the Anglo-American command structure would be revised for Overlord had been a feature of the letters and diaries of all the leading Allied military figures for many months. Montgomery, embroiled in a campaign in Italy that was becoming more unsatifactory and inconclusive as time passed, was keen that he should return to Britain and, like other possible candidates for top jobs, he lobbied discreetly for selection.

By the end of 1943 British military and industrial power was clearly on the wane while American strength was still growing by leaps and bounds. By D-Day the American air force in Britain would be half as large again as the RAF and, apart from in the early stages, the US Army would greatly surpass the British contribution to the invasion forces. British manpower resources, by contrast, were in decline and it was likely that army units would have to be disbanded and amalgamated in the event of heavy casualties being incurred. There was, therefore, no doubt that the Supreme Commander would be an American, and on his way back from the Teheran conference President Roosevelt chose General Eisenhower. Eisenhower would have preferred to have had Alexander as his senior British army subordinate but Churchill, strongly advised by Brooke, chose Montgomery. Any judgement of Monty's abilities should take account of this choice. Quite simply they decided that Montgomery was the most able and best qualified British general, even taking into account his known personal weaknesses and unpopularity with many of the leading Americans.

Appreciations for attacks on the French coast and studies of landing beaches and other matters had been made by the British since 1940 (ironically the first beaches studied were actually among those used on D-Day) but formal plans for a full-scale invasion were only started in the spring of 1943 with the appointment of a British officer, Lieutenant-General F E Morgan, as Chief of Staff to the

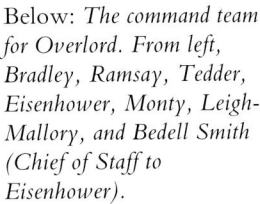

Below: *The command team for Overlord. From left, Bradley, Ramsay, Tedder, Eisenhower, Monty, Leigh-Mallory, and Bedell Smith (Chief of Staff to Eisenhower).*

A Good and Simple Plan

Supreme Allied Commander (designate), a cumbersome title usually shortened to COSSAC. No supreme commander was actually appointed until Eisenhower took up the job at the beginning of 1944. Morgan at first had only a single American deputy and one barely furnished office but in time he assembled a substantial organization that analyzed many of the factors involved in making a successful invasion. He and his staff studied offshore currents, local topography and beach gradients for potential landing sites all along the coast of France and the Low Countries; beach and inland defences; how well the areas inland favoured an advancing attacker or hindered the movement of defending reserves; where airfields could be built or captured; what special equipment was needed to make the landings possible; what scale of shipping was required to create and then support the beach-head; what ports could be captured and what were their capacities and how readily could they be repaired after being demolished, as they were sure to be, by the Germans; and many other matters. The invasion could not have been possible without this mass of preliminary work but it had limitations of which Morgan was only too well aware. Morgan had to make do with the forces he was told would be available and his calculations from these dictated that it was possible to attack only on the relatively narrow front of three divisions. He also called for the early appointment of a supreme commander who could decide finally on contentious matters and put more life into what was still a rather unreal staff exercise. Nonetheless the COSSAC outline plan was pre-

Above: *Monty with General Henry Crerar who would command First Canadian Army when it became operational in France. He and Monty never saw eye to eye.*

Left: *General Miles 'Bimbo' Dempsey (centre), who commanded Second Army in Overlord, and two of his corps commanders, Crocker (left) and Bucknall.*

Far right: Monty eyeing up a bowl of soup aboard his personal train in which he toured Britain to make his various morale-boosting speeches before D-Day.

Right: Air Chief Marshal Trafford Leigh-Mallory, Air C-in-C for Overlord.

Below: The outline plan for D-Day. The most controversial aspect in the final stages was the employment of the airborne forces with Leigh-Mallory arguing for a less ambitious scheme but being overruled by Monty and Eisenhower.

sented to the supreme Anglo-American military body, the Combined Chiefs of Staff, at the Quebec conference in August, and was approved.

Eisenhower briefly studied the plan before he left the Mediterranean at the end of 1943 and realized that it was unsatisfactory because the attacking force and frontage was too small. He said as much to Montgomery at a meeting before Eisenhower went off on a visit to the USA and Monty set out for home and his new job. No one, then, can claim that Monty's report to Churchill that New Year morning represented a singular inspiration (Churchill had not liked the plan either), but it is doubtful if any of the others involved had as clear an insight into what was wrong with the plan, why it was wrong, *and* what exactly should be done about it. During their short meeting Eisenhower had told Montgomery that he, Monty, was to be in charge of all army planning while Ike was away in the US. A proper presentation of the COSSAC plan was therefore arranged to begin on the day after Monty's return to England.

The COSSAC planners explained convincingly the reasons why Normandy had been chosen as the site of the attack, drawing on the sort of information outlined above, and this at least was effectively accepted from this point on. Monty began to take issue with them, however, when they passed to a description of the initial assault and the shipping limitations that restricted it to three divisions (essentially over the 'British' beaches actually used

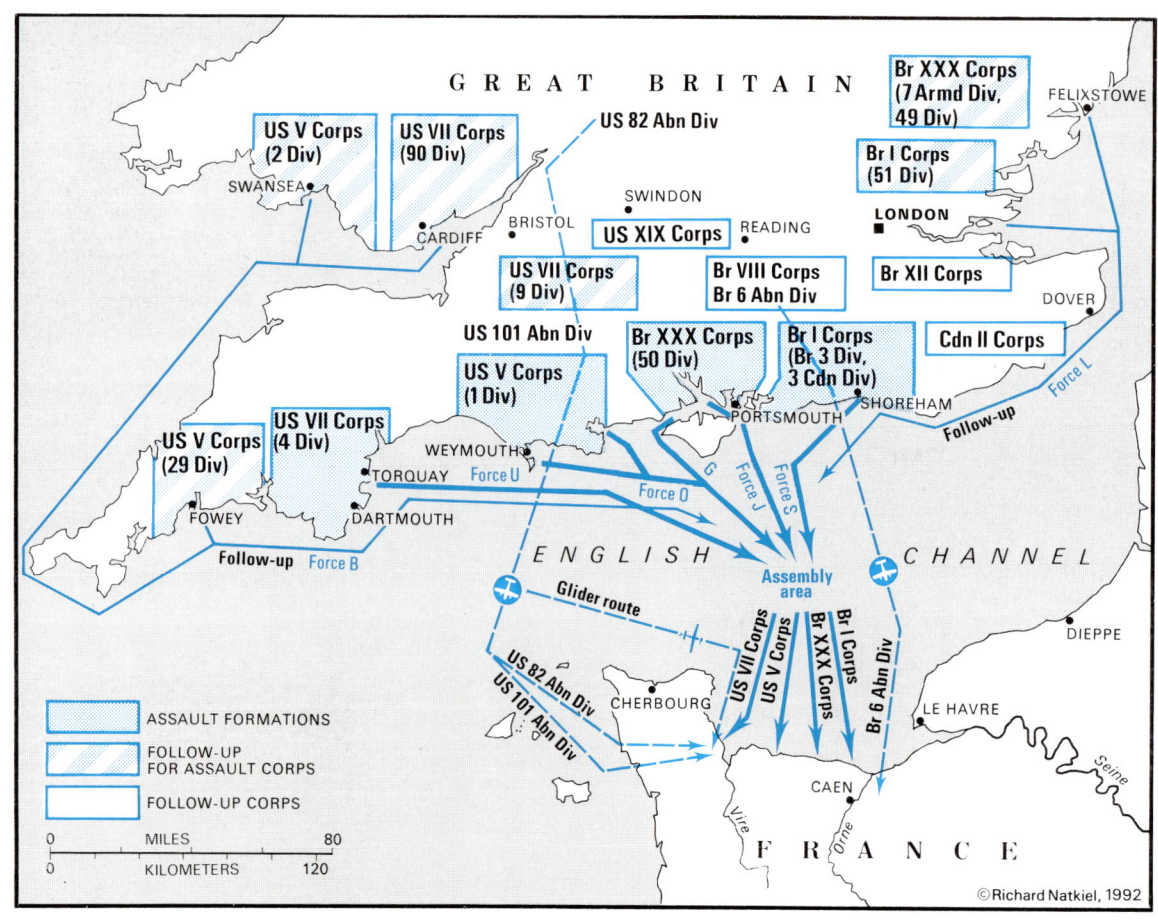

Right: *Monty during his pre-invasion tour. By allowing his men to stand at ease, Monty aimed to create a closer rapport between C-in-C and troops.*

Below right: *Air Chief Marshal Arthur Tedder, Deputy Supreme Allied Commander, who often crossed swords with Monty.*

on D-Day). In the COSSAC plan this would be followed by a drive inland to Caen and later a move west on Cherbourg. Implicit in this was a complicated command and administrative structure: US, British and Canadian troops in the assault were originally to be under First US Army but the British and Canadians were later to be transferred to their own army and would all come under 21st Army Group. The detrimental effects of this complexity for Montgomery would be compounded by the confusion certain to be caused when follow-up divisions and supplies for the various formations were subsequently landed on the original three overcrowded beach areas.

By the end of the third day of discussions Montgomery had imposed an entirely different and far more coherent structure. This made possible a sensible operational scheme to include what were likely to be the first three months of the campaign. He was persuaded that he was mistaken in his first idea, to extend the landings to the western side of the Cotentin peninsula, but insisted that a five-division seaborne assault was essential. This had the important benefit of giving a simple command and administrative structure – the British and Canadians to the east under their own officers with their particular supply requirements met over their own separate lines of communication, and the Americans to the west with their different procedures, ammunition, equipment, and rations. The British and Canadians were to penetrate quickly in-

land *beyond* Caen, capture the open ground to the south-east of the city so that airfields could be built there, and then hold off the German reserves which would be certain to move in from the north and east. In the meantime the US First Army would take the port of Cherbourg and then, joined by the US Third Army, attack south into the heart of

France while also clearing the Brittany peninsula. The next phase would see the British, Canadians and US First Army advancing to the Seine and Paris with Third Army covering the southern and inland flank. This tactical pattern confirmed the administrative neatness for not only did it make sense that the US forces operate on the west of the Allied armies since they had, by simple geography, usually been based in western Britain since they arrived, they would also be able to receive supplies and reinforcements through Cherbourg and the Brittany ports direct from the USA, once these ports were in Allied hands. Equally, the British would eventually advance along the Channel coast with its ports which were naturally the most convenient for supplies from Britain.

The important idea underlying the whole plan was that it was not the actual landing of the assault force that was likely to be the most hazardous. With proper detailed planning, equipment, preliminary bombardment and so on, this could be expected to succeed. The greatest problems would be in the succeeding phases as, first, the nearby German reserves would arrive to try to push the invaders back into the sea, and, second, if these attacks failed, the Germans would probably try to

Above: *Churchill visiting Monty's HQ on 19 May. This was a notable occasion for Churchill wished to question Monty's staff as to whether the administrative 'tail' of the armies was not excessive. Monty simply refused to allow this, saying that he had confidence in his staff and that was the end of the matter.*

Far left: *Valentine DD tanks, brainchild of Monty's brother-in-law, Major-General Percy Hobart, aboard a landing craft during training for D-Day. The canvas flotation screens shown erected on all but the tank nearest the camera enabled the vehicles to 'swim' ashore and could be dropped down on emerging from the water when the tank could immediately begin to fight normally.*

Left: *Patton, Bradley, and Monty were at pains to maintain good relations during the early stages of Overlord. De Guingand looks on anxiously hoping that the cordiality will last.*

'rope off' (Monty's phrase) the beach-head area. This would create the sort of stalemate that would become all too familiar to the Allied leaders looking at events at Anzio in Italy in those first months of 1944. Montgomery's achievement was in simplifying, tidying, and strengthening the Allied plan, to create the conditions in which these engagements of the build-up would probably be won; it was quite possible they might not have been with the original plan despite all the other factors in the Allied favour, such as their overwhelming air supremacy.

Much further debate would take place after Eisenhower's arrival in England before Monty's plan was finally accepted. The additional landing craft required to expand the assault could only be found at the expense of delay for Overlord or by taking them from other Allied campaigns. Since Admiral King of the US Navy would not disgorge enough from his massive stock in the Pacific, despite the Allied policy of putting the defeat of Germany as a higher priority than beating Japan, the lack of shipping could only be made good at the expense of the plan to invade the south of France at the same time as D-Day. The decision on how to resolve this dilemma was not Montgomery's to take but without his insistence that Overlord must be strengthened an unfortunate compromise might have been reached with Eisenhower agreeing to appease his bosses in Washington, who favoured invading the south of France simultaneously with the north. In April, it was agreed that the southern invasion would be postponed.

Also uncertain for some time was the structure of the Allied high command, Montgomery blithely announcing at an early press conference (reports of which were accordingly censored) that he had been appointed to command all the ground forces in the landing phase when in fact no such appointment had at that stage formally been made. Later it was indeed confirmed that Monty would have this role with Bradley of US First Army and Dempsey of

Above: *Among the specially-developed support ships were rocket-firing landing craft like this example. The whole bank of rockets could be fired in one massive volley to drench a potential landing area.*

SECRET

PROGRAM

PRESENTATION OF 'OVERLORD' PLANS

A. M. 15 MAY

Subject	Speaker	Time of Presentation
Introduction	Supreme Commander	10 minutes (beginning at 1000 hrs)
General Army Plan	C-in-C, 21 Army Group	90 minutes
General Navy Plan	ANCXF	90 minutes
General Air Plan	Air C-in-C, AEF	40 minutes
Strategical Air Forces Plan	Joint presentation Commanders USSTAF and Bomber Command	30 minutes
General Administrative Plan	C.A.O., SHAEF	30 minutes
Civil Affairs Plan	AC of S, G-5, SHAEF	20 minutes (Conclude presentation at 1330 hrs)

Total time allotted for presentation	3 hours 10 minutes
Intermissions for changing maps, etc.	[illegible]0 minutes
TOTAL TIME ALLOTTED	5 hours 5[illegible] minutes

P. M. 15th MAY

Subject	Speaker	Time of Presentation
NCWTF Tactical Plan	Admiral Kirk	1 hour (Beginning at 1430 hrs) (Division of time as agreed by the three speakers)
First Army Plan	General Bradley	
9th Air Force Tactical Plan	General Quesada	
NCETF Tactical Plan	Admiral Vian	1 hour (Division of time as agreed by the three speakers. Conclude presentation at 1730 hours.)
Second Army Tactical Plan	General Dempsey	
21 TAF Tactical Plan	A.V.M. Broadhurst	

Total time allotted for presentation	2 hours
Intermissions for changing maps, etc.	40 minutes
TOTAL TIME ALLOTTED	2 hours 40 minutes

SECRET

TOP SECRET

WITH THE COMPLIMENTS OF ALLIED NAVAL COMMANDER, EXPEDITIONARY FORCE.

Rear Admiral W.R. PATTERSON, C.B., C.V.O.
2nd Cruiser Squadron.

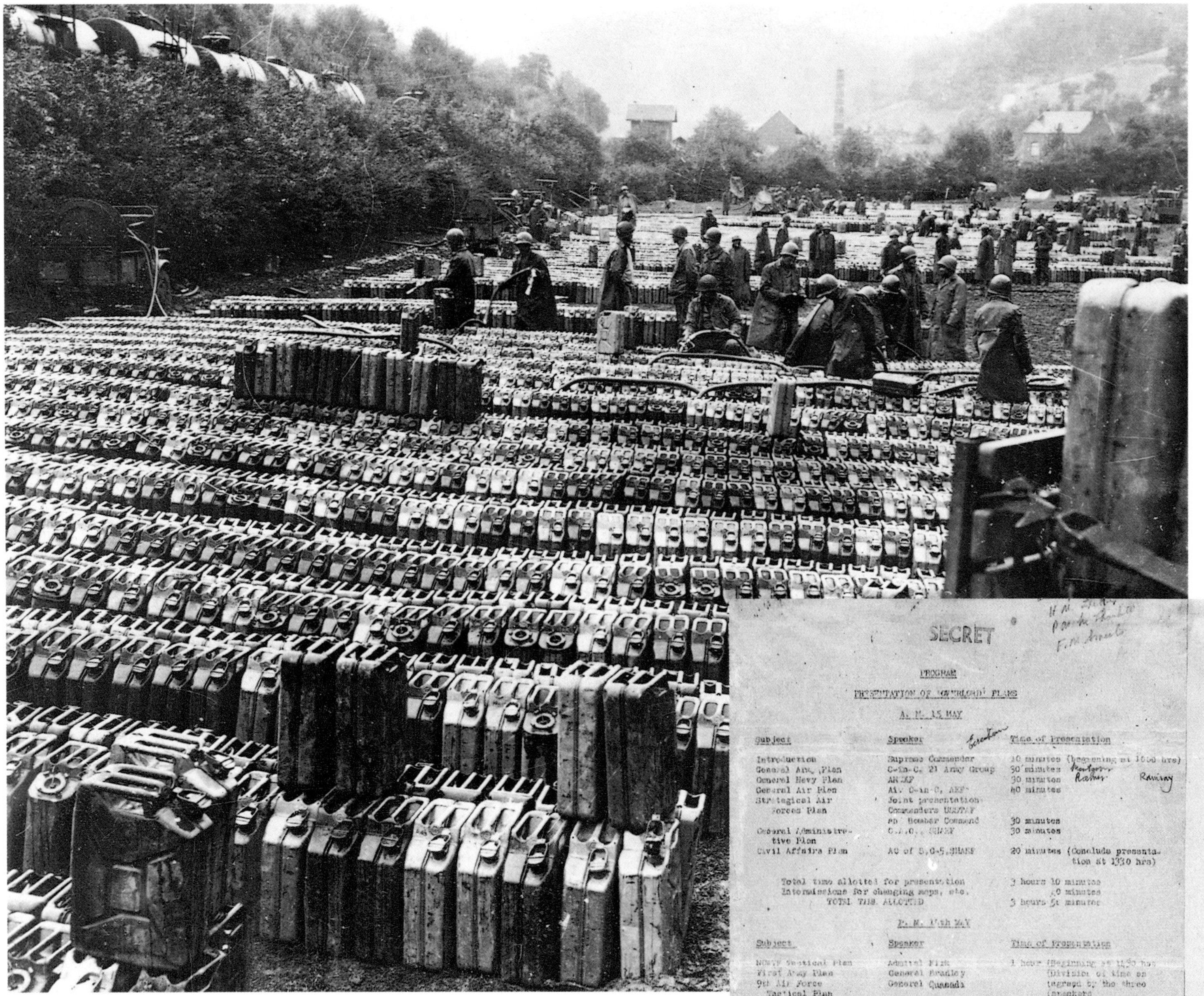

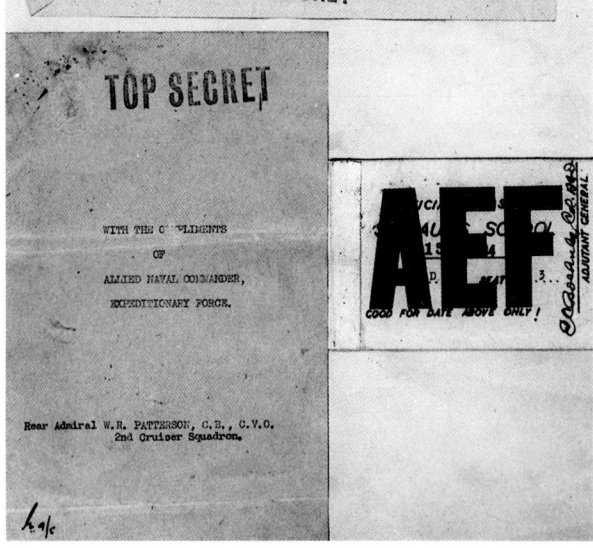

Above: *Over 20 million jerrycans were supplied to the Allied forces in the first three months of the invasion and more than half were lost or destroyed, often carelessly, leading to constraints on fuel supplies.*

Right: *The 'order of service' and a naval officer's pass for the famous briefing on 15 May.*

British Second Army reporting to him. It was always intended, however, when US Third Army (Patton) had gone to France that Bradley would take over the all-American 12th Army Group and Montgomery would then continue only as C-in-C 21st Army Group (by then also to include Crerar's First Canadian Army), while Eisenhower himself took over co-ordination of the land battle. A plan that had Monty first commanding Americans and then being 'demoted' clearly gave plenty of scope for disagreements.

There were also to be problems involving the air commanders and their relationships with each other and with the armies. A British officer, Air Marshal Leigh-Mallory, had been appointed Air Force Commander-in-Chief for Overlord but his authority was not accepted by either Spaatz or Harris, commanding respectively the US and British heavy-bomber forces. The whys and wherefores of this dispute are not all relevant to Montgomery's story but two consequences of it are. First, Spaatz

Above: *A briefing for Allied soldiers in England prior to the invasion.*

and Harris were generally grudging in response to calls to 'divert' (as they saw it) their forces from bombing Germany to operations to help prepare the invasion and later to support the armies in France. This made them ready allies for those opposed to Montgomery's ideas and methods, since such attacks were portrayed as only necessary because of Montgomery's caution or imcompetence. The second consequence of the problem was that Air Marshal Tedder was brought in as Deputy Supreme Commander, principally to co-ordinate the heavy bomber barons and the forces which would obey Leigh-Mallory. It was well established that Tedder was no admirer of Monty. There were also further potential sources of dispute lower in the air-force chain of command, for Air Marshal Coningham now led the RAF's Second Tactical Air Force and he was no friend to Monty either.

Even if all the personalities had been on good terms initially and events had exceeded expectations, such a set-up would have been fraught. Monty, as we have seen, would be wearing a variety of hats, metaphorically as well as literally, as land forces commander, C-in-C 21st Army Group, and close supervisor of British Second Army. In each position he would have to deal with a different air headquarters and often more than one. It would have been difficult for a tactful and politically sensitive man to avoid causing offence, and Monty was neither of these.

One of the unfortunate consequences of the airmen's internal squabbles was that the intimate ground-air co-operation, which had from time to time been a feature of the best-conducted Allied operations, was not fully realized in the earliest days of the Normandy landings. However, this is a very minor quibble indeed for, although they cannot be discussed in detail here, the effects of the preliminary air attacks and missions in support of the invasion once launched can hardly be overestimated. The Germans fought with astonishing skill and tenacity despite this huge handicap. Good generals or bad generals, Overlord would have failed without the Allied dominance in the air.

Not the least important of the air arm's achievements was the detailed reconnaissance of the assault area and the prevention of any equivalent German scouting of southern England - subjects which also introduce another vitally important facet of Overlord, the accompanying deception schemes (known collectively as Operation Fortitude).

In the main these were not of Montgomery's making or within his responsibilities but it is clear that he understood and appreciated their potential, which cannot be said of all the senior officers. He was horrified to find out in January that the RAF had begun intensive reconnaissance of the Normandy area without also beginning similar flights over other parts of France to hide the Allies' real intentions. This was put right, and, as a rule of thumb thereafter, the Allied air forces bombed or scouted two targets outside Normandy for every one in the invasion area.

The principal purpose of the various deception schemes was to suggest, before the invasion, that the Pas de Calais area, opposite the narrowest part of the English Channel, would be the Allied target area and, after the invasion had started, to continue by convincing the Germans that Normandy was a subsidiary operation and the Pas de Calais still the main target in attacks yet to begin. A wide variety of techniques was used, including false radio traffic and reports from double agents, and the plans were an astonishing success, keeping strong German forces idle and out of the Normandy battle for weeks, a vital contribution.

One minor respect in which Montgomery was involved in a deception was Operation Copperhead. An actor, M E Clifton James, was found who bore a close physical resemblance to Monty and, after a meeting with the general to help him get in character, was sent off to Gibraltar and North Africa at the end of May to have his presence there spotted, it was hoped, and reported to the Germans, with the implication that a Mediterranean offensive was planned. There is no evidence that

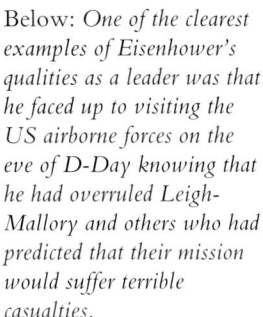

Below: *One of the clearest examples of Eisenhower's qualities as a leader was that he faced up to visiting the US airborne forces on the eve of D-Day knowing that he had overruled Leigh-Mallory and others who had predicted that their mission would suffer terrible casualties.*

the operation did the least bit of good but it does supply an interesting example of the more human and generous side of Monty's character that he took the trouble to insist, overcoming War Office opposition, that James, who was serving as a lieutenant, should receive a general's pay for the duration of the impersonation since he might be in unusual danger. Or was Monty rather being generous with someone else's money and enjoying baiting the Whitehall bureaucracy into the bargain?

With the plans working out to his satisfaction, Montgomery's next preoccupation was to attend to the morale of his soldiers. Immediately after that first formal presentation of the COSSAC plan Monty set out on the first of an exhausting series of visits to all the units under his command. The format he chose was the same throughout. The assembled gathering was usually several thousand strong and first he would walk slowly up and down their formed ranks, after having them stood at ease so that they were free to have a good look at him rather than face rigidly to the front at attention. Then he would climb up on top of his jeep and order them to break ranks and gather round to hear his speech. One writer has amusingly summarized the usual content of this as 'a simple gospel of Trust in Me; Trust in the Lord, and get your hair cut.' Other commentators have estimated the level of intellectual and emotional sophistication of these talks as equivalent to the usual valedictory speech at a school prize giving. Perhaps these comments are a little unfair but they do catch what seems to have been the correct flavour. Montgomery's message was indeed a simple one, simply delivered – that the high command was interested in the ordinary soldier and interested in particular in what was of greatest importance to every man, ensuring that everything possible would be done and every equipment provided to help him survive the coming battles. One exchange that has been reported had Montgomery ask a private what his most important possession was. 'My rifle, sir,' was the reply. Monty disagreed and said it was the soldier's life and he was going to do his best to look after it.

Below: *Admiral Ramsay, Eisenhower, and Monty aboard a warship off the Normandy beaches.*

Below: *Landing craft heading for Normandy seen from the headquarters ship of the Omaha landings, USS Ancon. Note the aircraft identification diagram beside the right-hand anti-aircraft position.*

Monty's was altogether a remarkable performance, creating a surprising rapport with British and American troops alike – it is worth noting that his first tour was to a group of American units and that equal numbers of the literally hundreds of thousands of men he spoke to were of those two principal nationalities.

Whether the morale boost he gave was deep and lasted into combat may indeed be questioned but there was no doubt of its effectiveness in the short term. Even the most cynical observer must agree that the attempt was worth the effort and that in making it Montgomery was demonstrating a better effort to understand the ordinary soldier than many of his more hidebound contemporaries.

One respect in which Montgomery was definitely encouraging of innovation was in his reception for the devices being developed under the

energetic command of his brother-in-law, Major-General Percy Hobart. Hobart's outspoken views on tank doctrine had ruined his career and the early part of the war had seen him serving, a retired officer, as a corporal in the Home Guard. One of the lessons drawn by the British from the Dieppe landings and other experiences was that there was a need for a range of specialized armoured vehicles to assist in crossing obstacles or breaching prepared

Above: *Anxious moments as a landing craft approaches the Normandy beach where it will disgorge its human cargo.*

defences. A variety of these was developed and organized as 79th Armoured Division with Hobart, back from retirement, in command. Monty enthusiastically welcomed these innovations when they were demonstrated to him and they would justify his praise on D-Day and throughout the coming campaign. By the end of the war the division had 20,000 men in its 17 regiments (which usually operated separately), and in excess of 1500 tracked vehicles against a standard armoured division's 14,000 men and 350 tanks.

Hobart's 'Funnies', as they were known, were demonstrated also to Eisenhower and Bradley and his staff but they were impressed with only one type. This was the Duplex Drive (or DD) conversion to standard battle tanks to enable them to 'swim' ashore from their landing ships. Part of the reason for the American rejection of the Funnies was that most of the other types were based on the British Churchill tank and they did not wish to complicate their supply arrangements by including these in an otherwise mechanically homogeneous force. This would prove an unwise and costly decision in the light of events at Omaha beach.

Monty, to his credit, got this one right.

The high value that Montgomery put on the 79th Armoured Division was related to another important and correct decision that he took – to make the landings shortly after low tide when the beach obstacles would not be under water but could be seen and dealt with by the engineers and Hobart's devices. DD tanks were to be landed to support closely the leading troops and compensate for the disadvantage of the wider beach they would have to cross under fire than if they had been landed at high tide. It was an added bonus that Rommel, now commanding the German armies defending the French coast, anticipated a high-tide landing and had adapted his defences accordingly.

As well as his tours to see the troops Monty also made a range of visits and speeches to workers in war industries and other civilian organizations. His messages to them were similar in many ways to those he expounded to the soldiers. For many it was surprising and pleasing enough that real top brass like Monty would condescend to come and see them but equally heartening was his theme: he saw the dockers and the railwaymen and the others

A Good and Simple Plan

Above: *Royal Marines of the 4th Special Service Brigade disembark on the beach near St Aubin sur Mer. The marine on the gangway is heading for a particularly wet landing in France.*

he addressed as part of the same team as his armies and that their individual efforts mattered just as much in getting the war over and won. Monty was so concerned that everything possible should be done to enthuse the whole nation for this last great effort that he also produced unlikely schemes for a National Day of Prayer which he urged in an extensive correspondence with the Archbishop of Canterbury.

Having set about putting the ordinary soldiers and the workers on the right track, Montgomery did not neglect to do the same for the senior officers. At the highest levels he was very definitely on his best behaviour, being as polite and charming as he possibly could be to Eisenhower, Bradley, and Patton among others. (From their memoirs and private papers it is clear that they were trying as hard along the same lines.) The story of the betting book mentioned in a previous chapter was part of a real attempt to create a friendly, informal, and sociable atmosphere. That it was a story that Montgomery chose to tell at some length in his *Memoirs* is perhaps also revealing of his need to be thought of as possessing these companionable qualities.

At the next level down there were the accustomed set-piece presentations of the plans. The two most important of these were the two-day Exercise Thunderclap on 7-8 April and the final senior officers' briefing on 15 May. The final briefing in particular was a unique assembly of leading Allied personalities. As well as all the Overlord commanders, those attending included the King, Churchill, Prime Minister Smuts of South Africa, the British Chiefs of Staff, and many more. At each occasion the senior commanders described their plans and intentions in detail and outlined the salient features of the German defences and their likely responses. All those present who have described Montgomery's contributions agree that they showed the greatest possible clarity and grasp of every facet of the very complex problems involved.

The earlier meeting was very much Monty's show and, apart from his lucid exposition of the plans he had fought so hard to set up, it is also remembered for another characteristic Monty story. Churchill and Eisenhower were due to arrive for one of the afternoon sessions and in the interval before this began Monty announced, without giving a reason, that smoking would on this occasion be permitted. Eisenhower was a heavy smoker and sure enough the Prime Minister was also clutching his trademark cigar when he arrived.

The seeds for one important future controversy were sown, however, at this meeting. Part of Montgomery's presentation featured a map with so-called phase lines drawn on it to show the positions that the armies could be expected to have reached at various times after D-Day. The evidence is absolutely clear that Montgomery did not set much store by this and never intended that it be anything other than a convenient summary of what might be possible. A rough idea of how far the front lines might be from the beaches at any point was obviously important to the logistical planners since, for example, this factor would directly in-

Below: *With German defences weakened, supplies could then flood on to the Normandy beaches.*

Right: *The hopeful evening headlines in a British newspaper.*

Bottom right: *One of the British airborne force's gliders successfully landed near the Caen canal.*

fluence fuel requirements among other matters. It would have been most unwise and unusual for any operational commander to commit himself to such precise targets and, if evidence to back this up is needed, it can be found in Bradley's annoyance that the phase lines extended to include the front of his First Army. Despite this definite limitation to the intended significance of the map, when progress in Normandy seemed to be slow, the phase-line predictions would be used in evidence against Monty to support claims that he was over-cautious and that his plans had failed.

It is worth digressing here slightly to mention some aspects of the logistical problem which show how clearly warfare and command in war had become dependent on administration and material factors. One important problem in the planning stage had been a dispute between British and American staffs over the capacities of various types of landing craft and assault ship. (It is not important here, but as it happened the British were correct in their more realistic estimates in the light of possible bad weather and other problems.) Again, when German E-Boats sank several tank-landing ships during a D-Day rehearsal the loss of sea-lift capacity, far more than the human casualties, had repercussions all the way through the planning process.

As noted above, the planners had to make certain assumptions as to progress ashore in order to prepare properly, as, for example, in their decision that up to D+15 fuel would be shipped in jerrycans and thereafter in bulk. Unfortunately the planners were ultimately too rigid in their schemes. Strict priorities had been established for the unloading of supplies over the beaches. These were abandoned on the second day when it was realized that more time was being wasted checking manifests and deciding which ship to unload first than would be spent simply unloading everything to hand and sorting it out on shore. For some time also only a tiny and inadequate percentage of supply tonnage was set aside to allow for emergency needs. Again jerrycans provide a good example of what might go wrong. During the eventual breakout from

Normandy a limiting factor for fuel supply was found to be that millions of these essential items had been carelessly lost or damaged. Another useful instance to remember for a generation accustomed to good roads and generally reliable motor vehicles was the discovery during the campaign that 1400 British trucks of a certain type all had defective engines – and all the replacement engines had the same fault. If Montgomery was concerned about the quality of the supply operation he had every reason to be.

Montgomery's last days before D-Day were spent in part in putting the final touches to his indoctrination programme, this time, as in previous battles, to all officers down to the battalion commander/lieutenant-colonel level. He gave the same speech to each gathering. The great Allied assets he said were possession of the initiative, well-trained troops, great fire-power, and 'a good and simple plan'. He rounded off his talk by quoting a verse written by the great seventeenth-century Scottish soldier, the Marquess of Montrose,

He either fears his fate too much,
Or his deserts are small,
Who dare not put it to the touch
To win or lose it all.

It is an interesting eulogy of boldness from what many have described as a cautious man – the verse was also part of the printed message issued to all D-Day troops and was later framed and proudly displayed in Monty's command caravan – and it is ironic in a man of such puritan habits that the quote comes from Montrose's poem 'To His Mistress'.

Perhaps the clearest example in the whole history of warfare of the moment when a single decision by a commander truly 'put it to the touch' was the moment when Eisenhower gave his order that the invasion would definitely go ahead despite his forecasters' uncertainties about the weather. D-Day had been planned for 5 June but bad conditions moving in from the Atlantic threatened to halt air operations and make the seaborne landings very difficult. The decision was not Montgomery's to make but it is once more revealing of a boldness that he was seldom credited with that his opinion was in favour of going ahead with the original plan, which Eisenhower decided against, and later also when Eisenhower finally committed to the 6th.

The events of D-Day itself could not be influenced either way by Montgomery once affairs had been set in motion. He spent much of the day in the garden at his HQ in England. By the end of the day the Allies had 150,000 men safely ashore. This was achieved by a combination of the elan of the two American and one British airborne divisions on the flanks; the solid progress of the British and Canadians on their three beach areas; the bravery and drive of the US First Army on the terrible Omaha beach; and the success at Utah, where the

Above: *Sherman tanks of a French armoured unit land in Normandy.*

Left: *Casualties from the fighting being evacuated to a hospital ship over one of the floating roadways in the British Mulberry harbour.*

advance inland was obstructed more by flooded ground than by the Germans.

Few of the objectives laid down had been attained and although there was cause for concern about the status of the thin Omaha gains, the other beach-heads were firmly established. The most notable shortfall was on the eastern flank where the British 3rd Division and its supporting 27th Armoured Brigade had been given the task of capturing Caen. They were halted well short of their objective, encountering difficulties in overcoming various German strongpoints as they moved inland and by attacks by Monty's old enemies from 21st Panzer Division. One of the writers most critical of Montgomery overall, R W Thompson, sums up the position well:

> The 'Objectives' of D-Day had not been gained, but these were not true guides to success or failure, nor on that day did anyone so regard them. They were not 'Objects' but thereafter they would be confused with objects by almost everyone except Montgomery and his generals.

Montgomery's generalship in Normandy has been the subject of as much debate as any historical issue arising out of World War II. The discussion usually centres around how far the events in Normandy corresponded to Montgomery's plans as set out before the invasion, how far these were modified as operations developed, and whether the eventual Allied success derived from Monty's leadership or was the inevitable product of material superiority. The assessment is complicated by the differing British and American perspectives – both in press reports and the private opinions of leading participants at the time and in later historical analysis. By its good communications and obvious importance to the progress of the war the Normandy campaign became most intensively reported, with correspondents, then as now, searching frantically for news of real advances, towns captured, notable leaders to idolize, and scandals to expose. In the event such progress as was made would often be a matter of a few fields and hedgerows at a time which did not make for great headlines. Nor, as General Bradley later pointed out, could Montgomery, 'spending his reputation in a bitter siege of Caen', draw attention to the much more powerful German forces opposing the British there than those against US First Army, unless he wanted to give his plans away.

Monty was also in some respects his own worst enemy with his insistence at the time, and later in his *Memoirs*, that everything had gone very much according to his master plan. This was his posture both in public and in private discussions with other senior officers with whom he could have been more frank about any doubts and difficulties he was suffering.

There is no question that the 'master plan' for the invasion was not followed in detail, whatever Monty might claim. The hope of capturing Caen on the first day was not fulfilled for weeks, nor was there any attempt to push armoured columns deep inland to disrupt the movement of German reserves, as Montgomery had advocated in his pre-invasion briefings. What he could more plausibly claim was that the shape the battles took corresponded to his initial ideas even if their locations were disappointingly near the coast. The difference was that the first plans had optimistically envisaged the Germans being compelled to fight desperately to try to regain Caen from the Allies because of its vital importance as a local communications centre; in reality Caen remained a focus because it was essential for the Germans, having retained it, to try to keep it.

The first German responses to the invasion were evidence that Caen would not indeed fall immediately and also started to set out the form the battle would follow for the next seven weeks. 21st Panzer Division was engaged from the beginning in the Caen sector. The young fanatics of 12th SS Panzer Division (*Hitler Jugend*) were next to arrive from reserve and were quickly drawn in against the Canadians near the Carpiquet airfield. Next again was the *Panzer Lehr* Division (particularly formid-

able since many of its personnel were former instructors in tank schools) and its units, too, found themselves drawn in to holding the line just west of Caen. Already, though, by the evening of the 9th, the Germans had been forced to postpone plans for a major counter-attack. Such plans were aborted for a further period by the virtual annihilation by air attack on the 10th of the headquarters personnel of Panzer Group West (commanded by Geyr von Schweppenberg who was one of the few to be only slightly wounded).

This Allied success occurred after the 'Ultra' codebreakers had precisely located the enemy position so that a major strike could be organized. It is worth digressing here, since this is often misunderstood, to show what Ultra information could and could not do to help the Allied armies and their commanders. It was very rare that codebreaking could give such precise tactical information as the location of an enemy HQ. It could tell a great deal about the German order of battle and was particularly important in reassuring the Allied leaders that strong German forces were remaining in the Pas de Calais as a result of the Fortitude deception (a deception which probably could not have been established without 'Ultra' guidance). It could tell Montgomery which panzer divisions were facing the British around Caen and which were their operational areas but it could not provide a way of attacking them cheaply – the battles still had to be fought and won. Useful information on German intentions could also often be gleaned. During the US advance on Cherbourg the Germans might have done better to fall back quickly to the port's fortified outskirts. Hitler forbade this, which the Allied generals knew, so they could adjust their plans to fit. The most important and famous examples of secret intelligence aiding the Allied generals in Normandy would be in meeting the German offensive at Mortain in August which shall be discussed shortly.

Montgomery hoped to gain quick compensation for the failure to take Caen on D-Day by mounting an encircling attack during the next few days but these hopes were disappointed, in ways which also gave significant pointers for the future. 51st Highland Division was intended to advance round the east side of the city. This move was soon halted by increasing German resistance. The second part of the encirclement was to be a paratroop attack a little

Left: *A Canadian engineer checks for mines. Ditches and verges of paths were favoured locations for booby traps since they were precisely the places where troops under fire would take cover.*

Bottom left: *Rommel inspecting a coast defence battery.*

Below: *A military policeman with a German paratroop unit keeps a lookout for Allied aircraft. Every German vehicle moving in daylight near the invasion front would have someone permanently on aircraft spotting watch.*

to the south and east of Caen. This was aborted on the insistence of Leigh-Mallory, fortunately as it turned out, but not before it earned the air chief the condemnation 'gutless bugger' in a letter from Montgomery to de Guingand.

The third segment of the advance (whose failure would have left the paratroops in trouble) was a tank attack by 7th Armoured Division through a well-detected gap in the German lines between Caumont and Villers-Bocage. Most of one of the division's tank regiments and a large part of a motorized infantry battalion were caught by a mere handful of German Tiger tanks and within a few minutes the British lost about 25 tanks and as many other vehicles. Because of this and other German blows 7th Armoured had to withdraw the next day after 50th Division had failed to make enough ground to join them.

This sequence of events had many lessons which should be taken into account in judging Mont-

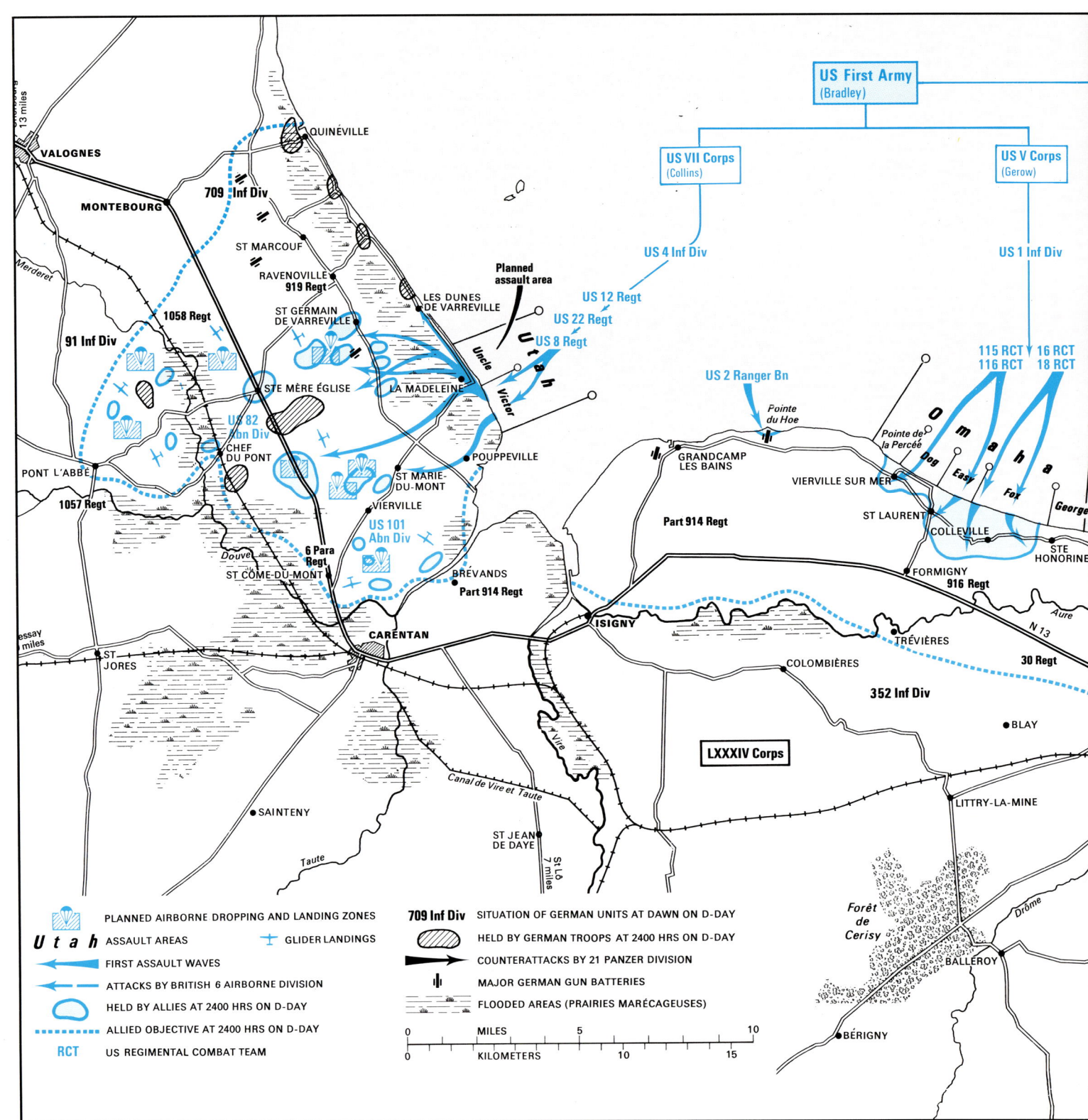

A Good and Simple Plan

gomery's achievements in Normandy. General Dempsey described the management of this battle by his senior subordinates as a disgrace. Bucknall of XXX Corps, Erskine of 7th Armoured, and Bullen-Smith of the Highland Division would all fairly shortly be dismissed. Next was the excellence of the German short range infantry anti-tank weapon, the *Panzerfaust*, given every opportunity to show its effectiveness, for example, in halting the tanks supporting the 50th Division attack, by the lack of close co-operation between the British infantry and armour. This was an important weakness which would only gradually be remedied as the units gained experience but an aspect in which the Germans retained superiority because of their usual practice and proficiency in fighting in *ad hoc* battle groups created for the mission to hand.

Among the lessons was the spectacle of SS Captain Wittman calmly driving alone in his Tiger from one end of the halted British column to the

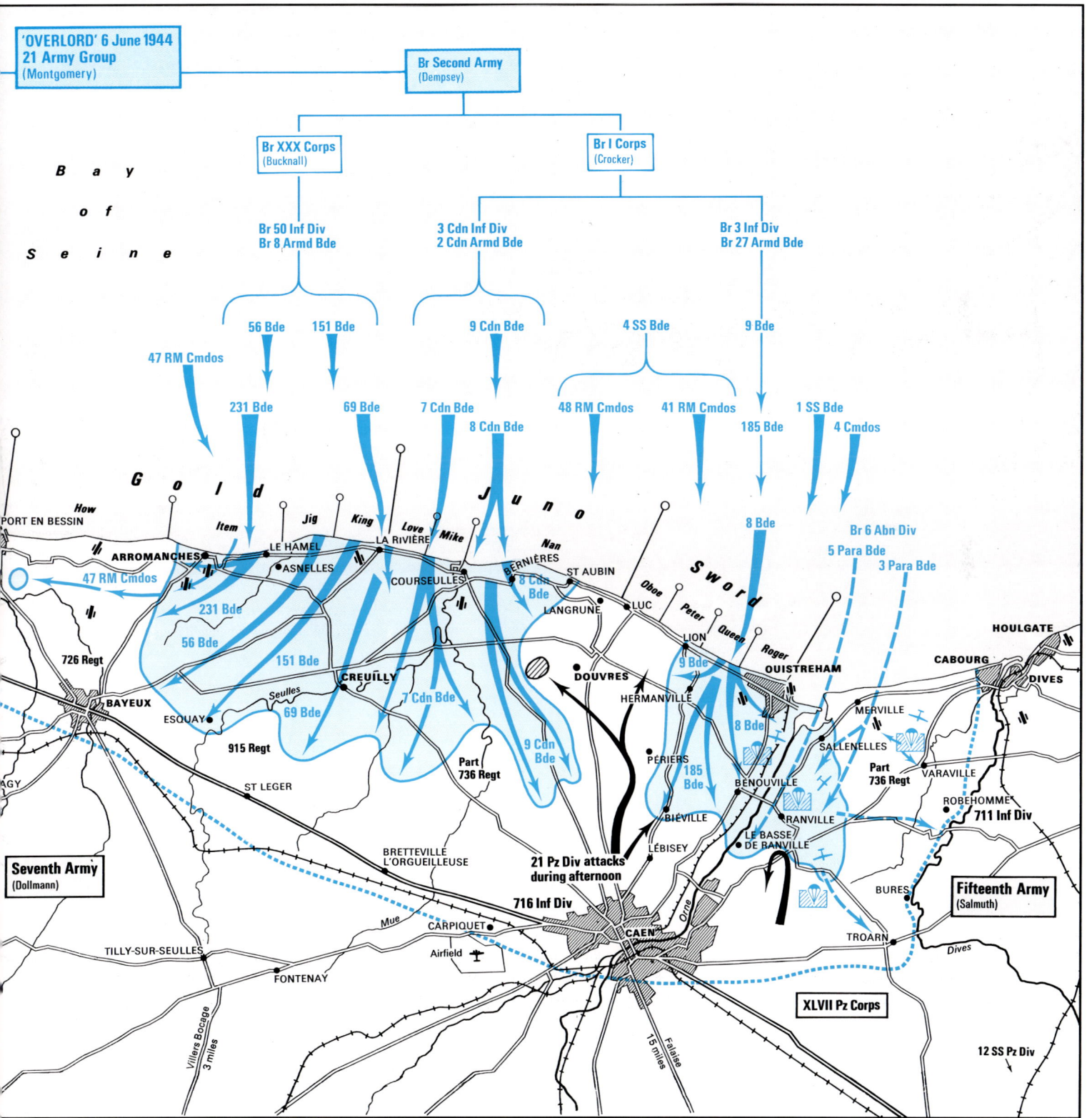

Below: *The Allied progress on 6 June.*

other, methodically destroying its tanks and vehicles as he went. Most of the tanks destroyed were Cromwells which mounted the same inadequate 75mm gun as the standard Sherman (the most numerous tank in British as well as American service) and with similar weak armour protection. Wittman's Tiger had little to fear from such opposition, neither had the more numerous German Panther tanks which were the most formidable on the German side. Later in June Montgomery would take steps to halt the circulation of official reports describing Allied tank inferiority, believing that these would be bad for morale. This was probably sensible enough but he could do nothing to stop the common gossip and its implications. What Montgomery did not do and could have done was to urge ceaselessly in his own private correspondence and reports to higher authority that the weakness be corrected (although this would obviously only be possible in the long term).

While the British were struggling with the great majority of the German tank forces, US First Army was intended to advance to Cherbourg *and* begin to move south on the west flank of the Allied line. Again there were problems. The near disaster at Omaha beach on D-Day meant that the drive for Cherbourg had to be deferred for the first few days in favour of solidly capturing Carentan to complete once and for all the link between the Allied beach areas. Then, when the drive to Cherbourg got under way, it could not be accompanied, as both Montgomery and Bradley hoped, by attacks to the south because of supply shortages. Only about half the supplies planned were landed for the American forces in the first week and for June as a whole only about 70 per cent. The Allies generally, and the Americans in particular, were victims of their own skill in providing so lavishly for their soldiers. Each US combat soldier was supposed to receive, for example, about twice the quantity of rations each day as his German counterpart. There was enormous waste in every category of supply and this capacity could more profitably have been devoted to ammunition which had to be rationed for some time in Normandy.

Like the British, the Americans also had problems with poorly trained and badly led units performing unsatisfactorily. Various commanders were soon being sacked, although some, like Collins whose VII Corps took Cherbourg, were very able and successful. The Americans were also to suffer from defects of their manpower policies although never from the overall shortages that haunted the British commanders. Although in all national armed forces the enterprising, the well-educated, the intelligent, and the physically and mechanically skilled tended to be sent or to gravitate to elite units, or aircrew posts, or other specialist military occupations, in the US army, more than in any other, the combat services were last in line to receive their manpower allocation. This did not reflect the complicated and demanding nature of the work and the fact that the infantry, above all, bore the greatest weight of casualties and those disproportionately on the natural leaders and better soldiers who were already in short supply. The US army also had an utterly demoralizing system of feeding replacements for casualties, both enlisted men and officers, from training back in the USA, through various depots and transit camps, to their eventual disoriented arrival, possibly months later with training half forgotten, in a front line unit composed totally of strangers. This was administratively simple but thoroughly destructive of the sort of teamwork and small unit cohesion essential to military efficiency in the close and difficult Normandy bocage. The Germans operated a more complicated system but one in which, whenever possible, men who were required to fight together had trained with each other and with at least some of the officers and NCOs who would lead them in combat.

As the Americans were making their slow pro-

Below: An illustration of the disadvantages of opening an attack with heavy air bombardments: Canadian troops pick their way forward over blocked streets in Caen.

gress toward Cherbourg, Montgomery was ordering his British commanders to prepare new attacks in the Caen sector. Unfortunately there was first another setback. From the 18th to the 21st the worst summer weather in the Channel for many years wrecked the Mulberry artificial harbour that had been built off the American beaches and badly damaged the British equivalent. In the long run this was less significant than might have been expected because landing supplies on the open beaches proved to be easier than the Allied planners had anticipated. In the short term the landing schedule for supplies and new troops lagged still further behind and Monty had to postpone his attacks. It is worth adding also that the weather for flying was often poor throughout the Normandy battles with low cloud hindering the pilots. On the 26th and 27th, for example, the first two days of Monty's new Caen offensive, practically no aircraft were able to fly from bases in Britain in support, although the forces by then established in Normandy played a full part. The air arm's achievement in Normandy was very great in protecting the cluttered beach-head, in operations over the battlefields, and in the unseen intervention to the rear which slowed and decimated the movement of German reinforcements and supplies. Nonetheless much more could have been done, given fine weather.

The new British attack, Operation Epsom, was delivered by the three divisions of VIII Corps with over 300 guns in support. The aim was to fight from around Bretteville l'Orgueilleuse, to the west of Caen, across the rivers Odon and Orne to the south. In four days of hard battling and fierce German counterattacks only a small bridgehead over the Odon was won and this was given up when Montgomery ordered an end to the offensive on the 30th.

On the surface this was a disappointment but there was considerable compensation. The advance had been held by the Germans only by the commitment of two more newly-arrived SS panzer divisions (9th and 10th, from Russia) along with part of 2nd SS Panzer which had been arriving in instalments from the Toulouse area for some days. (This was the formation responsible for the atrocity at Oradour-sur-Glane when many of the villagers were murdered in retaliation for resistance attacks which had slowed the division's march to Normandy). Montgomery was surely being disingenuous when he claimed that territorial gains did not matter in this battle. Its main purpose, as he stated, was certainly to draw in the German reserves while Cherbourg was finally captured (on the 27th) but this purpose could have been far better served by a more substantial movement and a real threat of a breakthrough, which was never developed. It did Montgomery no good that the chosen code name, known throughout the Allied high command, was

the name of a famous racecourse nor that his major effort in July, Operation Goodwood, would in the same way imply speedy progress in the cavalry tradition and the taking of a gamble.

By the end of June the criticisms of Montgomery for slow and sluggish advances were beginning to mount. The air chiefs, especially Tedder and Coningham, were deeply concerned that the comparatively small area under Allied control had meant that only about half the squadrons that should have been transferred to bases in France had gone, simply because there was insufficient room for their airfields in the packed beach-head. In particular they longed for the open ground to the south and south-east of Caen to be captured so that airfields could be built there. Certainly this would have made their task easier but Montgomery was correct in seeing that air supremacy had been won and was being very effectively exercised and that, in those circumstances, taking more airfields might not be an essential step on the way to the ultimate end of beating Rommel. The airmen, with their mistaken belief as to what were and were not cor-

Top: *One of the 79th Armoured Division's Churchill AVREs is passed by a convoy of Bren carriers in a Normandy village.*

Above: *British infantry advance during Operation Epsom.*

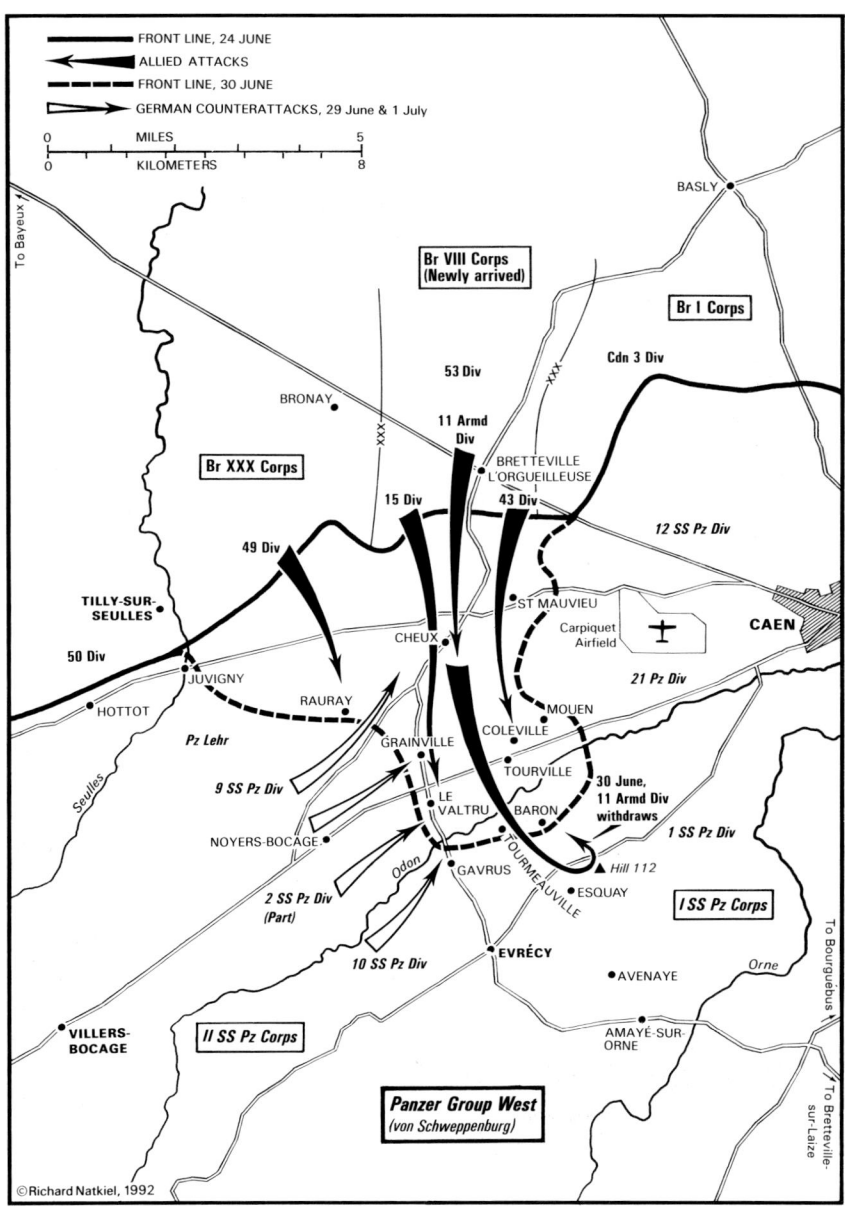

Above: *The disappointing progress made by Operation Epsom, but a closer look at the designations of the German units involved shows how the German armour was being held on the British sector.*

Above right: *US infantry come ashore on D-Day.*

Below right: *Tense moments for British paratroops as their aircraft approaches the drop zone.*

shambles himself. Von Rundstedt's advice for the future was simple: 'Make peace, you idiots, what else is there to do?' This much had been achieved under Montgomery's command.

With the fall of Cherbourg the US First Army could concentrate on advancing to the south at last. Their front line was still deep in the difficult bocage country with its small fields and near-impenetrable hedgerows tending to channel advances into lines all-too-readily predicted by the German defenders. On 3 July Bradley's men opened their new offensive to capture St Lô and, it was hoped, to gain the road between there and the coast at Coutances as the start line for the next phase which would be the real break-out. Although Montgomery's relationship with Bradley was much looser than the close supervision he held over the British and Canadian forces, this programme was still very much in line with Monty's policy as repeated in several directives he issued around this time. The advance unfortunately was slow and the casualty bill heavy, 40,000 from First Army before St Lô fell on 18 July. These losses were larger than those the British were taking and accordingly brought some criticisms of British commitment. There were also some ominous shifts of German forces to meet the American drive with new units arriving on the American sector. Among these was the *Panzer Lehr* Division (admittedly not at full strength after its experiences on the British front) which made a fierce counterattack on 11 July. This was soundly defeated, showing just how difficult an advance was for even the most experienced unit in this terrain. What the slow American progress meant for Montgomery was that there must be more attacks around Caen while the Americans were still pushing on. Bradley devised a new plan with a start line farther north, for what would be Operation Cobra and, with genuine understanding of American problems, Monty specifically told him on 10 July to take all the time he needed to prepare it.

By then there had already been further attacks on the British front. On the evening of 7 July 450 RAF heavy bombers attacked the northern outskirts of Caen which Montgomery had now decided should definitely be taken to confirm his grip on the German forces in that sector. The attack, by three divisions of I Corps, was not to go in until the early hours of the morning of the 8th which proved to be a mistake for, when it did, it was met by heavy German resistance and hindered by the destruction and rubble left by the bombing. Nevertheless, during the 9th, the whole of the city north and west of the Orne was in Allied hands. It had certainly not been a cleverly managed battle but again attention had been drawn to the Caen sector.

The next important step was Operation Goodwood, the largest offensive yet mounted by the British in Normandy. Pressure on Montgomery to score an important success had been growing

rect uses of airpower, did not realize that the only sure way to win the war was to beat the German army in the field.

Most of this chapter so far has described the difficulties and half-successes of the campaign from the Allied point of view. To assess Montgomery only on this basis would be misleading for, from the German side, a very different picture emerges. Shortly before the end of June both Rommel and his superior, von Rundstedt, the German Commander-in-Chief West (who was shortly to be sacked), went to see Hitler to ask permission to withdraw because they were certain that otherwise their front would collape disastrously. Instead, on 1 July after their return, a new directive from the Führer ordered that the existing line be held. Von Rundstedt had a caustic phone conversation with Keitel, Hitler's Chief of Staff, in which he described once again the Normandy problems and suggested sarcastically that, if Keitel did not believe him, he should take over and try to sort out the

A Good and Simple Plan

throughout the early days in July. As well as the cabal of his enemies among the air marshals, other officers, like Morgan, the one-time COSSAC now on Eisenhower's staff, were openly joining the ranks of Montgomery's critics. Churchill was pestering Brooke for more rapid gains (and being sharply told off for his trouble) and Eisenhower, understandably fretting at his weight of responsibility combined with his lack of opportunity really to influence events, was writing to Montgomery in terms that implied that he had either not understood Monty's plans or now unwisely wished to switch the main breakout effort from the American to the British sector.

The plan for Goodwood was to lead the attack with three armoured divisions of VIII Corps since there were ample reserves of tanks but a growing shortage of infantry. The attack was to be driven southward from the bridgehead on the east bank of the Orne between Caen and the sea, a bridgehead still confined to little more than the area that had been taken in the first few days of the landings. This confinement was to be an important weakness of the plan. Another was that the Germans, for once in Normandy, successfully anticipated the axis and site of the attack, despite every effort being made to preserve security and surprise. They created probably the most formidable defensive layout of the many powerful defences they built in Normandy, with strongpoints in various villages and five successive zones of defences based around dug-in tanks and well sited 88s. There was such depth to these defences that the farthest groups would be immune from any preliminary bombardment. This defensive plan has been described as Rommel's last military achievement for, on the 17th, during the battle, his staff car was caught and strafed by RAF fighters. It crashed and Rommel was badly injured. He would never return to the front. Instead he was murdered by the Nazis later in the year because of his marginal connections with the plotters who tried to kill Hitler on 20 July.

The crucial question about Operation Goodwood is whether it was Montgomery's intention to be content only with yet again drawing in and wearing down German forces on the eastern flank, or whether he was attempting a more decisive breakthrough. Since Montgomery's comments during as well as before the operation bear on this debate it is perhaps best to outline the actual events of the fighting first.

The Allied-controlled area east of the Orne was so small that, as part of the attempt to preserve surprise, the attacking divisions were held west of the river until the last moment. When the attack opened on 18 July with a massive air bombardment the armoured divisions and all their vehicles had to cross by only three bridges to begin their advance, and once over the river were further confined by British minefields as well as whatever the Germans might do. Only after the tanks had passed over could the artillery get across to take up firing positions sufficiently far forward to support the advance as it progressed. The first result was all-too-predictable: horrendous traffic queues amid clouds of dust reminiscent of the worst phases of Alamein, and the direct consequence of this was that the last armoured division to cross (7th) did not wholly get forward into battle on the first day.

Not all the bombing was accurately aimed and, after initial heartening gains, when the advancing armour began to move out of range of its supporting artillery, the significant surviving German forces fought back strongly. In two days of intense fighting which cost the British and Canadians some 400 tanks (over one third of their armour), only part of the Bourgébus Ridge, the principal objective, had been captured. The subsidiary Canadian attacks to the west of the main drive did succeed in taking the rest of Caen but also at a cost of significant casualties. Heavy rain fell on the 20th and it was clear by then that any continuation of the offensive was pointless. Goodwood had run its course and a new storm of criticism threatened Montgomery's position.

In public this arose from unwise remarks Montgomery made at a press conference on the afternoon of the 18th which gave a greatly over-optimistic view of progress up to that time and used such terms as 'break-through' and 'open country' which were faithfully repeated in the headlines in London and New York the next day. There was acute disappointment when the headlines a couple of days later read 'bogged down'.

The air marshals were still further outraged, Tedder promising Eisenhower that he would support him if he decided to sack Montgomery. They felt that there had never been a real attempt to make a decisive advance even though this had been promised by Monty when he persuaded them to

Right: *Field Marshal von Rundstedt, dismissed by Hitler in July for his all-too-realistic appreciation of the German position.*

Left: *Relaxing at a Normandy landing ground. The aircraft in the background is a Mustang fighter in British service but like all Allied aircraft painted with the distinctive black and white recognition stripes applied before D-Day.*

A Good and Simple Plan

'divert' the massed heavy bombers to support the army. Others like de Guingand later suggested, not that there was no intention to make a decisive advance, but that Montgomery deliberately exaggerated its prospects since this was the only way to persuade the air chiefs to support the offensive wholeheartedly. In either case the real villains of the piece must be the air marshals who should not have required any convincing at all to back an attack by the principal part of Britain's largest and most important army.

There is some justice in the claim that some of Montgomery's letters and signals did suggest a very optimistic prospect for Goodwood but others were much more cautious. He made sure that de Guingand gave Eisenhower a careful and moderate briefing and also sent one of his aides to give the same story to the War Office in London. In subsequent recollections both Dempsey and O'Connor, the commander of VIII Corps, firmly stated that they had not expected any spectacular victory.

This view is backed by an unambitious written order issued to Dempsey shortly before the offensive began. It was very unusual for Montgomery to issue such written orders – his usual method was to give simple oral instructions – so here one can interpret this in either of two ways. He may have thought the matter so important that he wished to be absolutely unambiguous or he may, more deviously, have been setting out an alibi, to be used later if required or quietly forgotten if all went really well.

Certainly, in terms of drawing in and weakening the German reserves, Goodwood was a success. In the first three weeks of July five fresh infantry divisions and one panzer division moved in against the British and Canadians; less than two full divisions joined the front on the American sector. Throughout these weeks British Second Army was facing an average of over 600 tanks with just under 200 opposite the Americans. And yet, it is difficult to be convinced that this sort of reward was sufficient for the

Below: *American infantry pass an abandoned Panzer Mk IV in a battered French town, August 1944.*

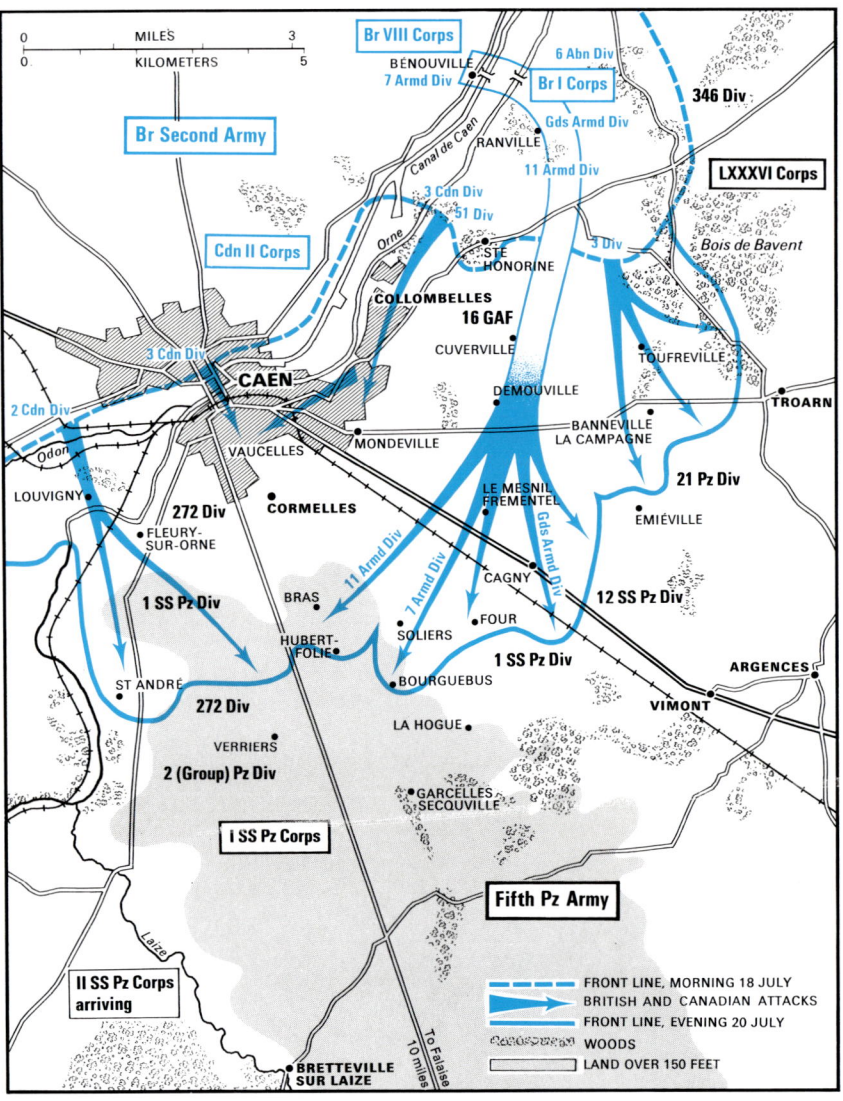

Above: *Operation Goodwood. The villages and the rail embankment in the path of the advance were employed in the effective German defensive system.*

effort put into Goodwood. One of the best recent writers on the Normandy battle sums this up well:

> to demand that history should accept that this was the sum of British ambitions is to suggest that a man sows wheat to harvest straw.

The same author, however, also very correctly draws attention to perhaps the most important point in Montgomery's favour – the clear and repeated connection in his thinking between the Goodwood advance and the awaited American Cobra attack, which he certainly expected should make substantial gains. As Max Hastings notes,

> after the war Bradley, the most unlikely man to provide spurious alibis for Montgomery, declared that he had never expected Goodwood to be anything other than a supporting operation for the American Cobra.

Cobra, which eventually began on 25 July, was first planned to start only a day or two after Goodwood opened and it is noticeable that Montgomery's descriptions of Goodwood's prospects tended to be toned down as Cobra was gradually deferred and the hoped-for close co-ordination ceased to be possible. It also seems to be the case that it was principally in the less formal, more spontaneous meetings and messages that Monty gave his most optimistic descriptions. His more soberly and carefully prepared pronouncements told a different story. This is an important clue, for it should be remembered, as we have seen, that Montgomery was a general who 'enjoyed fighting battles', as far as others could tell. He himself confirmed this view by writing to de Guingand just after D-Day that he was having 'great fun fighting battles again after five months in England.' His character was also one in which there was a pronounced trouble-making and risk-taking strain, usually fiercely repressed. It should be no surprise that, at this period when he was experiencing the most fulfilling employment possible for a military man of his ambitions, his sense of satisfaction and absorption in his work would expose the conflicts within his normally so controlled personality and loosen his tongue in a manner that he would come to regret.

To draw such a conclusion is, in a sense, to sit on the fence and say that both Montgomery's critics and supporters were partly right but what this strategic debate has often tended to obscure is the criticism that Montgomery deserves for the fact that Goodwood was not a well-constructed battle. Although the air attacks were better planned and conducted than those on 7 July, they were the sole attempt to modify what was otherwise an entirely unimaginative and predictable bludgeon against what were certain to be strong defences. Montgomery should have understood also that the congestion following the opening moves was almost inevitable and would significantly nullify the fleeting advantage given by the bombing, by allowing the Germans time to recover before the full attack developed.

In the aftermath of Goodwood Montgomery did his best to mend his differences with some of his superiors, happily receiving Eisenhower and Churchill in visits to his Tac HQ. It is worth turning aside here briefly to describe aspects of the arrangement at Tac HQ because these highlight the point previously made regarding Montgomery's growing tendency to isolate himself. In the course of the fighting in 1944–45 his HQ acquired an interesting menagerie including a cow (to provide the C-in-C with fresh milk), two puppies (named Hitler and Rommel), a horse (formerly Rommel's property), a collection of tropical fish and budgerigars (Monty also kept a noisy group of canaries in his caravan during the Italian campaign), and latterly a small flock of sheep. This collection was not, it may be said, unique. Eisenhower's HQ had, at one time, a puppy called Monty and the British XXX Corps also had a 'farm' which travelled with the HQ and among other things provided fresh

A Good and Simple Plan

Above: *Brooke, Churchill, and Monty, at Monty's HQ in Normandy.*

produce for the corps' field hospital. What Montgomery's collection does suggest is that, whereas Eisenhower and other senior American officers could relax together over Scotch and a game of bridge to the benefit of their working relationships (although Ike's entourage was also known to be a hotbed of malicious gossip), Montgomery tended to unwind with the junior officers of his personal staff or with his pets, to the neglect of his bosses and near-equals.

Ultimately he had no respect for Eisenhower as a potential battlefield commander although in his more sensible and generous moments he recognized and valued Ike's undoubted, essential contribution to the overall working of the alliance. (And if this account deals extensively with the quarrels between the Allied leaders and generals, it should be remembered that these were sweetness and rationality itself when compared to the ructions in the German high command.) Montgomery's fault was to fail to develop a relationship with Eisenhower that combined respect for the Supreme Commander's position with a willingness to keep him informed and involved. Instead, as Monty was soon astonishingly to note, Eisenhower 'is never allowed to attend a meeting between me and my army commanders and Bradley.'

By 20 July, when Goodwood was coming to an end, Bradley's First Army had reached the St Lô-Périers road which was to be the jumping-off point for Operation Cobra which, much delayed, began on the 25th. Although all its details were settled under Bradley's authority and so are not directly relevant here, Cobra was very much part of Montgomery's overall policy, so its results are of interest. During the 27th the German resistance began to cave in and their front disintegrate under the American attacks. On the 30th the advance took Avranches and from there could begin to turn west into Brittany and continue south and east into the heart of France. One feature of the advance was the much improved army-air co-operation. This was largely due to the efforts of General Quesada who was in direct command of the American tactical aircraft force. Like his British counterpart, Broadhurst, he put his more senior colleagues to shame by his genuinely co-operative attitude towards the army's needs.

As had long been planned, Patton's Third Army became fully operational on 1 August and he immediately began hustling its leading divisions ahead through the bottleneck at Avranches. With this change Bradley was promoted to command 12th Army Group, comprised of Third Army and

Above: *A variety of tanks of a Canadian armoured unit seen on 14 August during Operation Tractable. Churchill and light Stuart tanks face away from the camera on the far side of the road while on the road itself is a Churchill Crocodile towing the trailer which supplies fuel for its flamethrower.*

Right: *Field Marshal Gunther von Kluge, briefly Hitler's Commander in Chief West, who committed suicide when suspected of treachery.*

Bradley's old command of First Army, now under Hodges. First Canadian Army had become operational on 23 July under General Crerar and together with Dempsey's Second Army now made up Monty's 21st Army Group. Although it had originally been planned that Eisenhower would take over direct control of the land battle at this point, this move was deferred for the moment until a proper HQ could be established for Eisenhower in France. Instead Montgomery retained a supervising and co-ordinating role between the army groups, but with the continued burgeoning of American strength his relationship with Bradley was now essentially an equal one. These changes were not announced in the Allied press for some days and when they were it was badly handled, offending British sensibilities by suggesting a sudden demotion for Monty and, following this, annoying Americans by the suggestion that the British still wished to lord it over them. All of this would contribute to the background for the major strategic disputes to come, which are discussed in the next chapter.

As Cobra was developing, the British and Canadian forces were continuing to heave and beat away on the Caen sector, still aiming to convince the Germans that this was where the main Allied effort would be. Von Kluge, who had replaced von Rundstedt and also taken over Rommel's duties after his injury, spent 25 July on the eastern flank dealing with a new Canadian attack, thinking that Cobra was a diversion in its favour. Montgomery had ordered that this advance should go ahead even if the weather was unfavourable and Cobra had been postponed again – the clearest confirmation possible that his priority was to tie down German forces and not seek territorial gains.

The next major drive by 21st Army Group was Operation Bluecoat which began on the 30th. The conception of this offensive demonstrates Montgomery's battlefield skills at their best and also highlights the work of the excellent staff he had employed and developed. The six German panzer divisions were all deployed towards the east of the British line so Montgomery decided to make a difficult and ambitious shift in the weight of his forces to the west, nearer to their junction with the Americans, and attack from around Caumont towards Vire. Virtually every British and Canadian formation had at least to adjust its position if not move entirely. The ground, however, was as unpromising as any in the Normandy bocage and since this front had been quieter for some time the Germans had had an opportunity to bolster their defences with minefields. The area was also overlooked by the formidable crest of the Mont Pinçon ridge. Progress was slow, although briefly at one stage there was a possibility that 11th Armoured Division, whose commander, General Roberts, was reckoned to be one of the best British leaders, might take a quick breakthrough via Bény-Bocage. The opportunity was quickly denied by the Germans, partly through a fierce attack on 7th Armoured Division to the flank. This action finally earned dismissal for Bucknall of XXX Corps and the commander of 7th Armoured and two of his principal subordinates. Bucknall's replacement was Horrocks, one of Monty's old team, who had been out of action since being wounded at the tail end of the African campaign.

With the activation of his army Patton immediately began to demonstrate his best qualities in squeezing his leading divisions with remarkable rapidity through Avranches. The intended Allied plan, part of the scheme developed months before with Montgomery's original ideas, was to turn much of Patton's army west at this point to clear Brittany and open the major ports there. Now Montgomery was quicker than either Patton or Bradley to see that this was no longer wise and abandon the 'master plan'. After some hesitation Bradley and Patton committed most of Third Army to plunge south and east towards Le Mans.

The decision which sealed the Allied triumph in Normandy and made it into a truly crushing victory was taken by Adolf Hitler. On 3 August he ordered his commanders to prepare an all-out tank attack westward from around Mortain across the narrow neck through which Patton's men were pouring south. Helped by a few hours' warning given by Ultra information, Bradley met the attack with great confidence when it began on the 7th and, while it was being held over the next three or four days, with outstanding support from the British and American tactical air forces, he continued to pour more divisions through to follow Patton's spearheads.

Like all that had gone before in Normandy the two weeks that followed the opening of the Ger-

Above: *Monty, Churchill, and 'Rommel', 7 August 1944.*

man offensive at Mortain up to the final closure of what came to be known as the Falaise pocket, were and still are highly controversial sections of the careers of Montgomery and all the leading Allied generals. It is all too easy to judge, with the clear vision of hindsight, decisions that were taken at the time amid a welter of rapid movements in every direction and partial and often incorrect and misleading information. It would be particularly difficult for the Allied generals to appreciate quickly how long the German forces in the developing pocket would be held from retreating since this contradicted everything that they and the German generals (but not Hitler) well knew as militarily correct.

Even before the Mortain offensive began Montgomery and the American leaders realized the possibility that some at least of the German forces might be cut off by an encirclement from the British in the north and the Americans in the south. On 3 August Montgomery gave orders to the Canadian Army (which, in fact, had substantial non-Canadian elements) to attack south-east from the Caen area in what would be known as Operation Totalize. On 6 August he issued a directive to all the Allied armies which set the boundary between the army groups on an east-west line running just south of Argentan and anticipated the possibility of encirclements being made if the Germans were slow to withdraw. Any encirclement envisaged at this stage was to be a 'long hook' with airborne forces being dropped as far east as Chartres to help block any German retreat. This possibility remained part of Montgomery's and Bradley's thinking for some days.

Operation Totalize began in the early minutes of 7 August with an innovative and effective night attack by massed RAF heavy bombers. The attack was planned and commanded by General Simonds of II Canadian Corps, probably the most able of the Canadian generals. It was the familiar story of initial reasonable progress soon slowing as the German resistance stiffened. For many of the Canadian troops and the participating Polish Armoured Division this was their first battle and the inexperience told. Matters were not helped when a USAAF heavy bomber attack on the 8th was partly off target and caused friendly casualties. (Similar incidents had happened at the beginning of Operation Cobra.) By the 11th Totalize had ground to a disappointing halt well short of its target of Falaise.

By then, naturally enough, the ludicrous German offensive at Mortain had brought revisions to the overall Allied policy. Patton's XV Corps had taken Le Mans on the 8th and from there turned north to begin a 'short hook' through Alençon to Argentan. This was confirmed in a Monty directive on the 11th; the Canadians were to complete the encirclement with a new attack through Falaise to Argentan. The inter-army boundary, significantly, remained as before. By late on the 12th Patton's advance guard was in the Argentan area and he telephoned Bradley for permission to push on, allegedly offering to 'drive the British into the sea for another Dunkirk' – a joke which would have seemed in very poor taste to Montgomery and many of his subordinates who had been there. Bradley refused to allow Patton to advance any farther and did not contact Montgomery to discuss any boundary changes. So far Patton had not encountered any significant resistance to his advance which was militarily much less spectacular than the distances covered made it seem. Bradley noted that XV Corps in the lead was already dangerously isolated and that soon the formidable German

Right: *Across the Seine at last.*

Below: *The King listens to Monty's account of the tactical situation at a briefing in Monty's caravan.*

Below right: *Monty gives an informal talk to a group of soldiers from various units of 50th Division who are to receive decorations.*

forces to the west must begin to retreat. In that event he preferred a 'strong shoulder at Argentan' to pushing farther on and risking a 'broken neck at Falaise'. The drive to close the pocket thus remained a Canadian responsibility while in the meantime the Americans thickened their cordon to the south and pushed other forces on east into France.

The next phase of 21st Army Group's southward attack was Operation Tractable which began on 14 August. This time it was some of the RAF's aircraft which bombed short and disrupted the attack. Falaise did not completely fall until the 17th, after yet more confused and bitter fighting. Only on the 16th was von Kluge finally permitted to give the order for the German forces in the pocket to pull out. The last gap was loosely closed at Chambois on the 19th but it was not until the 21st that the pocket was truly sealed. In the intervening days there was great carnage as the remnants of the German forces first stampeded and then crept and infiltrated to the east, harried ceaselessly by the packs of Allied medium bombers and the low-level strafing of Thunderbolts and Typhoons.

Above: *Evidence of the crushing effects of Allied airpower over the German retreat through the Falaise Gap. Note also the survival of horse-drawn transport in the German Army: the British and Americans had long since been completely mechanised.*

Right: *A bloodstained young SS trooper makes his surrender.*

Significant German forces did escape from the encirclement and in retrospect this looks like something of a missed opportunity. Some of the criticism for this is often directed at Montgomery – for the slowness of the Canadian attack which was ultimately his responsibility, and, if this could not be corrected, for failing to recognize this and perhaps alter the boundary lines to permit the Americans to resume their advance. Beyond this it is difficult to say what might have been done, on the basis of the information that was available to the Allied generals at the time.

The battle for Normandy had been a great and decisive Allied victory. One example may serve to illustrate the state of the surviving German forces. The *Hitler Jugend* Division had gone into Normandy with 150 tanks and nearly 20,000 men; on 22 August its reported strength was 300 men, 10 tanks and absolutely no artillery. Since D-Day the Germans had lost about 400,000 men, half of them prisoners, as well as 1800 tanks and a great mass of other equipment.

All was not well with the Allied high command, however. The logisticians had proclaimed in July that Allied resources would not permit the advance to reach the Seine by D+90 as predicted in the original plan. Instead the Allied armies achieved this 'impossible' feat eleven days earlier and in only a few days more would be approaching the Dutch and German borders.

The Allied plans had been based on assuming a regular and methodical German retreat, as might well have been more prudent for the Germans. But instead there had been a prolonged stubborn resistance and then a sudden and unexpected total collapse. When this was combined with the genuine logistical difficulties (no matter how well the Allied armies might initially cope with these) it was obvious that a new strategy to deal with the situation might be required. Even before Falaise had fallen Montgomery was typically thinking ahead and developing ideas on what the Allies ought to do. The controversy that predictably resulted will be the principal theme of the next chapter.

A look back at the individual episodes in the Normandy campaign tells a pretty consistent story of partial successes and overall disappointment as hopes were not attained. Only the first few days of the Cobra offensive could really be described as a true success. The vicious battles fought in the bocage country and around Caen by the American, British, Canadian, and Polish forces showed only too well the astonishing resilience of the fighting men of all nationalities, and the fighting power of the German army combined with the shortcomings of the Allied training and equipment. Yet the campaign as a whole was far more for the Allies than the sum of its dubious parts. There was a clear and consistent Allied strategy throughout, devised and maintained by Montgomery. The events of the campaign derived directly from his 'good and simple plan' and the only large-scale attempt the Germans were able to make actively to disrupt this was the lunatic offensive at Mortain. The enemy largely danced to Montgomery's tune.

It is, of course, far easier now to see this whole than it was at the time. Montgomery's great failure was to do too little to explain his strategy to Eisenhower and convince Eisenhower and his other critics, who should have been in the know, of the value of the small steps being taken on the way to fulfilling it. No one finds it easy to believe a general who blithely insists that 'operations are going according to plan' and too often this seemed to be Montgomery's posture both in public and within the Allied high command. This attitude was doomed because it was all too plain to see that operations were not going according to plan in very many detailed respects – for several good

A Good and Simple Plan

reasons, many of them not of Monty's making or within his capacity to remedy – but this he was temperamentally unable to admit, in just the same way he had difficulty in being seen to take advice. The result was that he lost the trust of the top Americans as well as important senior British figures. On 1 September Eisenhower assumed direct control of the Allied land forces and, almost as some sort of compensation, Montgomery was promoted to Field Marshal.

Any summary of events between D-Day and September 1944 must recognize that the Allied land forces, under the command or at least co-ordination of the new field marshal, had won one of the decisive campaigns of World War II. Hundreds of thousands of prisoners had been taken, virtually the whole of France liberated, and the surviving enemy forces were still retreating in total disarray. Critics would mention the Allied air superiority, Hitler's undoubted blunders, and much more. There had been great controversy and many complaints about Montgomery's leadership and consistency of purpose, but ultimately the facts spoke for themselves.

If one substitutes 'plans' for 'words' then a passage from Lewis Carroll's *Alice Through the Looking Glass* can provide a very fitting concluding remark to this chapter:

'When I use a word,' Humpty Dumpty said in rather a scornful tone, 'it means just what I choose – neither more nor less.'

'The question is,' said Alice, 'whether you can make words mean so many different things.'

'The question is,' said Humpty Dumpty, 'which is to be the master – that's all.'

Below: *Watched by her English husband outside their hotel, a French woman welcomes the liberating British troops. Unfortunately in their enthusiasm their Union Flag has been hoisted upside down.*

Chapter Nine
Unrepentant Advocate

Left: *It was to take a bitter winter of hard fighting before the Allied leaders achieved the hoped-for German surrender.*

Above: *If the smiles seem a little forced it is no surprise for at this meeting at the end of November Monty again raised with Eisenhower the whole question of how the Allied armies should be commanded.*

Far right: *The leading US generals who saw the war in Europe through to its conclusion. Front row, from left, Simpson (9th Army), Patton (3rd Army), Spaatz (US Strategic Air Forces), Eisenhower, Bradley (12th Army Group), Hodges (1st Army), and Gerow (15th Army).*

Below: *Eisenhower and Bradley in conversation outside the latter's HQ in late August.*

Virtually every senior Allied figure is on record as having written or spoken during August or September 1944 of his belief that the war should be won within that calendar year. Montgomery agreed with this view both at the time and in retrospect, though in his opinion it was no foregone conclusion, but would depend on adopting the correct strategy and organization for the Allied forces. Montgomery began energetically promoting his ideas in mid-August and was still arguing at the end of March 1945 (though by then, of course, in very different circumstances) that mistakes were being made as his advice was disregarded. In one sense he was correct for in these later months of 1944 there was a very definite vagueness of purpose about the Anglo-American operations, though whether Montgomery's suggestions were superior or indeed even practical in themselves is one of military history's greatest hypothetical questions. Equally a subject of speculation is how disinterested Montgomery's motives were.

At various stages in this long-running argument Monty promised to stop what can best be described as (in his own phrase from other times) 'bellyaching' but repeatedly he renewed his agitation for changed policies. His critics have argued that the main part of his motivation was a self-seeking desire for personal publicity and aggrandizement. This is not convincing. Certainly Monty had a rather naïve enjoyment of his fame and was properly jealous of his reputation but this facet of his character dwindles to nothing when compared, for example, with Patton's gun-toting posturing and adolescent obsession with war's supposed glory and his personal share of it. The private papers of several of the top American leaders are also revealing. Their authors' motivation in the strategic debates comes over as being competition with Montgomery and with each other, almost for its own sake rather than as an incidental product of differing strategic views. It is probably more accurate to see Montgomery as being driven, not by his undoubted vanity, but by all his military experience and what he would have been happy to have described as his deeply professional attitude. It was this, not proud personal concerns, that virtually forced him again and again to insist on renewing his badgering of Eisenhower and his lobbying of his principal supporters in London. Certainly his strategic arguments broadly envisaged that a prominent part continue to be played by his own British and Canadian forces with some American sectors being downgraded in priority, but it is a general's job to detect and advocate the exploitation of what he sees as strategic strengths and opportunities within his area of responsibility. Montgomery's

stated objectives of the Ruhr and ultimately Berlin were justifiable on military grounds and, if others viewed the matter differently, to Monty this too was a reasonable part of the expected order of things – and it was part of Eisenhower's job to decide between the conflicting views.

Montgomery could not stand by and watch someone fiddling with a simple task but instead, infuriatingly, would virtually grab it out of an associate's hands to do himself, convinced he could do better. Everybody knows the type from trivial, everyday incidents in ordinary life and also knows how very annoying such behaviour can be. The contention here, however, is that Montgomery's motive was not simply to have his hand on the tiller come what may, but was instead based on his absolute conviction that affairs were being mismanaged and that he could indeed do better. The proof that he was genuinely disgusted with what was going on surely lies in his open offer in mid-October to serve under Bradley's command and his clear statements at other times that, if his own 'Ruhr strategy' was not to be followed, then all necessary resources should be put into the Saar offensive and the British in the north manage with what was left over. The only alternative to believing that Monty was sincere and altruistic in these offers is to suggest that he was making them for appearances' sake and expecting they would be refused – a very fine political calculation indeed, if true, since there must have been a good chance of him being taken at his word.

It is far more plausible that political naïvety rather than devious subtlety was the accompaniment of Montgomery's ideas from everything we know of him. He clearly found it difficult to accept that by August 1944 the US army's leaders in France and at home felt that their force had finally graduated to the major leagues with its efforts in the battle for Normandy, and that it would be professionally unacceptable to them not to be masters in their own house. In addition to purely military concerns the burgeoning of American power was

Above: *Patton, seen here at the crossing of the Rhine, was a great one for theatricals and revelled in the glory attached to his successes.*

as clearly evident to the American people and accordingly highly valued. It was therefore as politically inconceivable for Eisenhower to permit Montgomery to continue in command of America's largest armies, or openly control their strategies, as it would have been for a British government to accept an Allied plan in August 1944 that did not include early steps to overrun the launching sites in France and Belgium for the V-weapons that were being fired on London. It has often been said that strategy is the art of the possible and in 1944-45 Montgomery failed to accommodate his ideas to take account of the fact that, at the highest levels at which he was now operating, political factors had as definite an impact on military decision-making as the command organization and fuel supplies.

If Montgomery was motivated by anything other than the situation facing his armies on the ground it was by his knowledge of Britain's rapidly dwindling strength. British manpower resources had been stretched so far by the multitudinous demands of the long years of war that Montgomery's forces were literally the last army Britain could raise. In addition, as the campaign went on, the British forces could not be maintained at even their existing strength while casualties inevitably mounted. By the end of August Montgomery had already broken up one division to provide reinforcements for others and this process would continue. Montgomery was pressed by the knowledge that, if Britain was to have a real part in ending the war, then the sooner the better. Obviously every American leader looked to an early end to the war also, but not with the same sense of urgency that lost opportunities should never recur and that it might be worthwhile taking risks in the short term.

The first great round in the strategic debate began in mid-August as the Allied pincers moved in on Falaise and parts of Patton's Third Army drove eastward into central France. On 17 August Hitler sacked von Kluge as his Commander-in-Chief West and appointed Model in his place. On the same day Monty met Bradley to discuss future plans and proposed that all the Allied armies, 'a solid mass of some 40 divisions', should strike north-east together and burst over the Rhine north of the Ardennes to capture the Ruhr and thence to Berlin to win the war. Bradley seems to have agreed at this point but quickly began to change his mind in favour of a more easterly attack to Metz and the Saar area. The situation was left open by a directive Monty issued on the 19th, in his role as co-

Below: *A column of Bren carriers crosses the Seine at Vernon.*

ordinator of the Allied armies, but on the 21st Eisenhower held a conference at his HQ which began to resolve the position. This meeting confirmed that Eisenhower would indeed take over control of the land battles on 1 September and that both the Ruhr and Saar thrusts would be pursued. Hindsight suggests that, if the Allies did indeed have a chance to win the war in 1944, it was lost at this meeting.

Montgomery immediately erupted in protest when he heard of the decisions. He sent de Guingand to Eisenhower the next day arguing for concentration of effort under a single ground force commander, 'a whole time job for one man', and repeated this plea on the 23rd when he met Eisenhower personally. Monty had modified his ideas from the 'solid mass of 40 divisions' to a proposal that Second British and First US Armies make the Ruhr advance with Third Army alone remaining to Bradley's 12th Army Group. Eisenhower refused this, quite rightly telling Monty that it was a political impossibility, and must privately have felt Monty's claims to be unrealistic since US forces were already across the Seine and east of Paris and closing in on the French capital while the British were still only closing up to the river and preparing to make an assault crossing. Eisenhower did back

Above: *Monty and Lt-Gen J T Crocker observe shelling of German defences from a haystack somewhere near Caen.*

Left: *Belgian troops serving with the British forces receive a warm reception in their nation's capital. Monty did not think much of the occasion, writing that as far as he was concerned the Belgian troops could get drunk and stay that way.*

Left: *The sort of terrain over which the Allied armies had to make progress in Holland in the autumn and winter of 1944-45.*

Below: *Monty's HQ near Brussels.*

Monty to some extent but only with a poorly defined instruction that Hodges's First Army should operate on Monty's right flank with Monty having some powers of 'operational co-ordination'.

Politically impossible it probably was, but it is important to state that Montgomery could well have been right in purely military terms. Many senior German generals believed at the time and later that a powerful, concentrated offensive could have got to the Ruhr and won the war in 1944. The best subsequent historians' calculations of exactly the transport resources available to the Allies suggest that such a thrust could just have been supported logistically and point out that the distance from the British depots around Bayeux to Dortmund in the Ruhr is almost identical to the distance from Cherbourg to Metz, a distance over which Patton was supported to the disadvantage of Hodges and Montgomery.

Although an independent judgement could be expected to have seen the Ruhr as the most promising objective, to be successful a decision to concentrate on it would have to have been taken in mid-August and would have required astonishing insight from Eisenhower for, up to that stage, all the spectacular advances had been made by the US Third Army. It is worth adding also that the methods already being used by Patton's forces, with his open encouragement, to divert supplies to his front by literally hijacking them from other units would have made very difficult the sort of ruthless concentration Monty proposed. Patton's spectacular advances had a disgraceful and disruptive downside of supplies stolen and wasted and orders disregarded.

Once the British XXX Corps got across the Seine at Vernon on 27 August this picture of rapid advances only on the inland flank began to change. Monty still believed that the Allies were squandering an opportunity if they failed to concentrate their forces, but passed up the chance to see Bradley and Eisenhower together by supposedly being too busy to join them in Paris for the ceremonial entry

Above: *A wary British paratrooper takes aim during the fighting at Osterbeek near Arnhem.*

on the 27th. (When he had met Ike on the 23rd Ike, as usual, had had to come to Monty's HQ.) On 3 September, after a hectic advance, Brussels was liberated by the Guards Armoured Division and most of Antwerp, including the extensive and undamaged dock area, was freed on the 4th by the 11th Armoured Division. With his hand strengthened by these moves, Monty signalled to his chief, 'one really powerful and full-blooded thrust towards Berlin is likely to get there and thus end the German war.' He went on to say that only one such thrust could be supported logistically and that it should be the advance on the Ruhr. This was the definitive expression of Montgomery's views and, as far as he was concerned, the problem 'is very simple and clear cut.'

Eisenhower's reply was a careful statement of his ideas, far more consistently held and expressed than Montgomery every really comprehended, that the northern thrust should be the senior Allied attack but that the southern advance should also be strong. He stressed in addition that Le Havre and Antwerp should be opened to Allied use as soon as possible (both were in Monty's areas) since 'No reallocation of our present resources would be adequate to sustain a thrust to Berlin.' Eisenhower's ideas were in line with US military doctrine which laid great stress on the necessity for offensive action to be as unceasing as possible, crudely and unfairly summarized as 'everyone fights all the time.' This was contrary to British thinking in general and Montgomery's in particular, which preferred to pause to build up resources and then deliver a concentrated attack. Montgomery felt at a loss if he did not think he had a clear plan; the Americans delighted in improvisation. The lack of mutual understanding between Eisenhower and Montgomery was unfortunately compounded in this case by the fact that Eisenhower's reply was not received in an ungarbled form by Monty until the 9th, four days after it was sent.

Poor communication in every sense bedevilled the Allied planning around this time. The very rapid advances of August and the limitations of 1944 vintage radio and telephone equipment were bound to create problems but Eisenhower deserves every criticism for taking on control of the land battle from new headquarters whose communications systems were little better than those which had helped Gamelin lose the Battle of France in 1940. Montgomery was also right in that it was a full-time job for one man and, looking at the problems which descended on Eisenhower from all sides, it is easy to see on the one hand the genuinely massive burden he bore and on the other the many inessential calls on his time which he allowed. Simple physical problems also helped to keep the Allied commanders apart. Eisenhower had difficulty travelling for the early part of September because of a very painful knee injury. When he flew to see Monty on the 10th they had their meeting in Ike's aircraft because he could not comfortably leave it.

Monty may have been right in a way to refuse to

waste time on parades in Paris on 27 August and again on 8 September, and was furious when Crerar missed a conference on 3 September because of a Canadian parade in newly-captured Dieppe, but in the broader sense of communication between Monty and his peers these were vital opportunities to meet – and on neither day was Monty's input to operations at the front more crucial.

Monty genuinely believed in the British staff doctrine that, when meetings were necessary, the senior commander should always go forward to meet his juniors. He also firmly believed that conferences to discuss options and collect ideas were mistaken. He thought the top man should decide on a plan first and only then hold any necessary meetings to issue and elaborate his orders. Finally, Monty had no respect for Eisenhower as a battlefield commander and admitted to another British senior officer later in the war that, after the end of the Normandy battles, he did not report to Eisenhower in as much detail as he continued to do to London because he believed that Eisenhower and his staff were not capable of fully comprehending his reports. With this astonishing and irresponsible attitude, combined with his beliefs about correct staff procedure, it is no surprise that Monty hardly ever attended Eisenhower's conferences unless ordered to do so.

From 3 September Monty began to plan an airborne attack to assist his forces to drive yet farther north to cross the various branches of the Rhine at Nijmegen and Arnhem before moving on to the Ruhr. One effect of this change of plan, for this is what it was, was to downgrade the importance of operations to free the approaches to Antwerp. Preparatory attacks to establish a suitable start line for the new offensive (originally known as Operation Comet) took place from 6 September and made slow progress because of increasing and stubborn German resistance. By 10 September when Eisenhower and Monty at last met, Monty had evolved his initial modest scheme into one involving the whole of Allied First Airborne Army. Although Eisenhower would not support Montgomery in his arguments put forward at the same time for a single drive into Germany he did give the go-ahead for what now became Operation Market Garden. He did not give Monty the absolute priority of supply he wanted but on the 12th had something of a change of heart and sent Bedell Smith to Montgomery to allocate more resources. With this help the opening of Market Garden was advanced to the 17th but Monty was no longer thinking seriously in terms of reaching Berlin, only of a more limited bridgehead toward the Ruhr.

During Market Garden three paratroop divisions were to drop to secure a series of river and canal crossings between Eindhoven and Arnhem. The British XXX Corps was to attack from the south to link with them and, once over the Neder Rijn at

Unrepentant Advocate

Left: *The 'Bridge too Far'. The Arnhem bridge over the Neder Rijn, seen during the desperate fighting.*

Far left: *Even without enemy action, movement and transport had its problems as this scene of a ditched vehicle on the Beveland Isthmus in late October shows.*

Below: *The Germans did not hesitate to open dykes and sluices to flood large areas of Holland to aid their defence. This picture was taken in the Canadian sector near Bergen-Op-Zoom in November.*

Arnhem, would be well placed to turn east toward the Ruhr. Numerous books have described the problems encountered by XXX Corps in trying to advance; the brilliant success of the US 82nd Airborne at Nijmegen; and the ultimate gallant failure of the British 1st Airborne at Arnhem itself. The detail is unfortunately not a central part of Monty's story but the overall result is.

Market Garden was one of the least successful episodes of Montgomery's military career. The major Allied strategic reserve, the three elite divisions of the airborne force, were employed without any decisive effect. The British Second Army was the best supplied of the Allied armies at the time and its offensive power was used up and the clear initiative that the Allies had held since the Normandy landings dwindled away. Montgomery's perception of the progress of the battle did not fit with the facts. He sent various optimistic 'according to plan' reports as events unfolded and even signalled nonsensically to London on 26 September that the failure to capture the Arnhem bridge 'will not, repeat not, affect operations eastward against the Ruhr.' This not only deserves criticism in relation to the Arnhem operation, but also casts doubt on what is usually taken to have been his good judgement on other occasions in the past when he made similar pronouncements.

Some of the weaknesses of the Arnhem planning should not be laid at Montgomery's door and certainly did have an important influence on the result of the battle. Among these can be listed the poor co-ordination between the paratroop forces and the Allied air support, the decision to drop the British Airborne Division some distance from its objective and not right on top of it, the inadequate radios supplied to the British airborne forces which prevented them from communicating properly with the advancing XXX Corps and also delayed, for example, the provision of artillery support once XXX Corps was otherwise within range. None of these difficulties was Montgomery's error in the first instance.

Fundamentally, however, the whole concept of the battle was flawed. It had been hard enough in the ten days preceding the launch of Market Garden for XXX Corps to fight its way forward to its start line. To expect the advance to reach Arnhem in a couple of days thereafter was ridiculously optimistic. Consideration of the terrain would point to this since the nature of the ground would dictate that the frontage of advance would often be confined literally to a single road exposed above the surrounding waterlogged countryside. Intelligence that strong German forces were refitting in the Arnhem area, although admittedly incomplete, was disregarded at every senior command level. Other members of Montgomery's staff were none too enthusiastic for the plan and were similarly overruled and in this respect it was ill luck that de

Above: *Vickers machine guns ready to lay an indirect fire barrage on German positions, s'Hertogenbosch, October 1944.*

Top left: *Horrocks, Monty, and Sir James Grigg early in 1945. Grigg was Secretary for War (i.e. Army Minister) and one of Monty's more influential supporters.*

Left: *A mixed column of tanks, armoured cars, and other vehicles poised for the dash to Arnhem.*

Guingand, who had more influence and shared this scepticism, was briefly away sick.

If an airborne-backed advance was desirable it was at least arguable that it should have been made in a more easterly direction towards Wesel which would have provided better terrain and fewer water barriers to cross. This was turned down largely on the insistence of the airborne staff who thought the anti-aircraft defences in that area too formidable. This problem could have been overcome and the great advantage would have been that such an attack would certainly have been more wholeheartedly supported by US First Army on Monty's right. Unfortunately Monty's instincts were that, if he could not command First Army, and Eisenhower said he could not, then he would rely on his British forces (though he later complained about poor First Army support on his flank, blaming with some justice First Army weakness on too many supplies going to Patton's Third Army). In his *Memoirs* Montgomery frankly admitted that he made various mistakes in the planning of Market Garden but he said that with proper support it would have succeeded and that he remained its 'unrepentant advocate' – a phrase which could aptly be applied to his whole behaviour in these months. For all the drama and controversy surrounding Market Garden one fact stands out. At its conclusion Antwerp's great docks remained intact in Allied hands but still uselessly inaccessible.

One of the consequences of Montgomery's decision to plan Operation Comet on 3 September was that, after the success in capturing Antwerp the next day, 11th Armoured Division was moved inland to join the new advance. The less powerful infantry units that tried to push on past Antwerp in the following few days got practically nowhere. Both Horrocks, the corps commander, and Dempsey, the army commander, admitted after the war that they were so involved in the prospect of driving on into Germany that they did not properly consider how to make best use of Antwerp. Montgomery claimed in his *Memoirs* that the nature of his mistake was to believe that the Canadian army could free the approaches to Antwerp while the Ruhr attack was going on. This was no doubt true in part but there was probably also a greater element of the prevailing euphoria about the progress of the war in his decisions than he admitted, as well as a desire to compensate for his considerable frustration about the command problems.

His blindness about the importance of Antwerp was all the more remarkable since, in his directive of 26 August, for example, he had set out British

Above: *Infantry move down to the beach at Breskens on the south bank of the Scheldt to load for the final attack across the river that at last opened the port of Antwerp.*

Right: *The crossing of the Rhine and the final Allied advance through Germany.*

of 26 August, for example, he had set out British and Canadian objectives as including getting Antwerp into service and only then making the advance to the Ruhr. Again, on 6 September a signal to Crerar specifically intimated that he had taken note of the warnings from Ramsay, the naval C-in-C, that Antwerp itself was useless without control of the Scheldt estuary. Hitler recognized this with orders to hold positions both north and south of the river and to mine the channels, which he issued that very same day (and, if the hint were needed, copies of these orders were very quickly in Allied hands).

During September the Canadian Army was fighting for several of the Channel ports back along the coast as well as trying to drive the Germans out of the so-called Breskens pocket south of the Scheldt. Montgomery's relevant directive, issued on the 9th, did not allocate priority between these efforts and any positive input he might have had to these operations was limited by his frigid relationship with Crerar, never previously one of his favourites, after Monty had intemperately reprimanded him for his late arrival at the conference on the 3rd. Effectively only a single Canadian armoured division was fighting to reduce the Breskens pocket during the remainder of the month. Hitler had sent fresh troops south of the river to hold this area and to protect the retreat from the Pas de Calais of the German units which had not retired to the other Channel ports. Some 86,000 men escaped over the Scheldt during September to join the forces being cobbled together in Holland to oppose Monty and Hodges. Two divisions, assembled principally from among these escapees, took part in the attacks that several times cut the XXX Corps corridor north towards Arnhem. This withdrawal could not have taken place if 11th Armoured Division had advanced the few miles past Antwerp to the Beveland isthmus at the earliest opportunity, when this would have been easiest.

Eisenhower had never ignored the importance of Antwerp as completely as Montgomery did but had willingly agreed that it would not be top priority when Market Garden was being carried out. Unfortunately, even after the withdrawal of the remnants of the British airborne division on 25 September which marked the definitive failure at Arnhem, Monty did not concentrate on Antwerp. The Canadian Army was still finishing off the clearance of the Channel ports and from 27 September was also instructed to devote a large part of its strength to attacks north from the Antwerp area to assist the left flank of Second British Army, and not to concentrate in this area on attacks west along the estuary. Not until 16 October did Monty give the clearance of the Antwerp approaches priority in

UNREPENTANT ADVOCATE

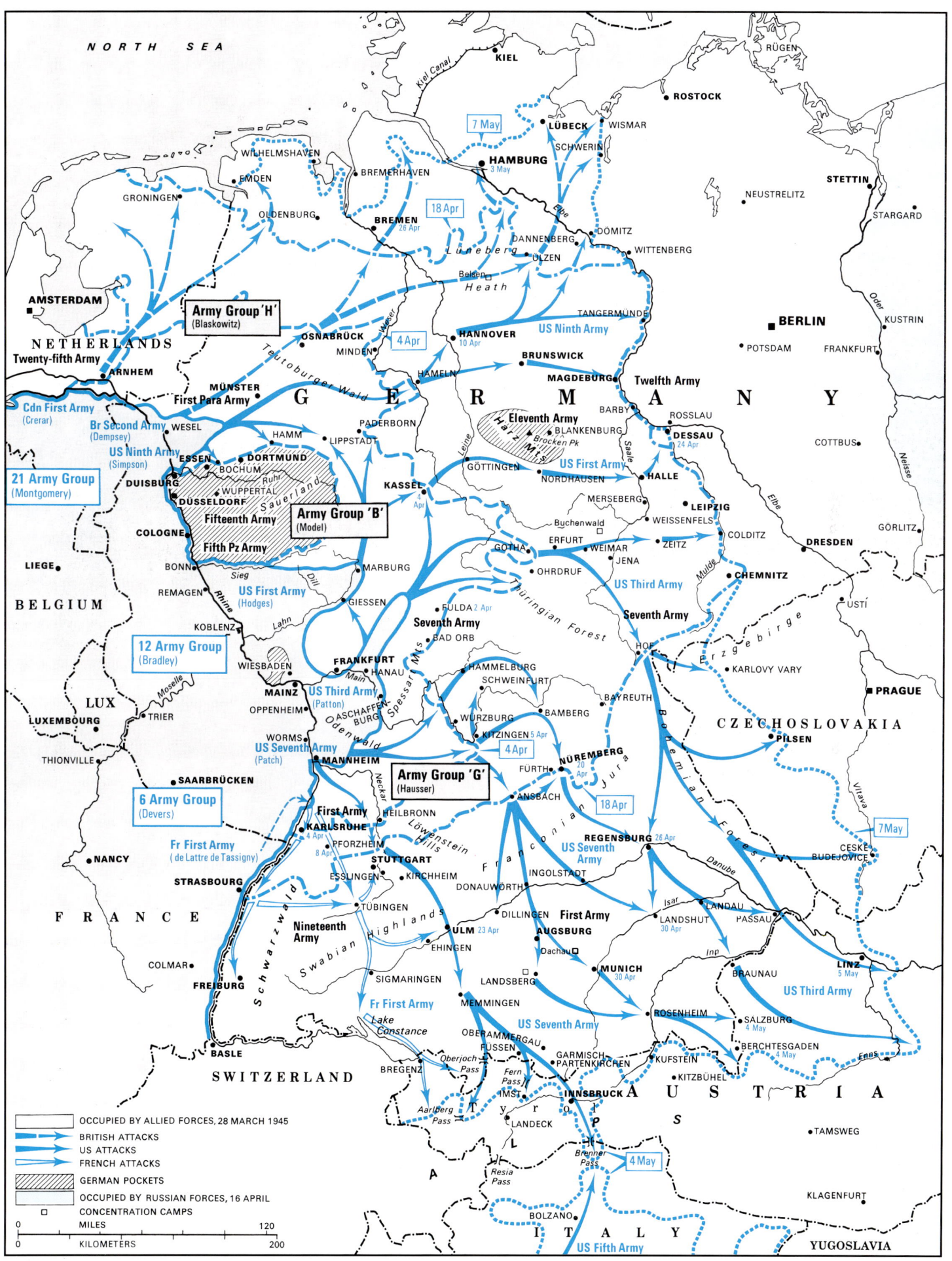

Above: *The Archer self-propelled gun married the 17-pounder anti-tank weapon with the chassis of the obsolete Valentine tank but because of the size constraints the gun was fixed to fire over the rear of the vehicle. This example is seen in Kleve in February 1945 during the final advance to the Rhine.*

his operations, as his directive of that day at last ordered, 'without any qualification whatsoever.' This decision emerged from the arguments over command and strategy which had never stopped and to which it is now appropriate to return.

The first important stage after Market Garden was a conference Eisenhower held at Versailles on 5 October. Monty still maintained the wholly unrealistic view that it was possible to reach the Ruhr before Antwerp was open. He was aware that the other Channel ports were beginning to come into service after their capture during September and with this and other improvements the supply position of 21st Army Group would soon be comfortable. But the American forces were not as well placed logistically, as he should have appreciated. Instead Third Army was involved in a vicious struggle around Metz and First Army around Aachen and the Hurtgen Forest, each suffering high casualties and making slow progress in battles which could have benefited from the sort of meticulous preparation that was Monty's usual trademark. Each Allied army, as Monty saw it, was fighting its own battles and he decided to make his most forceful protest yet to Eisenhower about the lack of a unifying command system, writing the Supreme Commander on the 10th that he should put either Monty or Bradley in sole charge of what should be the main Allied effort, to reach the Ruhr. Eisenhower replied decisively and correctly that the real issue at that point was Antwerp not the command system and, if Monty disagreed, they should submit the matter to their bosses for a final decision. Monty received this ultimatum on the 16th and immediately climbed down with his directive giving Antwerp priority and an apology to Ike, 'You will hear no more on the subject of command from me.' Monty kept this promise for roughly six weeks but had already sent home for his warm winter clothing, for the bright hopes of early September were long gone.

During the second part of October and early November the British and Canadian troops of the Canadian Army did succeed in dreadful conditions in clearing the Scheldt estuary at last, so that minesweeping could begin. The first cargo ship reached Antwerp on 26 November and all the Allied supply problems quickly began to fall away. There was little heartening progress on any of the other battle fronts, however, and Montgomery and his British bosses grew increasingly unhappy. After discussion with Brooke, Monty confronted Eisenhower with the command issue once again on 28 November, proposing as one alternative that Bradley should be made land forces commander. Montgomery thought he had at least partially won Eisenhower over to his point of view but after their meeting it was soon clear that he had not. The argument was still continuing (but now with Brooke leading the case for change) when it was overtaken by the news that a major German offensive had begun in the Ardennes.

This battle, usually described as the Battle of the Bulge, was the greatest setback suffered by the US Army during World War II and there were many aspects of its conduct in the initial stages which were not creditable to the US army or its leaders, although their recovery was forceful and effective. The Germans achieved complete surprise and quickly burst through one of the weakest sectors of

Top centre: *The bridge over the Rhine at Remagen unexpectedly captured by US First Army.*

Top right: *British infantry land on the east bank of the Rhine.*

Above: *Monty enjoys his first picnic on German soil with General Simpson (left), and, beside Simpson, Gen Collins.*

the whole Allied front. Hitler hoped to drive all the way to Antwerp. By thus physically cutting the Allied armies into two, he hoped to raise dissension between the British and Americans that would be decisive in the war as a whole. Antwerp was never a realistic objective but the outcome of the battle did bring Montgomery's relations with the senior Americans to their lowest point.

The initial reaction on the Allied side was confusion. On 19 December on his own initiative, Monty began sending his XXX Corps to guard crossings over the Meuse behind the retreating American front and already had a better picture of events than any other senior commander because of the efforts of his team of liaison officers. On the same day Montgomery personally went to visit First Army HQ only to find that it had been abandoned in a virtual panic without any information on its new location being passed. Bradley was out of touch, in part because he had ignored Eisenhower's wishes and kept his HQ well off to the south in closer contact with Third Army. On the 20th Eisenhower accordingly put Monty in charge of all operations north of the German salient with forces including US Ninth Army and part of First Army. Bradley was instructed to send Patton on what would prove to be a spectacular counter-attack from the south. Montgomery was given a strict warning by Brooke not to pass any disparaging remarks in any company that would seem to rub it in that he was being called in to salvage the situation.

It was the sort of battle in which Montgomery would be expected to be at his best and he was. He had an important steadying influence on Simpson of Ninth Army and Hodges of First Army who had been badly shaken by the turn of events. He made various minor withdrawals and regroupings to create a reserve and refused to make what he saw as premature counter-attacks. It was an outstanding battlefield performance in bringing order out of near chaos and it was certainly one achieved by Montgomery with little help or guidance from above. For much of the battle Eisenhower, and to a lesser extent Bradley, allowed themselves to be persuaded to take such excessive precautions for their safety from supposed German assassination squads that they were prevented from doing their jobs properly.

On 6 January Montgomery gave what turned

out to be a highly controversial press conference, supposedly because he wished to compliment the American forces for their fighting performance in stemming the German attacks. Initially this had good effects, with the *New York Times*, for example, reporting that 'No handsomer tribute was ever paid to the American soldier,' but this favourable reception quickly changed. The Germans broadcast a skilfully altered version of Montgomery's words and, when these were examined more closely even in the correct text, he was judged to have claimed far more credit for the British role in the battle and for himself personally than the events could possibly justify. This was probably never his intention but he had chosen his words with less care than he should and with far less sensitivity about the bad start made to the battle than he might if this had been a British failure.

Behind the scenes his relations with Eisenhower had also already gone through another very sticky patch. Convinced that circumstances had forced Eisenhower to create a better command system, Monty again reopened the arguments that there should be a single land commander in the northern parts of the Allied line for whatever reduction of the Ardennes bulge was to be made (Monty disagreed with the American generals and did not think it necessary to reconquer it entirely) and for the subsequent offensive into Germany. There are differing accounts of his meeting with Eisenhower on 28 December but the consequence was clear enough, for Eisenhower drafted a signal to the Combined Chiefs of Staff which essentially said 'him or me'. De Guingand managed to get Eisenhower to delay sending this, flew back quickly to Monty and successfully persuaded him to apologize, whereby he narrowly avoided dismissal.

This did not end the strategic debate, which continued up to meetings of the British and American Chiefs of Staff in Malta at the end of January while they were en route to the Yalta conference with the Soviet leadership. Eisenhower followed this with a conference of his own at Versailles on 31 January/1 February. The conclusion ironically was more favourable to Montgomery's ideas than it might have been, for US Ninth Army remained under his control for the coming battles.

These began on 8 February with the opening of Operation Veritable in which the specially strengthened Canadian Army attacked east and southeast from the Nijmegen area toward the Rhine at Wesel. Second British Army on their right had been greatly reduced to strengthen the Canadian force but, in typical Monty fashion, if its front was quiet, its staffs were deeply occupied in the detailed planning and preparation of the next battle, the crossing of the Rhine. On their right to the south was Ninth Army which was to complete a pincer movement with north-easterly advances to link with the Canadians in Operation Grenade.

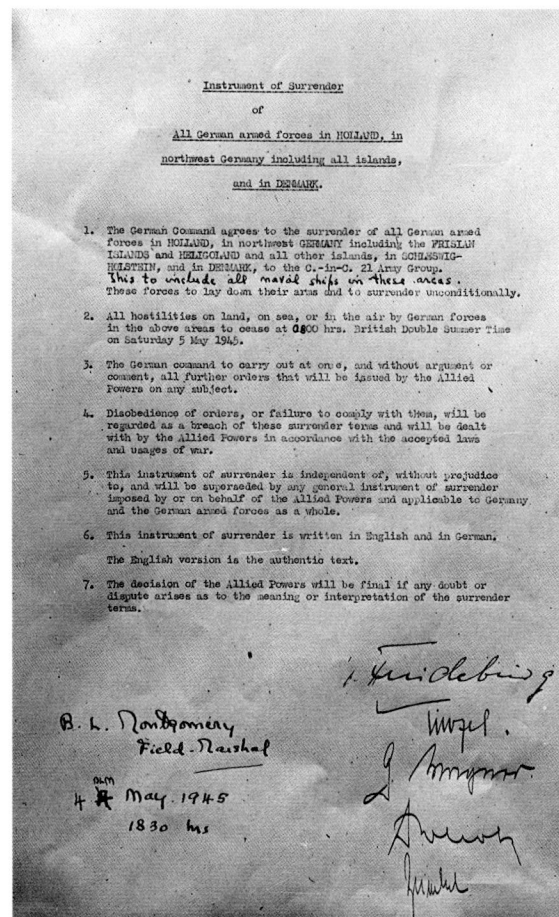

Operation Veritable is also better known as the Battle of the Reichswald and was simply described by Horrocks as 'twenty-eight horrible days.' Real progress, however, was gradually made and on 23 February the much delayed Operation Grenade got under way. By this time the Allied forces were all advancing successfully towards the Rhine and the German resistance west of the river collapsed all along the front in the next few days.

Top left: *The German surrender signed at Luneberg Heath. For many years Monty kept the original of this document despite demands in Parliament that it should be passed to public ownership.*

Above: *The end of Germany's war effort, some of the many thousands of German prisoners taken in the last weeks of the war.*

Left: *Watched by Monty, Admiral Friedeburg signs the surrender document.*

Montgomery was now ready to fight his last great battle and characteristically it was to be another elaborate set piece. Monty's crossing of the Rhine began on the night of 23/24 March with a bombardment by over 3000 guns. One British and one US airborne division were dropped on the east side of the river in the morning and among the thousands of vehicles and over 100,000 tons of supplies assembled to support the amphibious crossing were a number of Royal Navy landing craft that had been secretly and arduously brought forward from the sea by river, canal, and road.

Monty was taking no chances of failure as ever and this might now seem as having been over-insurance in the light of US First Army's success, including its brilliant exploitation of the unexpected capture of an intact Rhine bridge at Remagen and Patton's successful improvised assault crossing farther south still. This criticism of Monty is largely unjustified for these events could not have been anticipated when he was planning his attack and its end result did leave him fully capable of continuing his advance in full force to the east as it was meant to do.

Montgomery now began to speak of overrunning northern Germany and reaching out to Berlin but Eisenhower thought differently. With little guidance from his American masters (President Roosevelt was weak and would shortly be dead) Eisenhower decided to send much of his strength towards supposed German strongholds in the south and approached Stalin to co-ordinate the Anglo-American movements with the Russian offensives. The upshot was that any prospect of a British or American advance to Berlin was abandoned. Argument over this decision was ferocious at the top levels but after initial protests Montgomery stayed out of it. He instead concentrated on making the best of the tasks he was given with his remaining forces, for one of the consequences of these discussions was that Ninth Army was removed from his command.

Montgomery had one last triumphal moment in receiving the surrender of the German forces in the north at his HQ on Luneberg Heath on 4 May. That evening the teetotal non-smoker wrote to his old friend and mentor, Alan Brooke, that he 'was persuaded to drink some champagne at dinner' but he still went to bed early. In public it was a magnificent episode but in private there was still much that was sad about him. He took a short leave a few days later, but before setting out he wrote to his son's guardians, 'Do not tell any of my family I am coming home.'

One of the best known, but by no means the best, books on the campaign of 1944-45 bears the apt title *The War Between the Generals*. The episodes described above do not present a pleasing history, nor is it a story in which any of the major participants could be described as blameless. The concern here is with Montgomery, of course, who emerges ultimately as having done his cause more harm than good by his tactless manner and continual unwelcome returns to the same sensitive themes. Overall he was probably more correct in military terms in his advocacy of a concentrated Allied offensive than this counterparts but he personally failed to find ways of swaying their opinions that did not at the same time seem to belittle their abilities and justifiable ambitions. It was all too obvious that his ill-concealed opinion was that he was always right and that everyone who disagreed was 'quite useless'.

Even within the limitations imposed on him, by his own standards the Arnhem battle and the delay in opening Antwerp were serious mistakes. Some of the reasons have been discussed already but in essence by choosing the Arnhem advance in September, he was choosing to attack a stiffening defence with a dozen or twenty hastily supplied divisions while the remainder of the Allied armies struggled. The alternative might well have been to have had the whole Allied force of over 50 divisions fully supplied and able to advance well prepared in the middle of October. All Montgomery's experience would normally have indicated to him that the second course was the sounder one but, to complete the hypothetical analysis, if he had contrived to have the Allies follow this strategy, this book might now be discussing his habitual caution and a different set of lost opportunities.

Chapter Ten
A Very Full Life

Left: *Monty carrying the Sword of State at the State Opening of Parliament in 1958. Monty was given this honour twice more but was unable to complete the task through failing health on the last occasion in 1968.*

Above: *Monty in 1951 as Deputy Supreme Allied Commander in NATO. He is shown emerging from his official French residence, the Chateau de Courances near Paris.*

In a postwar lecture Montgomery commented that the Duke of Wellington had often failed to follow up his victories as effectively as possible. Many would suggest that this criticism would equally apply to its author, while others have described how Montgomery's battles tended to peter out with a diminuendo rather than reach a triumphal climax. Such a pattern also describes the final dozen years of Montgomery's career after 1945 and the period of private life leading up to his death in 1976. This sense of anti-climax becomes more pronounced when looking with the benefit of hindsight at Montgomery's long service with NATO and its forerunners for, with the collapse of the Soviet Union, we now know that the organization and preparations for which Montgomery worked and campaigned so hard will never be tested in any of the ways he envisaged. Equally, his time commanding British occupation forces in Germany and thereafter as Chief of the Imperial General Staff, the professional head of the British army, clearly belongs to a very different world, with most of its issues having long since been overtaken and set aside by later events. There is not sufficient space here to give a blow-by-blow account of Monty's doings during this period but it is appropriate to outline the basic facts of his career and highlight some revealing episodes.

Montgomery was Commander-in-Chief of the British occupation forces in Germany until May 1946 and became CIGS the next month. It is generally agreed that in Germany he was a success, emphasizing sensible and constructive policies to help towards recovery and, as usual, ensuring that the administrative aspects of his responsibilities were thoroughly carried out. As CIGS he is usually described as being very poor – unsurprisingly since he approached the job as he had all his others, unhesitatingly laying down the law on every subject he was involved in, and some that were none of his business, and caring little if his blunt language stirred opposition that might have been better smoothed over. Many of the causes for which Monty fought were in fact sensible even if his methods were not. He was absolutely right to argue (successfully) against the RAF and Royal Navy that Britain must plan to maintain a respectable army on the European continent if any meaningful anti-Soviet alliance was to be created. He was also forward-thinking in his advocacy of the creation of a post, similar to today's Chief of the Defence Staff, with tri-service authority – an important innovation that would be opposed by vested service interests until the 1960s.

When his period as CIGS ended in November 1948 he left several simmering controversies behind, to become Chairman of the Commanders-in-Chief Committee of the Western Union. When the Western Union defence organization was superceded by NATO he became Deputy Supreme

Allied Commander, serving once again under Eisenhower. Monty held this post from March 1951 under three more American Supreme Commanders until he eventually stepped down in the autumn of 1958. At NATO he was effectively an international inspector-general with every opportunity to exercise his great talents for training, chivvying, and criticizing but he was not directly in the principal line of command unless the Supreme Commander was incapacitated.

When he finally ended his active duty in September 1958 (although formally field marshals never actually retire) his proud claim was that his career of over 50 years of continuous service was possibly the longest in British army history and that he held the unique record of having commanded every possible formation in his career – platoon, company, battalion, brigade, division, corps, army, and army group.

As well as his pride in his military record he also happily showed off his range of contacts with other famous leaders, displaying in his home photos

Above: *Monty in 1955 at the concluding press conference for one of his effective NATO training exercises.*

Above right: *NATO Supreme Commander Gen Gruenther greets the Duke of Edinburgh during a royal visit in 1954. Behind the shaken hands is Gen Norstad, Gruenther's successor as Monty's boss. Monty looks on from the right.*

Right: *Far from fading away, the old soldier in retirement undertook a trying schedule of foreign visits. He is shown here in September 1961 with Chairman Mao of Communist China.*

given to him by such as Mao, Tito, the Pope, and, of course, the British royal family and Churchill. One of his collaborators in the writing of his book *A History of Warfare* has noted that Monty would often casually mention such 'very great friends' in conversation and ask if his listener knew them or had met them (which, inevitably, as a relatively young and unknown military historian, he had not). This comes across as the action of an essentially lonely old man who felt, deep down, that he was little loved and without true friends – and did not wish to admit it to himself. Montgomery once commented that, if he had so many distinguished friends, 'I must have led a very full life.' Indeed he had, but not, perhaps, in the sense in which he meant it then.

There is no doubt that Montgomery did have genuine friends but that he also had enemies or, at least, regular opponents. When Monty was CIGS Tedder was Chief of the Air Staff and their history of incompatability continued. Only very rarely did both attend any Chiefs of Staff meeting, each pre-

Above: *Monty at his son's marriage. Monty wrote with some pride in his* Memoirs *that none of his family had ever been involved in a divorce. He took it hard when David's marriage unfortunately ended in this way some years later.*

ferring instead to send a deputy if he knew that the other was definitely planning to be present. A similarly juvenile situation prevailed during Montgomery's time at the Western Union when the French General de Lattre was Land Forces C-in-C. They quarrelled over many matters but the final absurdity was that when together neither would make any attempt to speak the other's language – and Monty could certainly speak a little French.

An even more regular occurrence was Monty alienating those disposed to have a greater regard for him. Despite all their disagreements Monty and Eisenhower remained on fairly cordial terms after the war and during their work together when Eisenhower was NATO Supreme Commander, but Ike finally gave up on his difficult associate when Montgomery published his *Memoirs* with their outspoken criticisms of Eisenhower's military abilities. It is interesting also that, after the war, Monty seemed to get on less well with many of his wartime subordinates, perhaps seeing them as somehow potential professional rivals, except where, like his long-time intelligence chief Bill Williams, they were not regular soldiers but instead returned to civilian life.

The most notable such victim was de Guingand. When Montgomery learned that he was to become CIGS he persuaded de Guingand to return prematurely to service from sick leave and take up a post as Director of Military Intelligence in the War Office with the promise that he would become Vice-CIGS when Monty moved to the top job. As soon as Monty took over he changed his mind and appointed another officer, with little in the way of explanation or apology. There were other slights also, the final one being on the occasion of Monty's 80th birthday. Monty initially did not want de Guingand to be invited to a dinner being given in his honour. When other guests complained he changed his mind but the process lost him another friend for General Dempsey refused to come, in protest at what had gone on.

His relations with his family remained difficult after the war also. He was never reconciled to his mother and refused even to attend her funeral. The incident that typifies Monty's feelings of hostility occurred when he was being presented with the freedom of Newport in south Wales in 1945. Lady Montgomery had written to the town council saying that she would like to attend the ceremony and they had naturally, innocently, replied with an invitation. Montgomery was furious when he saw her and refused to go in to the celebration lunch until his mother had been removed. He also became estranged from his brothers and sisters for some years, apparently feeling that his family as a whole wished somehow to cash in on his fame. In later years he did mellow and resume more cordial contact with certain family members. Montgomery's relationship with his son was never an intimate one, on the father's side at least. He was proud and gratified when David did well in officer training during his national service, but was shocked, bitter, and aloof when David's first marriage ended in what his father saw as a disgraceful divorce. Again, though, father and son were reconciled in later years.

The tale of Monty's many public and private quarrels seems particularly sad when set against his often well concealed but nonetheless real capacity for genuine human warmth. The writer Bernard Levin, who is certainly no sycophantic admirer of the prominent and famous, has described in glowing terms his contacts with a charming, thoughtful, pleasant and considerate field marshal. Levin also recalls a fascinating occasion when he was interviewing Montgomery on live television and asked him how he dealt before his battles with the knowledge that, no matter how careful his preparations, many men would die because of his orders. Montgomery amazingly responded that he had never thought of it like that and fell silent for a few moments to do just that before rather disappointingly replying about the importance of the troops knowing that burials would be properly and reverently carried out.

Montgomery had obviously been brought up in an atmosphere of regular religious observance but seems to have drifted away from his faith during World War I and the years immediately thereafter. As a colonel, as already noted, he brought trouble on himself by doing away with compulsory church parades (and around the same time provoked a storm by ensuring that his medical officer inspected brothels used by his men). By the time of World War II he had returned to regular worship and as a senior officer always held and attended Sunday services at his HQ, often participating in the service

Above left: *Old warriors together, Monty and Churchill.*

Above: *Lady Montgomery, Monty's mother, from whom he was completely estranged in later life.*

by reading the lesson. His public messages usually included rather simplistic references to the aid he prayed for from 'the Lord Mighty in Battle' but, however naïve his religious symbolism, there is no question of the sincerity of his convictions.

Regular features of Montgomery's postwar life both before and after his 'retirement' were his many trips overseas to meet foreign leaders. These were often controversial. While he was still serving he would often blithely exceed his brief and introduce matters his political bosses either reserved to themselves or did not want discussed at all. After he retired he happily proclaimed that he was only a private individual with no official status but clearly he thought he did have great influence.

His contacts with the communist world provide good examples both of his naïve and idiosyncratic behaviour and of his independence of judgement. On one occasion he was crossing the Atlantic on the same liner as the then Soviet Foreign Minister Andrei Gromyko. Montgomery wanted to meet Gromyko but this was refused, so instead he hid on the liner's deck and successfully ambushed him during his early morning walk. On another occasion Montgomery decided to liven up a dinner with Stalin and other Soviet leaders by clumsily teasing Molotov. Stalin's malicious humour was all too readily gratified by the unnecessary embarrassment of one of his subordinates. Yet following this same visit (in 1947), Montgomery concluded that the Soviets did not want and would be unable to fight a major war for many years to come – a conclusion that now seems a great deal more plausible than it did at the time and from which many benefits might have proceeded if it had been more widely recognized. Similarly Montgomery was one of the first senior Western figures to advocate the realistic policy of recognizing the communist regime in China and was one of the first to visit, when he went there in 1960 and 1961.

There were other surprises as well. At a comparatively early stage he described the US involvement in Vietnam as unwise on practical military grounds. There was controversial criticism also of British military intervention when, during a visit to Egypt to tour the Alamein area in 1967, he made

Left: *Deep in thought in the grounds of the Chateau de Courances. One of Monty's most firmly held principles was that a commander should always ensure that he had time to himself to think problems through.*

Below: *In old age at his home in Hampshire.*

a speech describing British conduct during the Suez crisis in 1956 as morally wrong.

During this Egyptian visit Montgomery also toured the Alamein cemeteries, both British and German, and was openly upset. He had never been happy when visiting hospitals and hated funerals, avoiding them whenever possible. He failed to attend Churchill's funeral, pleading rather unconvincingly that ill-health prevented him returning from a trip to South Africa.

It is worth mentioning that he was a frank supporter of the apartheid system of government in South Africa, although it should be remembered that in the 1960s, when Montgomery's visits there chiefly took place, such views were not as widely regarded in Britain as reprehensible as they would be now.

By the later 1960s Monty's health and vigour were clearly failing. While he was attending his 80th birthday dinner his home was burgled and his field marshal's baton and other unique items were taken. Nothing was ever recovered despite a rather sad and pathetic public appeal by Monty in which he clearly came across as old, tired, and disappointed. It was doubly sad, for this was the second

Above: *With Khrushchev in Moscow in 1959. Monty insisted that he was visiting the USSR as an ordinary citizen but clearly he privately thought he was a great deal more important than that.*

such mishap in his life. In 1941 virtually all his private possessions including most of his momentos of his late wife had been destroyed when a German bomb hit the warehouse where they were in storage.

One of his last public duties was at the State Opening of Parliament in 1968 when Monty sought and was granted the honour of carrying the Sword of State. Holding the heavy sword up during the lengthy Queen's Speech proved too much for him and he nearly collapsed. Another peer quickly took over and, after a brief rest, Montgomery slipped quietly away.

In his last years he was virtually housebound and his mental abilities also dwindled. Latterly he even had difficulty spelling the word Alamein when signing his name and title. He died on 24 March 1976. For the many veterans of his battles who attended his state funeral on 1 April it was a deeply emotional occasion. Tributes came from all over the world and following the public ceremonies Montgomery was buried in the village churchyard at Binsted near Isington which had been his home since the war.

In the preface to his book *A History of Warfare* Montgomery very characteristically quoted verses from the Bible (I Corinthians, 14) which are worth repeating in these closing remarks,

> If the trumpet give an uncertain sound, who shall prepare himself to the battle?
> Except ye utter by the tongue words easy to be understood, how shall it be known what is spoken?

This aspect of leadership is without doubt one that Montgomery mastered and, as his almost instanteous transformation of the morale of the Eighth Army in 1942 and his pre-invasion work in 1944 proved, this is a skill of inestimable worth. A central part of this was the ability to strip a complex problem to its essentials. As Montgomery very clearly realized, one of war's essentials is that a general must win battles; here we see the other side of the coin to his vanities and dogmatic assertion of his personal achievements: his equally clear acceptance of his own responsibilities.

It is conventional in military biographies to compare the subject with other great historical figures. This shall not be attempted here but remarks by two of Britain's other military heroes will be used to conclude other significant themes.

A short time before the Battle of Trafalgar Lord Nelson told his captains, 'Nothing is sure in a Sea Fight beyond all others . . . but no Captain can go very wrong if he places his ship alongside that of an enemy.' 'Words easy to be understood' indeed but firmly and correctly based on the conviction that the British ships, or rather their crews' training, were overwhelmingly superior to their opponents'. Montgomery had no such advantage. Throughout his years in high command there is no question that, division for division, the German army usually remained significantly superior to similar British or American formations in operational technique and in most areas of fighting equipment. In later life Monty made the rather dubious claim that he selected divisions for particular operations according to their particular aptitudes,

Above and top: *Monty's funeral. His beret with its two badges and his field marshal's baton lie on top of the coffin. Five other field marshals were among the official mourners.*

in night fighting for example. This claim can scarcely bear detailed examination but what is certainly true is that his habitual methodical approach implicitly recognized the limitations of his forces and gave the greatest opportunity to develop the artillery power and overall material strength which were the facets of land warfare in which the Allied armies could compete with and outdo their enemies. For the British, too, this insistence on controlled and prepared operations was essential in the difficult manpower situation of 1944-45 and it would have been the greatest possible condemnation of Montgomery if he had failed to take this vital national interest into account.

Nelson hoped by his instruction to bring about a 'pell-mell' battle, quite happily accepting that 'nothing is sure' in such circumstances. Montgomery's greatest strength was his ability to make things certain, often out of an atmosphere of confusion. His greatest weaknesses emerged at the times when he abandoned this policy and tried to improvise.

Shortly after the Battle of Waterloo the Duke of Wellington is reported to have said 'I don't think it would have done if I had not been there.' Many students of the battle would agree with the Duke's remark. Can we say the same about Monty? This is of course a hypothetical question but one to which the answer on many occasions must be yes. Montgomery's personal faults and military mistakes have been discussed at length in various places in this book. Against these can be set the occasions when, without Montgomery, 'I don't think it would have done.' This list for the present author begins at Alamein, takes in the landings on Sicily, but above all includes the plan for D-Day and the battle for Normandy. Without Montgomery's contribution in the first eight months of 1944 it is easy to imagine D-Day a half success followed by a long stalemate and the war ending in 1945 with Soviet forces on the Rhine.

When Churchill and Montgomery met for the first time in 1940 Churchill had not known how the war might be won. He later recollected that immediately after Pearl Harbor, for all the problems and difficulties that were sure to lie ahead, he was certain that, with the USA in the war, victory was simply a matter of the 'proper application of overwhelming force.' It is seldom difficult with hindsight to pick holes in the reputation of famous men, Montgomery more than most because of his awkward and often unpleasant private character. He may very well have been provided with overwhelming force but his public achievements in its proper application were not matched in scale and success by any other British soldier of the war and no subsequent criticism has modified these in other than minor details. His obituary in *The Times* may have the last word, 'He knew his dark trade better than anyone else in his time.'

INDEX

Page numbers in *italics* refer to illustrations

Alam Halfa 56, 61, 63, 66
  battle of 55, 60, 61, 62-3, 65
Alamein, *see* El Alamein
Alamein to Zem Zem (Douglas) 77
Alanbrooke, Viscount *see* Brooke, FM Sir Alan
Alexander, Gen Sir Harold 27, 41, 51, 54, *55*, 56, 66-7, 75, *106-7*, 109, 124
  deputy to Eisenhower 87, 89, 90, 97, 99, 106, 111, 114
  and First Army 107
Allied First Airborne Army 170
Anderson, Betty 19, 25
Anderson, Lt Gen K A N 90
anti-tank weapon *Panzerfaust* 147
Antwerp 169, 170, 173-4, 176, 177, 179
Anzio landings 131
Ardennes 36, 39, 176-8
Arnhem *169*, 170, *171-2*, 172, 174, 179
artillery, British/Allied 71, 91
  5.5-inch *72*
  6-pound anti-tank *69*
  17-lb 90
  25-lb anti-tank *70*
  Archer 17-lb SP anti-tank *176*
artillery, German 71, 97
  anti-tank '88' 68, 71, 95
Auchinleck, FM Sir Claude 14, 46-7, *47*, 54-8 *passim*, 66, 83, 86
Australian forces 7, 74, *86*
  9th Australian Divn 68, 69, 71, 73, *74-5*, 75

Badoglio, Marshal P 114
Barnett, Correlli, qu. 82
Beda Fomm 82
Bedell Smith, Gen Walter 7, 89, 107, *124*, 170
Belgian troops 40, *167*
Berlin 165, 166, 169, 170, 179
Bilotte, Gen P 38
Bismarck, General 62
Bradley, Gen Omar N 7, 110, 111, *124*, *131*, 131-2, 138, 139, 140, 143, 148, 150, 154-8 *passim*, *164-5*, 165, 166, 167, 176, 177
Briggs, Maj Gen H R 81
British army,
  IN WORLD WAR I
    British Expeditionary Force *9*
    Second Army 16
    IX Corps 16
    33rd Divn 16
    47th Divn 16-17, *18*
    112th Inf (later 104th) Bde 16
    East Yorks Regt 17
    Royal Fusiliers 17, *19*
    Royal Warwickshire Regt 13-14
  IN INTER-WAR YEARS
    8th Infantry Bde 25
    17th Infantry Bde 24
  IN WORLD WAR II
    21st Army Group 128, 132, 133, 156, 159, 176
    First Army 87, 90, 96, 97, 99, 103, 106
    First Canadian Army *see under* Canadian forces
    Second Army 132, 133, 153, 156, 167, 172, 174, 178
    Eighth Army 5, 6, 7, 14, 36, 38, 50, 54-8 *passim*, 61, 62, 66, 67, 68, 70, 71, 72, 76, 76, 77, 80-83 *passim*, 85, 86, 87, 89-93 *passim*, 95, 96, 97, 99, 100, 102, 103, 107, 108, 110-115 *passim*, 117, 120, 187
    CORPS
    I 150
    II 34, 40
    V 44, 115
    VIII 149, 151, 153
    IX 97, 99
    X 67, 68, 71, 74, 80, 85, 91, 93, 95, 97, 114
    XII 44
    XIII 61, 62, 67, 73, 74, 110, 111, 114, 115
    XXX 67, 68, 71, 74, 80, 90, 91, 92, 110, 111, 120, 147, 154, 157, 168, 170, 172, 174, 177
    New Zealand Corps 92, 93, 94
    DIVISIONS
    1st Airborne 114, 172, 174
    1st Armoured 71-4 *passim*, 81, 91, 93, 94, 97
    1st Canadian *see under* Canadian forces
    1st South African *see under* South African forces
    2nd New Zealand *see under* New Zealand forces
    3rd 30, 31, 34, 36, 38, *38*, 39, 40, 41, 45, 143
    4th Indian *see under* Indian Army
    5th 114, 120
    6th Armoured 97
    7th Armoured 61, 62, 72, 73, 74, 84, 85, 90, 91, 92, 99, 146, 147, 152, 157
    8th Armoured 71
    8th Indian 120
    9th Australian *see under* Australian forces
    10th Armoured 61, 66, 68, 71, 72, 73, 82
    11th Armoured 157, 169, 173, 174
    44th Infantry 57, 61, 66
    50th 91, 92, 95, 146, 147, *158*
    51st Highland 69, 71, 73, 76, 77, 84, 85, 86, 90, 95, 111, *111*, 145, 147
    56th 99
    78th 118, 120
    79th Armoured 138, *149*
    Guards Armoured 169
    Polish Armoured 158
    BRIGADES
    4th Armoured 120
    5th New Zealand 97
    8th Armoured 61, 73, 81, 90, 95
    9th Armoured 71, 76, 77
    22nd Armoured 58, 61, 62, 63, 65, 83
    23rd Armoured 61, 62, 92
    27th Armoured 143
    132 Brigade 61
    151st 91
    Guards Brigade 90
    Long Range Desert Group 91
    Special Air Service *92*
    organization 34, 38
    battle group tactics 57-8
Broadhurst, AVM Sir Harry 7, 93, *93*, 99, 108, *109*, 155
Brooke, FM Sir Alan 18, *19*, 20, 27, 31, 34, 38, 40, 41, 47, *51*, 77
  as CIGS 54, *55*, 74, *106*, 124, 151, *155*, 176, 177, 179
  on Montgomery, 36, 41, 103
Brussels 167
Bucknall, Lt Gen G C *125*, 147, 157
Bulge, battle of the 176-7, 178
Bullen-Smith, General 147

Caen 128, 143, 144, 145-6, *148*, 152, 156, 160
Canadian forces 6, 111, *113*, *117*, 128, 129, 141, 144, *145*, *148*, 150, 152, 153, 159, 160, 164
  First Canadian Army 132, 156, 157, 170, 173, 174, 176, 178
  II Canadian Corps 158
  1st Canadian Division 103, 108, 111, 114, 120
Canterbury, Archbishop of 139
Carroll, Lewis, qu. 161
Carver, Betty *see* Montgomery, Betty
Carver, Dick (stepson) 27
Carver, Jocelyn (step daughter-in-law) 27
Casablanca Conference 87, 102, 106, *106*
Chamberlain, Neville *31*, 38
Cherbourg 128, 145, 148, 149, 150
Churchill, Winston S 13, *18*, *34*, 40, 47, *48-9*, *106*, *121*, 129, 183, *185*, 186, 188
  and North Africa 54, 55, *55*, 66, 74, 86-7, *87*
  and Overlord 121, 124, 126, 139, 151, 154, *155*, 157
Clark, General Mark 103, *116*, 120
Collins, Maj Gen J Lawton 148, 177
Combined Chiefs of Staff 178
Coningham, AVM Sir Arthur 7, *59*, 60, 93, *93*, 107, 133, 149

Crerar, Lt Gen Henry *125*, 132, 156, 170, 174
Crocker, Lt Gen J T *125*, 167
Cunningham, Admiral Sir A B *106*, 114

D-Day 69
de Guingand, Gen Sir F W 29, *107*, *109*, *131*, 146
  as Chief of Staff to Montgomery 56, 57, 67, 72, 81, 91, 93, 107, 153, 154, 167, 173, 178
  first meeting with 25
  Montgomery's treatment of 20, 184
de Lattre de Tassigny, General 184
Dempsey, Gen Sir Miles 27, 110, 111, *125*, 131, 147, 153, 156, 173, 184
Desert Victory, film 99
Dieppe raid 50-51, *50-51*, 110, 137
Dill, Gen Sir John 44
Dorman-Smith, Maj Gen Eric 55, 56
Douglas, Keith 77
Dunkirk 39, 40, *40-41*, 41
Dunn, Henry, picture by *15*

Eden, Anthony *106*
Edinburgh, Duke of *183*
Egypt 51, 54, 56, 60
Eisenhower, Gen Dwight D 7, 103, *106-7*, *123-4*, 139, 182
  portrait of Montgomery by 19-20, *21*
  as Supreme Commander, North Africa and Sicily 87, 106, 113, 114
  as Supreme Allied Commander 124, 125, 126, 131, *134-5*, 138, 141, 151-6 *passim*, 161, *163-5*, 165, 166, 167-8, 173, 174, 176, 177, 179
El Agheila 82, 83, 84, 85, 91
El Alamein 44, 54, 57, 60, 61
  First Battle of 54, 56
  Second Battle 65, 71-6, 86, 94, 99
  comparative strengths 71
  planning for 67-8
  pursuit following 81-2
El Alamein to the Sangro (Montgomery) 97
Enfidaville 97
Eric, or Little by Little (Farrar) 10
Erskine, Maj Gen G W E J 147
Europe, NW, conditions endured in 6

Falaise pocket 157, 150-60, *160*, 166
Farrar, Rev Frederic William 10-11
Feisal I, King, of Iraq *28*
Free French forces 7, *143*
French forces 34, 36, 38, 39, 40, 44
  1st Army Group 38

Freyberg, Gen Sir Bernard 62, 75, 92, 93, 94
Friedeburg, Admiral Hans Georg von *178*
Fuller, Gen J F C 27
Gabes gap 85
Gamelin, Gen Maurice *34, 36, 38*, 169
Gatehouse, Maj Gen A H 68, 82
Gazala Line 54, 60
George VI, King *7, 19, 99*, 100, *102*, 139, *158*
Georges, Gen A 38
German army 36, 39, 44, *53-4*, 58, *64*, 66, 71, 75, 76, 77, 80, 84, 90, 96, 100, 110, 112, 114, 117, 118, 148, 151, 157, 159, 160, 187
Deutsches Afrika Korps 62, 65, 66, 67, 71, 72, 81, 85
Panzerarmee Afrika 54
DIVISIONS
2nd, 9th, 10th SS Panzer 149
10th Panzer 96
12th Panzer (*Hitler Jugend*) 144, 160
15th Panzer 62, 66, 73, 74, 91, 94, 95
21st Panzer 62, 66, 73, 74, 91, 92, 94, 96, 143, 144
90th Light 62, 66, 73, 91, 95, 97, 99
164th Light 75, 91, 92, 94, 97
Panzer Lehr Division 144, 150
Gerow, Gen Leonard *165*
Gneisenau, armoured cruiser 14
Gorringe, General 17
Gort, General Lord *34, 34*, 38, 40, 41, 44
Gott, Lt Gen W H E 54
Graham, General *107, 109*
Grigg, Sir James *172*
Gromyko, Andrei 185
Gruenther, Brig Gen A M *183*
Gunn, James 19
Gurkha troops 95, *95*
Gustav Line 117

Harding, Maj Gen John 72
Harris, ACM Sir Arthur 132-3
Herbert, A P and Gwen *28*
Highland Division's Farewell to Sicily, The 113
History of Warfare, A (Montgomery) 183, 187
Hitler, Adolf 29, 36, 60, 76, 80, 81, 110, 113, 145, 150, 151, 157, 161, 166, 174, 177
Hobart, Maj Gen Percy 25, 27, 136-7, *138*
Hodges, Gen C H 156, *165*, 168, 174, 177
Horrocks, Lt Gen Sir Brian 40, 61-2, *65*, 67, 85, 93, 94, 97, 99, *102*, 157, *172*, 173, 178

Indian army 7, 13, 67
4th Indian Divn 74, 76, 81, 91, 93, *95*, 97, 99
8th Indian Divn 120
Infantry Training Manual, Part II 28

Ireland, in early '20s *22, 25*
Ironside, FM Sir W E *34, 34*
Italian army 60, 66, 71, 77, 80, 119
First Italian Army 90, 96
XX Corps 62
DIVISIONS
Ariete armoured 66, 74
Folgore 97
Littore armoured 66, 74
Pistoia, Spezia 91, 97
Trieste 91
Young Fascist 91, 97
Italy 96, 109, 113-15, 117-18, *118, 120*, 120-21
conditions endured in 6, 114, 118, 120
landings in 114, *115*
maps 118-19
surrender 113, 114

James, M E Clifton 134-5
John, Augustus 19

Kasserine battle 89, 90, 96, 110
Keitel, FM W 150
Kesselring, FM Albert 112, 117
Khrushchev, Nikita 187
King, Admiral E J 131
Kirkman, Brigadier 67
Kitchener, FM Earl *14*
Kluge, FM Gunther von 156, *156*, 159, 166

Le Cateau, battle of 14
Leese, Lt Gen Sir Oliver 27, 67, *67*, 72, *87-8*, 90, 91, 95, 107, 111, *121*
Leigh-Mallory, ACM Sir Trafford *7, 124, 126*, 132, 133, 146
Levin, Bernard 184
Lewin, Ronald 65, 97
London, air raid precautions in *35*
Luftwaffe 39, 54, *56, 61*, 97
Hermann Göring Division 110
Lumsden, Lt Gen Herbert 67, *67*, 68, 72, 82

Maginot Line *34, 36*, 38
Malta 54, 77, 82, 106, 107, 108
Mao, Chairman *183*
Mareth Line battle 90-94, 95, *96, 97*
Marshall, Gen G C *106*
McCreery, Gen Sir Richard 75
McNaughton, Gen A G L 103
Medenine battle 90
Memoirs (Montgomery) 13, 14, 21, 27, 34, 39, 49, 55, 81, 83, 89, 94, 99, 120, 139, 143, 173, 184
Messe, Gen Giovanni 90, 94
Messina 110, 111, 112
Milligan, Spike 45
Model, FM Walter 166
Molotov, V M 185
Monte Cassino 117
Montgomery, FM Viscount
EARLY YEARS 10-14, *12*
birth 10, 11

Anglo-Irish background 10
in Tasmania 11, 12
paternal influence 11-12
relationship with mother 12, 13, 20
corporal punishment for 12
at St Paul's School 12-13, *13*
determined on army career 13
at Sandhurst 13, *13*
gazetted into Royal Warwickshire Regt 13
in India 13-14
promoted lieutenant 14
IN WORLD WAR I
adjutant, later platoon commander, temporary captain and company commander 14
wounded 14
awarded DSO 14, *17*
promotion through to Lt Col GSO1, 8, 16-17, *18*
INTER-WAR YEARS *26-8*
in Cologne, Major GSO2 17
Battalion Commander Royal Fusiliers 17, *19*
at Staff College 17, 24
death of wife 18, *27*
friendship with Betty Anderson 19, *25*
Bde Major 17th Infantry Bde 24
joins 8th Infantry Bde 24-5
meets de Guingand 25
Staff College instructor 25, 27-8, 67
Swiss holidays *25*
wedding to Betty Carver 25
posted to Egypt 27
brevet Lt Col 29
return to Royal Warwickshires 25, 28
in Palestine 28, *28*
posted to India 29
Chief Instructor, Indian Staff College, colonel 29, *29*
returns to England as commander 9th Infantry Bde 29-30
commands army side of amphibious exercise 29
Palestine posting in command of 8th Division 30
illness 31
returns to England to take over 3rd Division 31
Davell on 31
IN WORLD WAR II 1939-42
advice to troops on VD 20
commands 3rd Division 30, 31, 34, 36, 38-41, 44, 45
on Gort *34*, 44
temporary command of II Corps 41
promoted Lieut Gen commanding V Corps 44, 45, 46, 47
transferred to XII Corps and South Eastern Command 44, *44*, 46, 50
dealings with Auchinleck 14, 46-7, 55, 56

dealings with Churchill 47-8, *87, 129, 155, 157*, 188
anti-invasion policies 47, 50
and Dieppe raid 50-51
IN WORLD WAR II 1942-4
his take over of Eighth Army 54, 55, 56-8, *65*
Alam Halfa defensive plan 55
libel threat from Auchinleck 55
in Malta *107*
cooperation with RAF 59, 60, 66, 93, 108
no retreat policy 58, 61, 62
and Alam Halfa battle 61, 63-5, 66
relations with Alexander *65*, 66-7, *98*, 109
organizational changes 67
planning and training for Alamein 67-70
deception plans 68-9
and Alamein battle 71-7, 80, 188
pursuit after Alamein 81-5, *83*, 100
entertains von Thoma *80, 81*
Rommel compared with Montgomery 81, 82
and El Agheila position 84
at Tripoli 86-7, *87, 102*
bet with Bedell Smith 89, 96
advance from Tripoli 90
Kasserine 90
and Mareth Line 90-94
Wadi Akrit position
preparations for Husky 96, 97
Enfidaville 97, 99
promoted Lieut Gen 100
knighted 100
incidents with McNaughton and Mark Clark 103
planning for Sicily operation 106-10
planning for Italy 106, 113-14
coordination with Patton 110, *110, 131*, 139
preparation for Overlord 110, 129, 121, 126, 128-9, 130-31
operations in Sicily 111-13, 188
operations in Italy 114-15, 117, 120
administrative difficulties 117-18
farewell to Eighth Army 120-21
in North Africa *55, 67, 79, 88, 95, 99*
in Sicily *5, 105, 109-10*
with Mark Clark *116*
IN WORLD WAR II 1944-45
reaction to COSSAC plan 121, 126, 128
Montgomery plans and stragegy 128-9, 131, 143-4, 157, 160, 188
Allied command structure 124, 128, 131-3, 14304, 157, 160, 188
Allied command structure 124, 128, 131-3, 166, 167, 176, 178

INDEX

relations with Eisenhower 20, 126, *134,* 139, 155, 160, *163,* 164, 167, 169, 170, 178, 184
unpopularity with senior RAF personnel 93, 133, 149, 152-3, 183
deception operations 134-5
morale-building visits *128, 133*
specialized vehicles 136-8
invasion phase-lines 139-40
indoctrination programme 141
D-Day message to troops 141
Normandy operations 145, 146-7, 148-61, *167,* 188
on Leigh-Mallory 146
and Caen sector 145-7, 149, 150
and tank inferiority 148
Operation Goodwood 149, 150-54, 155
his Tac-HQ 154-5, *155, 168*
and Operation Cobra 155, 156
and Bluecoat 156-7
and Totalize 157-8
Falaise pocket 160
promoted Field Marshal 161
strategy for ending war 164-6, 179
offer to serve under Bradley 165
and political factors in Allied strategy 165-6, 167, 168
his Ruhr strategy 165, 166, 167-70, 172, 173, 174
Operation Market Garden 170, 172-3, 174, 176, 179
relationship with Crerar 174
and Ardennes offensive 177-8
Rhine crossings 178, 179
receives German surrender *178,* 179
at Berlin victory parade *2-3*
LATER YEARS *1,* 184-7
carries Sword of State *180,* 187
friendship with Lucien Trueb 20, *20*
service with WU and NATO 181-3, 182-4
as CIGS 182, 183, 184
view of Soviet Union 185
failing health 186-7
death and funeral 187, *188*
PROFESSIONAL CHARACTERISTICS
anti-Indian Army prejudice 14
battlefield skills 157
bravery 14, 31
controversial behaviour 20-21, 185-6
dealings with Auchinleck 14, 46-7, 55, 56
difficulties in dealing with equals or superiors 20, 31, 46-7, 155
emphasis on night operations 28
emphasis on training, instruction and preparation 11, 19, 25, 28, 29, 31, 49-50, 69, 182, 188
generalship 25, 28, 31, 36, 80, 83, 94, 110, 143, 187-8
importance of air dominance 149
importance of communication skills 17, 31, 36, 50, 70, 170
leadership 7, 21, 40, 49, 62, 70, 161, 170, 187
his liaison officers 102, 177
military critics and criticisms of 100, 102, 115, 149, 151, 152, 154, 160
'no belly-aching' 56-7, 72
obsessional military interest 18-19, 21
Patton-Montgomery rivalry 112
personality cult 46, 50
his principles and methods of command 16-17, 40
professionalism 18, 49, 50, 164, 188
relations with Eisenhower 20, 126, *134,* 139, 155, 160, *163,* 164, 167, 169, 170, 178, 184
relations with US leaders 89, 111, 124, 177
relationship with younger men 20, 155
ruthlessness 45-6, 67
self-advertisement 57, 62
skill in formal presentations 11, 19, 49, 50, *60, 90,* 139
solitariness 183
speech and writing style 19
treatment of subordinates 20, 103
two cap-badge gimmick *6,* 19, *62, 74*
unconventionality 11, 19, 21, 25, 28
use of fixed defensive positions 57
value of physical fitness 18, 45, 49, 62
PERSONAL FEATURES
anecdotes about 12, 19, 40, 45, 48, 49, 103, 139, 184, 185
attitude to Farrar ancestry 10
character assessment 179, 187-8
as a child 12
difficult to like 10, 20, 25, 182
distance from relatives 27, 179, 184
enjoyment of sports 13, *13,* 18
his marriage 18, 20, 21, 25, 27, 29, 103
portraits of 19, *21*
relations with mother 12, 13, 20, 27, 184
relations with son and guardians 27, *103,* 184
religious sense 184-5, 187
Montgomery, Betty (wife, formerly Carver) 24, 25, 27, 29
Montgomery, Brian (brother) 20

Montgomery, David (son) 27, *27, 29, 103,* 184
wedding of *184*
Montgomery, Donald (brother) 12
Montgomery, Very Rev Henry (father) 10, *10-11,* 11, 12, 27
Montgomery, Maud (née Farrar, mother) 10, *10-11,* 11, 12, 13, 27, 184, *185*
Montgomery, Sir Robert (grandfather) 10
Montgomery, Sybil (sister) *11*
Montrose, Marquess of 141
Morgan, Lt Gen F E 124, 125, 151
Morshead, Gen Sir Leslie 68
Mortain, German offensive at 145, 157, 158, 160
Mulberry harbour *142,* 149
Mussolini, Benito 112, 113
Nash, John, painting by *15*
Nehring, Gen Walter 62, *63*
Nelson, Admiral Lord 187, 188
Nevinson, C R W, painting by *14*
New Zealand forces,
New Zealand Corps 92, 93, 94
2nd New Zealand Division *55,* 61, 62, 65, 66, 71-5 *passim,* 81, 85, 90, 91, 92, 95, 120
5th New Zealand Brigade 97
Nijmegen 170, 172, 178
Niven, David 45
Norstad, General 182
North African campaign 54-8, 60-63, *63,* 65-77, 80-87, 89-97, 99-100, 102-3
conditions endured in *6, 85*
Nye, Lt Gen Sir Archibald 27

O'Connor, Lt Gen Sir Richard 27, 82, 153
Operation Bluecoat 156-7
Operation Cobra 150, 154, 155, 156, 158, 160
Operation Epsom 149, *149,* map 150
Operation Fortitude 134, 145
Operation Goodwood 149, 150-54, *154,* 155
Operation Husky 96, 106-10
Operation Market Garden *169,* 170, *171-2,* 172-3, 174
Operation Overlord,
Anglo-American command structure 124, 128, 131-2
deception plans 134-5, 145
importance of air dominance 133-4
landings *136, 138-41, 150*
logistical problems 140-41
maps 126, 146-7
Operation Torch 51, *82*
Operation Totalize 157-8
Operation Tractable *156,* 159

Paget, Gen Sir Bernard 27
Palestine 28, 30, *30*
Park, AVM Sir Keith 108

Patton, Gen George S 87, 96, *102,* 103, 108, *109-10,* 110, 111, 112, *131,* 132, 139, 155, 157, 158, 164, *165,* 166, 168, 173, 177, 179
on Montgomery 87
Pienaar, General 68
Plumer, General Lord 16
Polish troops 160
Polish Armoured Division 158
Portal, ACM Sir Charles *93*
Poston, John *65*

Qattara Depression 61
Quesada, Maj Gen E R 155

Ramsay, Admiral Sir Bertram *7, 124, 134,* 174
Ramsden, Maj Gen W H 56, 67
Renton, General 62, 72
Reynaud, Paul 40
Reynolds, Major and Mrs Tom 27, *103,* 179
Rhine crossing *165,* map 175, *177, 178,* 179
Roberts, Maj Gen G P B 62, *65,* 157
Robertson, Field Marshal Sir William 24
Rommel, FM Erwin 47, 54, 56, 58, *58,* 60, 61, 62-3, 65, 66, 68, 72-7 *passim,* 81-5 *passim,* 90, 94, 100, 138, *144,* 150, 151, 156
Roosevelt, Franklin D *121,* 124, 179
Royal Air Force 124, 132, 134, 182
Desert Air Force 93, 108
2nd Tactical Air Force 133
in N Africa and Mediterranean 54, *57,* 60, 62, 93, *101, 107, 114*
in Normandy 149, 150, 151, *152,* 154, 158, 159
Royal Marines *139*
Ruhr strategy 165, 166, 167-70, 172, 173
Rundstedt, FM Gerd von 150, *152,* 156
Ruweisat Ridge 60, 61

St Mark's church, Kennington 11
Salerno landings *112,* 114, 115, 117
Salisbury, Frank, portrait by 19, *21*
Sassoon, Siegfried, qu. 19
Schweppenberg, Gen Geyr von 145
Sicily *5,* 87, 96, *104,* 106-13, *113-15*
conditions endured in *6*
invasion of 110-13
Simonds, Lt Gen G G 158
Simpson, Lt Gen W H *165,* 177, *177*
Smuts, FM Jan C *107,* 139
Somme offensive (WWI) 16, *19*
South African forces *7,* 69, 71, 74

1st South African Division 68, 69, 71, 74
Spaatz, Lt Gen Carl A 132-3, 165
Staff College, Camberley 17, 24, *24*, 27-8
Stalin, Josef 54, *121*, 179, 185
Stalingrad 80
Stirling, Lt Col David *92*
Stumme, General 72
Syracuse 108, 110, 111

Tanks, British 34, 73, 74, 76
   Churchill *51*, 138, *149, 156*
   Cromwell 148
   Crusader *67, 82*, 100
   Duplex Drive conversion 138
   Grant *58*, 61, *66*, 71, *75, 79, 91*
   Honey *94*
   Sherman 69, 71, *81-2*, 92, *143*, 148

Stuart *156*
Valentine 61, 92, *93, 130*
tanks, French *39*
tanks, German *37, 39, 52, 57, 65, 73, 76*
   Mk III Special 62, 71
   Mk IV Special 62, 71, *153*
   Panther 148
   Tiger 146
Taranto, landing at 114
Tedder, ACM Sir Arthur 7, *93, 93, 106,* 107, *124, 128,* 133, 149, 152, 183
Teheran Conference *121*, 124
Thoma, General R von 72, *80*, 81
Thompson, R W 143
Tobruk 54, 60, 82, 110
Tripoli 60, 80, 84, 85, 86, 87
   victory parade in 86, *87*
Trueb, Lucien 20, *20*

Tuker, Maj Gen Francis 27, 95
Tunis 80, 97, 99, *99*
Tunisia 84, 87, 90

Ultra intelligence 145, 157
United States Army 80, 89, 108, 124, 128, 148, 176, 187
   12th Army Group 132, 155, 167
   First Army 128-9, 131, 140, 141, 143, 148, 150, 155, 156, 167, 168, 173, 176, 177, 179
   Third Army 128, 129, 132, 155, 157, 166, 167, 168, 173, 176, 177
   Fifth Army 103, 114, 115, 117, 120
   Seventh Army 109, 111, 112
   Ninth Army 177, 178, 179
   II Corps 90, 91, 96, 110, 111
   VI Corps 114

VII Corps 148
XV Corps 158
82nd Airborne Division 172
United States Army Air Force 124, 132, 158

Wadi Akarit battle 94-6, 97
Wadi Zigzaou 90, 91
War Between the Generals, The (Irving) 179
Wavell, FM Sir Archibald 19, 29, 30, *31*, 83, 86
   on Montgomery 31
Wellington, Duke of 10, 182, 188
Wilder's Gap 91, 92, 94
Williams, Bill 184
Willkie, Wendell 74
Wittman, SS Captain 147, 148

Zhukov, Marshal Grigori *2-3*

ACKNOWLEDGMENTS

The author and publishers would like to thank the designer Mike Rose, Ron Watson for compiling the index, the editor Damian Knollys, the picture researcher Elizabeth Montgomery, and Richard Natkiel for supplying all maps. Our thanks also to the Imperial War Museum for providing all photographic material except as follows:

The Bettmann Archive: 22-23, 25, 40, 51(below), 65(top), 132(top), 161
BPL: 52, 53, 56, 64, 97(both), 101(top), 109(top), 151(top).
Bundesarchiv: 37(both), 39(bottom), 54, 63(both), 68, 93(top), 145, 152(top), 162
Hulton-Deutsch Collection: 8, 12(left), 13(top), 17(lower), 24(right), 103, 181, 186(top)
John Frost Newspapers: 45(left), 76(top), 141(top)
National Archives: 112(bottom)
National Army Museum: 172(bottom)
Public Archives, Canada: all prefixes as follows DND/PAC —
   H G Aikman (PA 132856, 116510, 131221) 144(top), 148, 170-71
   Ken Bell (PA 138423) 170(insert)
   D I Grant (PA 116525) 156(top)
   Terry F Rowe (PA 141671) 120
   J H Smith (PA 138269)
   A M Stirton (PA 114482) 117(top)
   also C-14160: 51(top)
UPI Bettmann Newsphotos: 4-5, 7(top), 20, 28(bottom), 29(top), 30, 32-33, 34(both), 35, 40(top), 42-43, 45(right), 46-47(top), 47(top right), 48(insert), 48-49(main pic), 59, 67(top), 73(top), 74(lower), 78-79, 80, 83(bottom), 84(bottom), 87(lower), 88(top), 90(top), 90-91(bottom), 93(bottom), 95, 98, 99(bottom), 106, 110(both), 112(top), 114, 115(both), 116, 123, 125(top), 127, 128(top), 133, 134, 138, 142, 143, 144(bottom), 155, 159(bottom), 167(top), 172(top), 178(bottom), 180, 182, 183(both), 184, 185(both), 187, 188(both)
US Army: 102(bottom), 107(top), 122, 124, 135, 153, 163, 164, 165(both)
US Navy: 83(top), 136-137